Culture and Climate in Health Care Organizations

Contents

Tables

Figures

Box

Acknowledgement

We gratefully acknowledge the work of Ms Deborah Debono at the Centre for Clinical Governance Research, Australian Institute of Health Innovation, University of New South Wales who unstintingly gave her time and expertise in coordinating the efforts of the editors and authors, and ensuring the copy and proofs were of high quality. Ms Margaret Jackson proof-read the entire manuscript and we record our appreciation to her, too.

Notes on Contributors

Lawrence Benson is senior Fellow in the Health Policy and Management Group at Manchester Business School, Manchester University. He gained his PhD from the University of Bradford studying partnership working within Primary Care Group boards. His recent projects include evaluating NHS networks commissioned by the NHS Institute for Innovation and Improvement and an evaluation of the assistant practitioner during its introduction to the NHS commissioned by Greater Manchester Strategic Health Authority. Lawrence started his career as a NHS planning and commissioning officer in London and West Yorkshire.

Jeffrey Braithwaite is Professor and Director, UNSW Institute of Health Innovation and Director, Centre for Clinical Governance Research, University of New South Wales, Australia. His research inquires into the changing nature of health systems, particularly the structure and culture of organizations, attracting funding of more than AUD $ 32 million. He has published multiple times in the *British Medical Journal, The Lancet, Social Science & Medicine* and many other prestigious journals. Jeffrey has received numerous national and international awards including a Vice-Chancellor's award for teaching from UNSW and his paper on organizational restructuring, published in Health Services Management Research, was one of the top 50 management articles in 2006.

Joanne L. Callen is Coordinator of the Master of Health Informatics (MHI) program at The University of Sydney, Australia. She has published a considerable body of research including the first international study which quantitatively showed the relationship between culture and use of a clinical information system. She has developed and published an information system implementation model, the *Contextual Implementation Model*, which has an underlying theme of diversity at three levels: the organizational, departmental and individual level. Dr Callen has executed a leadership role in health informatics education and recently led the review and curriculum re-design of the MHI program.

Ann Casebeer is Associate Professor in the Department of Community Health Sciences, and Associate Director of the Centre for Health and Policy Studies, both at the University of Calgary. She is also Academic Co-Director for SEARCH Canada. She combines an applied practice background with an academic grounding in organizational learning and systems change. Her understanding of innovation and broad social policy mechanisms for change within complex environments is grounded by ten years in the UK National Health Service, and in over a decade with SEARCH (a public service organization targeting knowledge development for health gain). Research expertise includes the use of qualitative and mixed methods in action-oriented contexts and for knowledge exchange and use.

Ann Dadich is a registered psychologist and a Research Fellow at CInIS whose research passions lie in the related areas of social policy, health and mental health service systems, knowledge transfer, and community psychology. She is experienced in conducting community-based research that is complex and involves many distinct stakeholder groups. Before entering academe, she worked in both the government and non-government sectors with people who experience mental health issues. These experiences continue to inform her research interests and her approach to conducting research that is both empirical and respectful.

Huw Davies is Director, Knowledge Mobilisation and Capacity Building for the Service Delivery and Organisation R&D Programme (SDO) of the National Institute for Health Research (NIHR). Huw Davies holds a personal chair at the University of St Andrews, and directs the Social Dimensions of Health Institute (SDHI) at the Universities of Dundee and St Andrews, as well as working with the SDO Programme at the NIHR. His research interests are in public service delivery, especially health care, encompassing evidence-based policy and practice, performance measurement and management, accountability and governance. He also has a particular interest in the role of organizational culture and organizational learning in the delivery of high quality services, and in developing greater understanding of the working relationships between service professionals and service managers. Huw has published widely in each of these areas. His most recent book is *Using Evidence: How Research Can Inform Public Services* (Nutley, Walter and Davies, Policy press, 2007).

Helen Dickinson is a Lecturer in Health Care Policy and Management at the Health Services Management Centre at the University of Birmingham. Helen heads the health and social care partnership programme at HSMC and her primary research interests are in inter-organizational collaboration, leadership, evaluation of public services, policy implementation and critical theories.

Joan Durose is a Senior Fellow at the Health Services Management Centre at the University of Birmingham. Joan co-directs an MSc. in Leadership for Service Development and her main research interests include the theory and practice of team and organizational development. Prior to joining HSMC Joan worked as an organizational health consultant with a wide range of national and international healthcare organizations, with a particular interest in supporting OD practitioners and senior teams in organizational change using a range of team based and whole system techniques.

Kathy Eljiz, Centre for Industry and Innovation Studies (CInIS), University of Western Sydney. Kathy Eljiz, BBC (Hons) is a PhD Candidate with the Centre of Industry and Innovation Studies at the University of Western Sydney. Kathy's PhD is examining how beds are allocated in hospitals, using both formal and informal relationships. Her interests are in organizational culture, informal networks, and the use of social capital in hospitals.

Louise Farbus is a Post-Doctoral Research Fellow in the School of Allied Health Professions, University of Plymouth. Her interests are predominantly in the evaluation of education, health and social care. Hence, she has published in *Psychology Teaching Review, Journal for the Royal Society of Health Promotion*, and *Practice Nursing*. She is currently involved in the English NHS Service Delivery and Organisation R&D Programme 'The management and effectiveness of professional and clinical networks'.

Anneke Fitzgerald is the Research Studies Coordinator in the College of Business and a member of CInIS. Her research interests and efforts are predominantly in the field of Organizational Behaviour and in the context of Health Services Innovation and Clinical Leadership. She is particularly interested in organizational and professional culture, professional identity construction, as well as operations management and process improvement research in acute health services. Her experiences as a health manager continue to guide her research and teaching interests.

Tim Freeman is lecturer in Health Policy at the Health Services Management Centre, University of Birmingham (UK). He is director of doctoral studies and co-director of research, and also sits on the UK NHS Service Delivery and Organisation (commissioning) research panel. While his PhD applied psychometric scaling to the measurement of clinical governance, he has over time become increasingly interested in post-structuralist approaches to public-sector governance. Consequently, his recent work includes a Q-methodology study of public sector leadership discourses, and he holds an Economic and Social Research Council conference award for interpretive policy analysis.

John Gabbay is Emeritus Professor at the Wessex Institute for Health Research and Development at the University of Southampton. He has a longstanding interest in the social and organizational aspects of clinical knowledge and is currently researching the role of communities of practice and collective "mindlines" in knowledge utilization in primary care.

Kathy Germ is an independent organizational researcher, writer, and consultant. She specializes in the areas of working and well-being, health promotion, public health, and the processes of learning and changing in organizations. Kathy is also an adjunct assistant professor at the Centre for Health Promotion Studies (Public Health Sciences) at the University of Alberta. Kathy holds a PhD in organizational analysis (University of Alberta School of Business) as well as a master's degree in health promotion and an undergraduate degree in nursing. Prior to her academic and consulting career, Kathy worked extensively in Alberta's health system.

Stanley Gold is a psychiatrist and psychoanalyst with special interest in small and large group work. He has worked as consultant on group relations conferences in the UK and Australia, where he was a founder member of the Australian Institute for Socio-analysis. Over the last ten years he has worked as Organizational Consultant particularly in the areas of health care promotion and delivery. He was previously Senior Lecturer and Chair of the Centre for Psychodynamic Studies, School of Psychology, Psychiatry and Psychological Medicine, Monash University and remains an Honorary Senior Lecturer. He is a Member of the Victorian Ass. Psychoanalytic Psychotherapy, the Australian Ass. of Group Psychotherapists and The Group Analytic Soc. London. He is an Associate of the Bayswater Institute London and is a board member of the International Society for the Psychoanalytic Study of Organisations where a recent contribution was: Swimming with Sharks: The Politics of Survival in the Large Group.(*Socio-Analysis*, 2004, 6: 1–19). He is an Associate Editor of *The International Journal of Organisational and Social Dynamics*.

Karen Golden-Biddle is Professor of Organizational Behavior and Everett Lord Distinguished Faculty Scholar at Boston University's School of Management. In her research, she explores two areas: the cultural, relational and identity processes in organization-based change with special emphasis on health system innovation and change; and theorizing in organizational studies.

David Greenfield is a Senior Research Fellow and adjunct lecturer in the Centre for Clinical Governance Research at the University of New South Wales. David's research focus is the development and enactment of practice and how organizations shape and mediate learning and knowledge management. His research interests include community of practice, innovation and change in health services, organizational culture and climate, learning and knowledge management and health service accreditation.

Wendy Harding (PhD) is a Senior Lecturer in Organisational Dynamics with the COS Group at RMIT University. Her particular interests are in large group dynamics and relational theories. These interests are utilized and developed through consultant work in a variety of organizations.

Stephen Harrison is Professor of Social Policy at the University of Manchester, where he heads the organizational research programme within the National Primary Care Research & Development Centre. He was formerly Professor of Health Policy and Politics at the University of Leeds. Steve's main research interests are in the health policy making process and in the politics of health policy and health service organization. His most recent book is *The Politics of Healthcare in Britain* (with Ruth McDonald: Sage, 2008).

Bob Hinings is a Professor Emeritus in the Department of Strategic Management and Organization, Faculty of Business, University of Alberta and Senior Research Fellow in the Centre for Entrepreneurship and Family Enterprise. He is currently carrying out research into regionalization of health services in Alberta and the introduction of primary health care innovations. He has a long record of studying professionals in organizations. He is also involved in research into the organization of the Canadian wine industry.

Paula Hyde is Senior Lecturer in Leadership and Experiential Learning at Manchester Business School, University of Manchester. Her research interests include workforce modernization, human resource management and psychodynamic approaches to understanding organizational life. She co-edited the previous book in this series with Lorna McKee and Ewan Ferlie about organizing and reorganizing health care (Palgrave Macmillian) and has published on workforce development, role redesign, and organizational dynamics in health care.

Rowena Jacobs is a Senior Research Fellow at the Centre for Health Economics, University of York, UK. She has a PhD in Economics from the University of York and a Masters degree in Economics (cum laude) from the University of Cape Town, South Africa. She has recently been awarded a Postdoctorate fellowship funded by the Department of Health's R&D Programme to examine performance measurement in mental health care services. Her research interests include health policy reforms, incentives and performance measurement.

Mary A. Keating is Senior Lecturer in Human Resource Management at Trinity College Dublin. An occupational psychologist, she has consulting experience in the area of Human Resource Management, specifically in management recruitment and compensation. She is a member of the Top Level Appointments Committee in the Irish public sector. Mary is a Research Fellow of the International Institute for Integration Studies (IIIS) at TCD and a Fellow of the Salzburg Seminar.

Frederick Konteh is a Research Fellow at the Centre for Health and Public Services Management, York Management School, the University of York. His main research interest is evidence-based, in the social and geo-demographic dynamics underpinning the provision and access to public services. Frederick is also interested in analysing the cultural implications of policy, quality and performance in health care management and delivery using both quantitative and qualitative methods. Frederick was principal investigator for a World Bank funded 'Willingness to Pay' (for Water) study (1995) and a DFID funded 'Corruption and Governance' study (2002) in Sierra Leone.

Susan Long is an organizational researcher and consultant. She is an adjunct Professor at RMIT University in Melbourne Australia where she supervises research students and conducts organizational research. Originally trained as a clinical psychologist and psychotherapist, she has worked as a group and organization consultant and researcher for over 25 years. As an organizational consultant she works with organizational change, executive coaching, role analysis, team development and management training. She has worked with government departments, hospitals, prisons, professional associations, financial institutions, insurance companies, airlines and the travel industry and a wide range of service industries. She is currently President of the Psychoanalytic Studies Association of Australasia, Past President of Group Relations Australia, a past President of the International Society for the Psychoanalytic Study of Organisations (ISPSO), past Executive member of the Australian and New Zealand Academy of Management and past member of the clinical college of the APsS. Her research interests involve participatory action research projects in industry, government organizations, health, education and correctional services and have attracted grants through the Australian Research Council and industry. She has published five books and many journal articles.

Sarah MacCurtain is Co-Director of the Health Services Performance Research Group. She received her PhD from Aston Business School. She teaches Organizational Behaviour at the University of Limerick. Continuing research interests include top management team effectiveness, trust and organizational performance, bullying, employee stress and well being in the health services, organizational climate and innovation. She has co-authored publications inclusive of books, monographs, book chapters, journal articles and conference papers. Her books and monographs include *High Performance Work Systems: The Economic Evidence* (2005, National Centre for Partnership and Performance); *Principles of Organizational Behaviour, An Irish Text*, Gill and Macmillan, 2004; *Managing Knowledge Based Organizations: Top Management Teams and Innovation* (2002, Blackhall); *Effective Top Management Teams: An International Perspective* (2001, Blackhall). Her articles have been published in journals such as *Management Revue, Personnel Review, International Journal of Human Resource Management* and *Irish Journal of Management.*

Juliet MacMahon is a lecturer in Human Resource Management and Employment Relations at the University of Limerick. She is a member of the Chartered Institute of Personnel and Development (CIPD) and a fellow of the Irish Institute of Training and Development. She has a wide range of consultancy experience in HR in both public and private sector particularly in voluntary health care sector. Current research interests include work on climate in health care organizations, employment legislation, bullying and harassment, employment relations in small enterprises, women and occupational change in Ireland and work life balance issues. She has published in journals such as *Employee Relations, Administration Journal, Journal of European and Industrial Training.* She is currently engaged in a study of bullying among health care workers in Ireland. This research is being done in partnership with two Irish trade unions.

Aoife McDermott is a Lecturer in Human Resource Management at Dublin City University Business School and a member of the Learning, Innovation and Knowledge (LInK) Research Centre at DCU. Her research interests include health services research, particularly in the areas of organizational change and the role of the HR function.

Russell Mannion is Director of the Centre for Health and Public Services Management at the University of York and Senior lecturer in Health Policy and Management in the York Management School. He was based at the Centre for Health Economics at York between, 1995–2006. He has authored several books and over 100 journal articles, book chapters and scientific papers, and provides advice to a range of national and international agencies, including the WHO, International Society for Quality in Health Care, HM Treasury, The UK Department of Health, The Healthcare Commission and the UK National Patient Safety Agency. He is a Visiting Research Fellow at Bocconi University and a Visiting Professor in the Faculty of Medicine, University of Oslo. Russell was recipient of the 2005 Baxter book award presented by the European Health Management Association for – *Cultures for Performance in Healthcare.* Mannion, R., Davies, H. and Marshall, M (2005) OUP Press, 2005.

Andrée Le May is Professor of Nursing, in the School of Health Sciences at the University of Southampton. Her research includes studies of organizational change and knowledge management. She is editor of the new book, *Communities of Practice in Health and Social Care* (2008) which explores how communities of practice can make service development and quality improvement in health and social care easier to initiate and more sustainable.

Edward Peck is Professor of Public Services Development at the University of Birmingham, UK, where he endeavours to lead the College of Social Sciences efficiently, effectively and efficaciously.

Dan Penny took up the position of Director of Cardiology at The Royal Children's Hospital, Melbourne in 2001. He is also the Leader of Heart Research at The Murdoch Children's Research Institute and a Professor within The Department of Paediatrics of The University of Melbourne. Dan is a clinical paediatric cardiologist. He is interested in the interface between research and clinical care. He currently supervises/co-supervises five doctoral students. He is a founding director of The Australia and New Zealand Children's Heart Research Centre, which is a research collaborative for cardiovascular research in children across Australia and New Zealand. He is one of the editors of the upcoming third edition of *Paediatric Cardiology* which is one of the definitive texts in the field. He spends time in Vietnam where he has been involved in developing a new cardiovascular institute in Hue city. In addition to his day-to-day management roles, he has a particular interest in Program Development and Quality and is completing a Masters of Health Administration in Latrobe University, Melbourne.

Catherine Pope is Professor of Medical Sociology in the School of Health Sciences, University of Southampton. Her research interests centre on the organization and delivery of care, organizational change, and professional practice; she is currently working on projects about the use of computer decision support in urgent and emergency care and a study of ambulance crew handover routines.

Trish Reay is an Assistant Professor in the Department of Strategic Management and Organization at the University of Alberta, School of Business. Her research interests include organizational and institutional change, organizational learning and knowledge transfer. She has published articles on these topics in *Academy of Management Journal, Organization Studies, Journal of Management Studies and Human Resource Management*. Her most current research investigates how organizations are learning to provide better primary health care services.

David Reeves is Senior Statistician at the National Primary Care R&D Centre, University of Manchester. David's main research interest is in the evaluation and enhancement of the quality of patient care. To this end he has developed a special interest in the application of quantitative Social Network Analysis methods to the measurement of care networks, for the purpose of better understanding how health, social and other professionals work – or do not work – together in providing care to patients with complex needs, and of how to organize multidisciplinary working to maximize health outcomes for patients.

Kent V. Rondeau holds a BSc Honours and a Bachelor of Laboratory Technology degrees from the University of Regina, an MA in public policy and administration, an MBA from Concordia University, and a Doctorate in health administration from the University of Toronto. Prior to joining the Department, Dr Rondeau taught in the School of Health Services Administration at Dalhousie University for eight years. His research interests include the design of health care organizations and systems, health care workforce reduction, strategic human resource management, and the management of health care quality.

Jill Schofield is the Somers Chair of Healthcare Management at the University of Edinburgh Business School. Her research interests include the implementation of policy initiatives and the operation of the policy process across the not for profit and public sectors and in particular how managers learn to adopt new working practices and what motivates them to do so. A second major strand to her research involves understanding the operation of intersectoral and interagency working particularly around the organizational consequences of partnership and collaborative activity. Her most recent projects have included a study of professional partnerships in health care and the management and effectiveness of health care networks.

Rod Sheaff is professor of health and social services research in the University of Plymouth, UK. His main interests and publications concern health system reform, health system organization and management, especially in primary care, health care ethics, marketing for health services and the working of public sector quasi-markets. He has researched and taught in a number of health systems, including France, Germany, Russia, Poland, Romania, Saudi Arabia and the USA besides the UK.

Terrence Sloan, Centre for Industry and Innovation Studies (CInIS), University of Western Sydney. Terry is an active member of the Centre for Industry and Innovation Studies (CInIS) and a member of the School of Management. Along with research into benchmarking of hospital operating theatres operations and patient flow in emergency departments, Terry's teaching and research interests include innovation, knowledge management and logistics in supply chains.

Michelle O'Sullivan is a Junior Lecturer in Industrial Relations in the University of Limerick, Ireland. She holds a BA (Public Administration), a PhD and a Diploma in Employment Law. Michelle previously worked as a trade union official with the Irish Medical Organisation. Her main research interests are in the areas of trade union membership and recognition, employment law, bullying in the workplace, minimum wage regulation and migrant workers. She has published widely in books and journals including *Personnel Review, Employee Relations, Industrial Relations Journal* and *Labor Studies Journal.*

At the time of writing **Elizabeth Wade** was a Senior Fellow at the Health Services Management Centre (University of Birmingham), where she led the department's work on health and social care commissioning. With a background in NHS management, Elizabeth has a particular interest in identifying and developing the skills and competencies required by public service commissioning managers. She is currently a Senior Policy Manager for the NHS Confederation, the independent membership body for NHS organizations across the UK.

Terry H. Wagar is Professor of Human Resource Management at Saint Mary's University in Halifax, Nova Scotia. He is co-author of *Canadian Human Resource Management: A Strategic Approach,* now in its 8th edition. In 2006, Dr Wagar received the International Personnel Management Association's (IPMA Canada) President's Award for outstanding contributions to the field of human resource management. Dr Wagar's research is primarily in the areas of human resource management, labour and employment law, and workforce reduction/organizational restructuring.

Kieran Walshe is an academic with some 20 years experience working in health services research. His main research interests are centred on quality and performance in health care organizations, and have included topics such as the development of clinical audit and clinical governance; clinical negligence and patient safety; inquiries into major failures in care; organizational failure and turnaround; and regulation and inspection in the health care sector. A key interest for him throughout his academic career has been to build a more effective linkage and exchange between the academic/research and policy/practice communities. He began his career as an NHS manager in 1985, and has worked at a research unit at the Kings Fund (1989–95); at the University of Birmingham (1995–2000); at the University of California at Berkeley as a Harkness Fellow (2000–1); and since 2002 at Manchester Business School, where he co-directed the Centre for Public Policy and Management for three years. He is now director of the Institute of Health Sciences at the University of Manchester, which exists to promote collaborative and interdisciplinary research in the health sciences.

Johanna Westbrook is Director of the Health Informatics Research & Evaluation Unit, University of Sydney. Her research centres on designing innovative, multi-method approaches to measure how effectively clinical information technology delivers desired benefits, and improves the quality and safety of health care. She has led significant studies of the impact of electronic ordering and medication management systems on error rates and health professionals' work, studies of telemedicine applications, and examined the role of interruptions in clinical error production. Professor Westbrook has published over 140 papers and attracted in excess of $17M in research funding. She has received several research awards and in 2005 was elected as a Fellow of the American College of Medical Informatics.

Mary Westbrook is Conjoint Associate Professor at the Centre for Clinical Governance Research, University of New South Wales. She was previously Associate Professor in Behavioural Sciences, Faculty of Health Sciences, at the University of Sydney. Her main areas of research are health organizational behaviour, safety in healthcare, health professionals' careers, and the psychology of illness, disability, ageing, ethnicity and gender. She has published over 120 research articles in peer reviewed journals, is a Fellow of the Australian Psychological Society and was appointed a Member of the Order of Australia for 'services to education in the field of health sciences research'.

Preface

This preface to the sixth book to emerge from the Organisational Behaviour in Healthcare (OBHC) conference, considering as it does Culture and Climate, also demonstrates that the community which comes to OBHC is now a subculture of the organizations studies discipline (Mark & Ferlie 2008). The selected papers represent rich empirical research, theoretical insights, and international perspectives, and join a designated series, a status bestowed by the publisher Palgrave, in confirmation of this distinct cultural identity of research represented by the OBHC community.

As this collection shows, culture remains a problematic concept, but is as critical now as it was to the late Professor Barry Turner who wrote the seminal text *Exploring the Organizational Subculture* in 1971 that led to his co-founding of the Standing Conference on Organisational Symbolism (SCOS). SCOS began as a subculture of or perhaps a counterculture to the European Group for Organizational Studies (EGOS), which itself was founded as a European equivalent to the American Academy of Management – illustrating the point that, to understand an organizational culture we must first know something of its history. It also highlights the continuing distinction between the European and American approaches to research that finds a creative tension in the apex provided by the antipodean context in Sydney in 2008. The distinction between culture and climate reinforces such differences, deriving as they do from qualitative and quantitative perspectives respectively; the distinction suggests that no method is superior to any others, but rather reflects just the culture or subculture within which it sits. It is a dynamic field of study, so, for example, we know ethnography is re-emerging through an anthropological model in which culture, identity, and power are key concepts, confirmed by the OBHC conference in Aberdeen in 2006, with focus on power, and Sydney in 2008, on culture.

Indeed, the chapters which follow reflect the ebb and flow of debate rather than a linear progress towards definitions in the field of organization studies which may as Schein suggests, still be in a "pre-Darwinian state of development"(Schein 2006). This need for greater theoretical understanding, especially in relation to culture, also explains concern with problems such as managing change rather than on the paradigms or ways of seeing that need to develop; such instrumentality in approach also highlights how culture itself is seen as an artefact for manipulation by differing interests within the organization, rather than something less amenable to control.

However progress has been made by the relevance culture now has in understanding patient safety in health care, which coincidentally reiterates the link with Turner's work on industrial safety (Turner & Pidgeon 1997), and is the motivation of many of the contributions to this book. It also gives a practical focus for debates on theory and the relationship to practice in what otherwise might become a chasm of misunderstanding into which patients will ultimately fall – but those problems will be addressed by the 2010 OBHC conference, in Birmingham UK.

ANNABELLE MARK
Middlesex University London
5th May 2009

References

Mark, A. and Ferlie, E. (2008) 'So far so good? Or organisational Behaviour in healthcare the development of a field', Keynote address to SHOC, OBHC Sydney.

Schein, E. H. (2006) 'From brainwashing to organizational therapy: A conceptual and empirical journey in search of "systemic" health and a general model of change dynamics. a drama in five acts', *Organization Studies*, 27 (2), 287–301.

Turner, B.A. and Pidgeon, N.F. (1997) *Man-Made Disasters*. 2nd edn. Oxford: Butterworth Heinemann.

Introduction: Why Focus on Culture and Climate?

Catherine Pope, Jeffrey Braithwaite and Paula Hyde

This book brings together a series of papers which detail recent international research on the theme of culture and climate in health care organizations. It is the sixth edition in the Palgrave series of edited collections on organizational behaviour in health care and was developed from the highly successful Organizational Behaviour in Health Care Conference held at the University of New South Wales, Sydney in March 2008.

This conference is a key biennial meeting for members of the Society for the Study of Organizing Health Care (SHOC) and it attracts scholars from across the globe who share an interest in health care organizations and change. The theme of the sixth conference in Sydney was 'Culture and Climate: Cracking the Code'. The topic of culture and climate was chosen for the Conference to encourage participation by a range of different interest groups – researchers, health care managers, practitioners, and policy makers aiming to explore climate in changing health systems, relationships and collaboration, and culture and climate research and its interface with practice. This clearly sparked interest. The conference was very well attended, with over 71 submitted papers presented as well as lively panel discussions and plenary addresses. This volume provides a historical record of some of the best papers at the Conference and an opportunity to advance the concepts of culture and climate in health care organizations. It provides a showcase for international research about health care organizations which we hope will continue the debates and conversations begun at the Conference, and which will help move critical academic debates forward.

The book builds on the structure of the conference. The chapters in Part I take a critical look at the concepts of culture and climate and related organizational constructs in the context of change within health systems and services. These twin concepts are much used but difficult to pin down and define. The idea of organizational climate has been mobilised in organizational research to signal an interest in the environment within organizations, and has lead to work exploring the attitudes of members of groups and the relationships within and between teams. Much of this work has

been influenced by social psychology and has utilised psychometric measurement and statistical analyses. While there is corresponding quantitative
research on organizational cultures, the concept of culture has particularly
drawn on more qualitative approaches such as ethnography and face to face
interviews. This in part reflects the anthropological and sociological origins
of the concept, but is also suited to capturing data about meanings, norms
and values, and routines and rituals – all phenomena that are variously
collected under the heading 'culture'. The three chapters in Part I provide
a welcome opportunity to re-explore the concepts of culture and climate.
Braithwaite et al. open the debate by showing the interrelationships between
these concepts, using an empirical case study of the Australian health service organizations. The next two chapters, by Mannion et al. and Freeman
and Peck, provide different examples of the operationalization of the concept of culture in the context of organizational and managerial change in
the NHS.

Part II looks more closely at relationships and collaboration to help understand how these create and challenge organizational culture and climate.
Here we have chapters examining conflicting relationships in health care
organizations, including an account of difficulties posed by the dual roles
of clinician-managers (Fitzgerald & Dadich), the tensions between Human
Resource managers and clinical managers (Hyde) and the special difficulties
experienced in bullying cultures (MacMahon et al.). Other chapters tease
out a range of factors associated with culture and their influence on organizational behaviour and change, ranging from the impact of individuals and
place on an organizational innovation (Pope et al.), to the role of interpersonal relationships in managerial decision-making (Eljiz et al.). The chapters
by Rondeau and Wagar on human resource management practices and by
Callen et al. on team climate highlight the ways in which culture and climate can hinder or support organizational performance and change. This
section concludes with two chapters looking at collaboration, one based
on creating organizational networks (Sheaff et al.) and the other looking
at attempts to foster learning cultures (Casebeer et al.). All these chapters
provide rich and detailed descriptions of relationships and collaboration
in health care organizations. What they also do is draw on a range of different conceptual models, theoretical and methodological approaches to
understand the processes and structures of the interactions which influence
organizational cultures and climates.

Part III presents four chapters which shine fresh empirical light on how
cultures and climates manifest in practice. McDermott and Keating provide
a case study of the links between organizational climate and the capacity
for change. The chapter by Long and colleagues reflects on their, often difficult, participatory action research approach to organizational change and
they provide some useful lessons for those that wish to use this approach
to get research into practice. A different kind of collaboration is highlighted

in the chapter by Greenfield which looks at how a clinical group worked together to change the culture and climate of their clinical practice. This book concludes with a chapter from Dickinson et al. exploring cultural performance.

The chapters collectively represent work by a range of scholars from diverse disciplinary backgrounds and working in different countries and health systems. The methods deployed demonstrate the wide variety of approaches to studying organizations, from in depth observation and interviews, focus groups, surveys and questionnaire based measures. This book also offers strong, but diverse theoretical perspectives, calling on the likes of Butler on performativity (Freeman and Peck), Lefebvre on place and space (Pope et al.), Mitchell on stakeholders and Timmermans and Berg on technologization (Greenfield). The case studies and research settings on which the chapters are based reflect very different types of health care organizations and focus on the work of people at all levels – clinicians, managers, practitioners. They provide rich empirical evidence about the importance of understanding culture and climate in health care organizations and, we believe, take us some way along the path to cracking the code for understanding culture and climate in health care organizations.

Part I

Culture and Climate in Changing Health Systems

1

Converging and Diverging Concepts in Culture and Climate Research: Cultate or Climure?

Jeffrey Braithwaite, David Greenfield and Mary T. Westbrook

Introduction

Are culture and climate different aspects of organizations, or are they the same general construct? In one sense, there is an easy way to cut through the tangled thicket of this question. It depends on the definitions used to explain the concepts, and the perspectives taken in characterizing them. In this paper, we briefly trace the roots of the terms culture and climate, and discuss their manifestations and conceptualizations in contemporary theory and research. Although it is clear that much depends on how culture and climate are defined, we emphasize the commonalities and explore the links between them. We introduce some evidence drawn from an Australian study of 22 randomly sampled, stratified health care organizations. This was part of a large-scale national research project into health sector organizational behaviour. The findings provide a gateway into understanding contrasting and converging views of culture and climate, particularly in terms of statistical relationships between the two concepts. The implications of this for research, practice, and teaching are discussed.

The roots of culture and climate

Historically, culture and climate are sometimes seen as distinct organizational variables; sometimes, as arising from differing academic traditions; and sometimes, as rival theoretical concepts. Alternatively, they have been viewed as two sides of the same coin, reflecting similar manifestations of 'the way things are done around here' representing the shared perceptions, values and meaning-making that people employ to co-construct their organizational worlds. No one, so far as we are aware, has conjoined the concepts by advancing a hybrid term such as cultate or climure.

Conceptually, although it is not as easy as it might seem to cleave the two constructs, climate emerged from an early concern for the measurement of individual attitudes, and has often been of interest to industrial or social psychologists. One question testing climate researchers historically was the relationship between data on individual attitudes obtained via questionnaire surveys and aggregations of these data. Climate has since expanded to be viewed by many as a systems-wide, organizational-environmental construct, metaphorically akin to the weather.

More often than not, culture is also conceived broadly, not so much as an organizational variable but as a way of understanding or expressing organizational life holistically, that is, the sum total of enacted behaviours, meanings and attitudes. A problem challenging culture researchers is the way in which many cultures manifest; is it feasible to see one meta-organizational culture, multiple sub-cultures, or many micro-cultures? Culture has traditionally been the domain of anthropologists, sociologists, or sociologically oriented scholars of organizational behaviour. Although it is not as clear-cut as the table suggests, and without claiming to be exhaustive, we can synthesize what scholars have said by looking at contrasting and converging views of culture and climate (Table 1.1).

Having presented the divisions this way, it should be stressed that many scholars have concluded that whatever distinctions there once were between the two concepts, these are now muddied and they essentially examine similar organizational features. Both attempt to describe organizational members' experiences with, and construction of, their workplace landscapes. Perhaps those investigating climate focus more on psychometrics, and cultural investigators ethnographically explore the world of people's lived experiences, but for many commentators it is difficult to distinguish between culture and climate, and some leading thinkers, including those in the *Handbook of Organizational Culture and Climate* (Ashkanasy et al., 2000) have shown how hard it is to maintain these differences.

Manifestations and conceptualizations of culture and climate in contemporary theory and research

Theoretical models – culture

We can consider culture and climate further by examining models which, according to the predilections of the writers, have been used to capture the main explanatory variables. A tripartite model has been advocated by Schein (2004), who suggests that there are levels of visibility to which observers of a culture can attend. Figure 1.1 shows the Schein model with examples from a hypothesized general practice.

Table 1.1 Contrasting and converging views of organizational culture and climate

	Culture	Climate
Researcher tendencies or stance	Explore: what is culture?	Measure: what is climate?
	Point of view: the participant's	Point of view: the researcher's
	Sociological or anthropological approach	Psychological or social psychological approach
	Traditional qualitative preference over quantitative	Traditional quantitative preference over qualitative
	Focused on how the emergent nature of culture and socialization processes occur	Focused cross-sectionally on the climate of the here and now
	Theoretical foundation: social constructionism; critical theory	Theoretical foundation: behaviour as a function of person and environment
	Interested in: deeply held assumptions, myths, rituals	Interested in: actual practices and patterns of behaviour
Selected characteristics of the concepts	Originated in sociology of work and organizations and the anthropology of contemporary behaviours	Originated in Gestalt psychology
	Some related concepts or interests: meaning-making, stories, embedded behaviours	Some related concepts or interests: workplace safety, policies, procedures, service delivery
	Recurring metaphors: community of practice, glue that holds people together, change mechanism	Recurring metaphors: atmosphere, environment, weather, social milieu

Sources: Adapted from Alvesson 2002; Ashkanasy et al. 2000; Denison 1996; Martin 2002; Payne 2000

Martin (2002) sees culture differently, construing it as an expression of a wide range of complex variables. She presents three conceptual perspectives. The integrationist perspective attends to the consistencies and agreements that manifest. The differentiationist perspective looks at inconsistencies that emerge, for example in terms of subcultures. The fragmentationist perspective sees culture as ambiguous and transitory. One seductive way to understand this model is by mapping the three perspectives to an organization's levels. At the level of the whole organization, cultural features which are shared, or often promoted normatively by the occupants of the executive suite, are organizational-wide and reinforced by corporate policies and imposed or articulated values. At the meso, or intermediate organizational level, differences in terms of gender, profession, between departments or across various groups, teams and networks

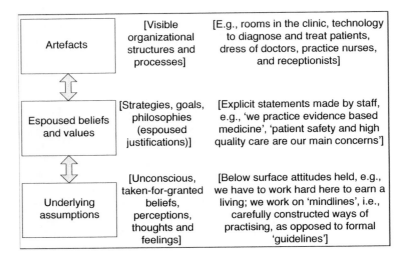

Figure 1.1   Schein's levels of culture with examples drawn from a general practice

Source: Adapted from Figure 2.1. Levels of Culture in Schein, Edgar H., Organizational Culture and Leadership, 2004:26 (Reprinted by permission of the publisher John Wiley & Sons Inc.).

Table 1.2   Martin's three cultural perspectives applied to a teaching hospital

Level	Integration	Differentiation	Fragmentation
Whole organization	A consensus-oriented hospital; clinicians, managers, and patients are relatively aligned	The hospital is divided, with considerable differences across sub-cultures	Little organization-wide accord pertains; hospital issues are constantly shifting sands
Sub-cultures	Different groups (e.g., professions, wards, departments) exhibit few sub-cultural differences	Sub-cultural groups interact in complex, distinctive ways with distinguishable values, beliefs and behaviours	Sub-cultural groups and their inter-relationships are pliable, shifting and ambiguous
Individual	Many doctors, nurses, allied health staff, managers and patients are individually aligned to the broader hospital's values	Individual personalities are comprised of pluralist sub components, unique characteristics and modules	Individuals are in flux with fragmented perspectives within a milieu of multiple political positioning and behavioural repertoires

Source: Adapted from Martin, 2002.

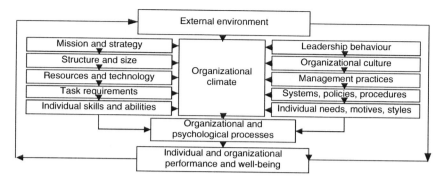

Figure 1.2 An integrated model of organizational change with climate as the central construct

Sources: Burke and Litwin 1992; Isaksen et al. 2001 (Reprinted by permission of the publisher (Taylor & Francis Ltd, http://www.tandf.co.uk/journals)).

can be seen. At a micro level, fragmented individuals and their interactions emerge through personalities, friendships, enmities and cliques; all is in flux. Martin holds that the three perspectives can be seen in discrete levels of analysis. Table 1.2, adapted from Martin, shows how the perspectives map to three levels of analysis, in this case of a hypothetical teaching hospital.

Theoretical models – climate

Turning to climate, it has been noted (Schneider, 1975; Schneider et al., 2000) that in practice, this concept is often related to another variable. Indeed for some commentators, climate invariably needs to be linked or applied to another concept, as the idea of climate in isolation is incomplete, so it is a 'climate for X' that is mobilized. For example, Isaksen and colleagues (2001) integrated a range of frameworks, particularly the work of Burke and Litwin (1992) into a multi-faceted model for organizational change which has climate as the main variable (Figure 1.2); this becomes a 'climate for change' framework.

Applied to a National Health Service (NHS) acute trust or an Australian area health service, we can discern, according to this model, that climate is at the centre of change, and is the core determinant of it, with various organizational and individual elements playing a role in promoting or inhibiting health reforms or service change. The external environments, and individual psychological processes, are also highlighted.

In other work, Ekvall (1991; 1996) developed ten dimensions held to be key in enacting a climate for creativity. Table 1.3 summarizes these dimensions

Table 1.3 Ten dimensions, definitions, and health system manifestations of a climate for creativity

Dimension	Definition	Health System Manifestation
Challenge	How challenged, emotionally involved, and committed are employees to their work?	Clinical professions' levels of engagement with and participation in service delivery
Freedom	How free are staff to decide how to do their job?	Relative levels of autonomy of doctors, nurses and allied health staff
Idea time	Do employees have time to think things through before having to act?	Pressure of work and patient throughput can inhibit thinking or available staff development time
Dynamism	How eventful is organizational life?	Organizational and clinical triumphs and tragedies; interest in hospitals created e.g. by active press or major enquiries
Idea support	Are there resources to give new ideas a try?	Beyond clinical and infrastructure budgets, special-interest funding can support new initiatives
Trust and openness	Do people feel safe speaking their minds and offering different points of view?	Health care managers, policy-makers and ministers can help facilitate a psychologically safe environment
Playfulness and humour	How relaxed is the workplace? Is it okay to have fun?	Despite the serious nature of health care provision, emphasis can be placed on workplace enjoyment and pleasure
Conflicts	To what degree do people engage in disagreements, quarrelling, or warfare?	Promoting less combative within-group and across-group relations amongst clinical and managerial stakeholders
Debates	To what degree do people engage in lively debates about the issues?	The extent to which mechanisms exist for open dialogue and healthy discussion
Risk-taking	Is it okay to fail?	Empowerment of clinical staff to make decisions and learn in a non-blaming milieu

Sources: Adapted from Ekvall 1991, 1996.

and the definitions of them, and considers health sector manifestations of these constructs.

Empirical studies

Four recent empirical studies help illustrate aspects of these models. Health care organizational culture has been examined in Australia (Braithwaite, 2006a, b; Braithwaite et al., 2005) and the English NHS (Mannion et al., 2007; Mannion et al., 2005). Braithwaite and colleagues compared two large teaching hospitals matched for size, budget, structure and case-mix for cultural differences via a triangulated methodology using observational studies and a questionnaire survey (Braithwaite et al., 2005). They employed Schein's and Martin's theoretical schemas to contextualize their data. This study showed how deeply culture varies across superficially similar organizations. Important factors included leadership, involvement of clinicians in decision-making processes, and the ways in which communication, change, finances, and human resource practices emerge and were handled.

Mannion et al. (2007) examined current and projected use of tools to measure culture in the English NHS. They canvassed the views and needs of stakeholders (clinical governance managers, representatives of agencies, regulatory bodies and colleges, and patients, carers and their supporters), and conducted two case studies of NHS trusts in deploying instruments to assess culture. They identified 70 such tools with varying degrees of utility and purpose, and noted there was considerable opportunity for health sector organizations to harness the benefits of diagnostic, assessment, and improvement tools to enhance organizational and clinical performance and service delivery. Factors to be considered in the selection of tools include commitment of senior managers to quality initiatives, supporting the values and ethos of the public service, emphasizing patient-centred care, engagement of clinicians, capacity for organizational learning, an environment supportive of risk-taking and innovation, less blaming and more workplace justice, more standardized care, an emphasis on teamwork and involvement of patients in decision-making.

Two recent, instructive studies which the authors labelled as climate investigations are those of Patterson and colleagues (2005) and Wiley and Brooks (2000). The Patterson group designed and validated a climate scale, the Organizational Climate Measure (OCM), testing a sample of 6,869 respondents drawn from manufacturing. Although neither the study data nor the instruments were related to the health sector, the OCM is grounded in considerable literature and appears to be *prima facie* suitable generically across industries. The framework to which the sub-scales in the instrument were mapped was the Competing Values Model (Gifford et al., 2002; Quinn and Rohrbaugh, 1981; 1983) which hypothesizes that values underpin culture in four broad domains: human relations (essentially, how well are people treated, developed, and involved), internal processes (to what degree things are inward-looking, rules-oriented, controlled and stable), open systems (the extent to which the organization focuses externally, is flexible and receptive to change and innovation), and rational goals (how the organization sets and pursues objectives, efficiency, improves productivity, manages performance, and provides feedback on these).

Wiley and Brooks assessed research using linkage approaches whereby the relationship between employees' judgements of their work environment were mapped to organizational performance. In effect, they asked, do employee ratings and descriptions of their workplaces predict and translate into better service to customers and better organizational performance outcomes? They found several key variables from their synthesis of multiple studies in several industries: the importance of leadership in reinforcing values and supporting improvement, effective communication, a vision of the future, and clear priorities. In their summary, Wiley and Brooks suggest a key question in creating a positive organizational climate is whether the organizational leadership instils confidence in the staff and the organization.

A study of culture and climate in Australian health organizations

Taken together, the empirical work and the conceptual models discussed show some of the many ways to understand culture and climate in organizational, particularly health organizational, settings. To further illustrate how these variables manifest and interact, we report findings from our current research examining the culture and climate of Australian health service organizations in a national study of health sector organizational behaviour. In this study, we took a definitional position on the two constructs based on relevant literature (Alvesson, 2002; Ashkanasy et al., 2000; Martin, 2002; Parker et al., 2003; Schein, 2004; Scott et al., 2003; Svyantek and Bott, 2004; van den Berg and Wilderom, 2004), settling on culture as 'a set of shared organizational meanings, values and norms that guide interactions' and climate as 'the broader environment within which culture and micro-cultures operate'.

Method

We operationalized our definitions, constructing indicators of culture and climate, including the dimensions *staff wellbeing, communication, team orientation, decision-making* of individuals and teams, *leadership* and *management* and *standards of care* enacted. Our sample consisted of 22 stratified, randomly sampled health service facilities. The health services were broadly representative of Australian health care: all of the states and one territory were represented. The sample was stratified with regard to size (10 small, six medium and six large health services), public and private mix (16 public, five private and one mixed public-private provider) and location (eight metropolitan, three regional, seven rural and four remote participant organizations). The research team examined the sample over a three-year period and conducted intensive fieldwork throughout 2006 and early 2007. Fieldwork comprised week-long structured observations at each site along with 386 semi-structured field interviews totalling over 900 hours. Field notes were transcribed, and a report for each organization created. Following the RAND-UCLA two step method of judging social data (Fitch et al., 2001), the organizations' documentation was ranked individually by an expert panel

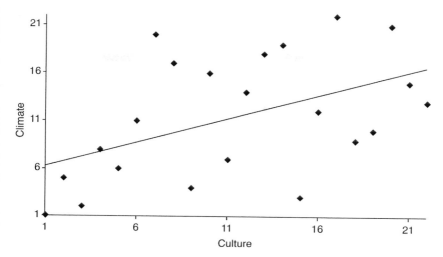

Figure 1.3 Correlations of culture and climate of 22 health care organizations

of four (with training in health services research, administration, social psychology and sociology) from best to worst in terms of the goodness and productiveness of the cultures and climates. After the panellists assessed the field notes and interview transcripts separately, they met to review all scores, discuss differences, and reduce inconsistencies. Once they agreed on the final rankings, their scores were averaged. A Spearman's rank order correlation was calculated between the indices of culture and climate.

Results and analysis

The Spearman's rank order correlation between the rankings on culture and climate yielded R = 0.49 (n = 22, p = 0.02) indicating a significant association between the variables, but not complete overlap. Figure 1.3 shows the strength of the correlation coefficient. These findings mean that although any particular researcher might see culture and climate as separate constructs, on the definitions we offer, they are significantly related empirically. If they differ, they share a common core.

Discussion

There are tools available by which to measure culture (see Mannion et al., 2007) and climate (see Patterson et al., 2005) which are under-utilized in research and industry. The benefits of using diagnostic and assessment tools include securing knowledge of respondents' views, obtaining baseline and comparative data on key organizational constructs, having the capacity to measure changes to culture and climate longitudinally or benchmark data across organizational types, and providing ways of relating stakeholder views to aspects of service and performance (Wiley and Brooks, 2000). Health care organizations with otherwise matched features differ on relative cultural characteristics (Braithwaite et al., 2005) and in regard to climate features (Ashkanasy et al., 2000). Our recent work (Figure 1.3) shows culture and climate are related even if they are not one and the same construct. Understanding the key differences and similarities is important if improvement strategies are under consideration.

The models, including Schein's (2004) and Martin's (2002) on culture, the Isakesen/Burke and Litwin climate for change framework (Burke and Litwin, 1992; Isaksen et al., 2001), and Ekvall's (1991; 1996) climate for creativity dimensions, each point to distinct aspects of culture and climate, and emphasize different clusters of variables. They have utility in theoretically and conceptually bringing relevant features of culture and climate to the foreground, and provide opportunities for researchers to order and explain their data within the scope of the selected model or models.

The implications for research, practice, and teaching

There are implications for our work. The implications for researchers are that measurement tools with capacity to provide predictive data, and theoretical models by which to frame this data, are increasingly available, and are being designed and refined by a succession of scholars. Fresh data on culture and climate, including the data provided here, are available. For practitioners, assessment tools and models can help with the improvement activities such as organizational development or workplace enhancement. Teachers of undergraduate and postgraduate students, and of students pursuing research degrees, can access a wider range of exploratory tools and models, and explanatory data, than previously. These help illuminate aspects of behaviour in health organizations for the benefit of the next generation of practitioners and researchers.

Conclusion

Organizational behaviour as a discipline, including health organizational behaviour as a sub-discipline, has new ways of examining and understanding people's *in situ* interactions. Depending on the perceiver – researcher, practitioner, teacher – culture and climate may be one and the same or separate variables. Whether or not they are, the answer to this puzzle seems subordinate to the understanding to be gained from exposing for analytic inspection the behaviours, values and meanings of health sector stakeholders in their organizational settings.

Shall we move then to describing the thorny concepts of culture or climate as either cultate or climure? There is no ready metric by which to determine this. There will always be taxonomic lumpers and splitters amongst us, particularly in research. You decide.

References

Alvesson, M. (2002) *Understanding Organizational Culture*. London: Sage.

Ashkanasy, N.M., Wilderom, C.P.M. and Peterson, M.F. (eds) (2000) *Handbook of Organizational Culture and Climate*. Thousand Oaks, CA: Sage.

Braithwaite, J. (2006a) 'Analysing social structural and cultural change in acute settings using a Giddens-Weick paradigmatic approach', *Health Care Analysis*, 14, 91–102.

Braithwaite, J. (2006b) 'An empirical assessment of social structural and cultural change in acute settings', *Health Care Analysis*, 14, 185–93.

Braithwaite, J., Westbrook, M.T., Iedema, R., Mallock, N.A., Forsyth, R. and Zhang, K. (2005) 'A tale of two hospitals: Assessing cultural landscapes and compositions', *Social Science & Medicine*, 60, 1149–62.

Burke, W.W. and Litwin, G.H. (1992) 'A causal model of organizational performance and change', *Journal of Management*, 18, 523–45.

Denison, D.R. (1996) 'What is the difference between organizational culture and organizational climate? A native's point of view on a decade of paradigm wars', *The Academy of Management Review*, 21 (3), 619–54.

Ekvall, G. (1991) 'The organizational culture of idea-management: A creative climate for the management of ideas', in Henry, J. and Walker, D. (eds), *Managing Innovation*. London: Sage, 73–9.

Ekvall, G. (1996) 'Organizational climate for creativity and innovation', *European Journal of Work and Organizational Psychology*, 5 (1), 105–23.

Fitch, K., Bernstein, S.J., Aguilar, M.S., Burnand, B., LaCalle, J.R., Lazaro, P., van het Loo, M., McDonnell, J., Vader, J. and Kahan, J.P. (2001) *The RAND/UCLA Appropriateness Method User's Manual*. Santa Monica, CA: RAND.

Gifford, B.D., Zammuto, R.F. and Goodman, E.A. (2002) 'The relationship between hospital unit culture and nurses' quality of life', *Journal of Healthcare Management*, 47, 13–26.

Isaksen, S.G., Lauer, K.J., Ekvall, G. and Britz, A. (2001) 'Perceptions of the best and worst climates for creativity: Preliminary validation evidence for the situational outlook questionnaire', *Creativity Research Journal*, 13 (2), 171–84.

Mannion, R., Davies, H., Konteh, F., Jung, T., Scott, T., Bower, P., Whalley, D., McNally, R. and McMurray, R. (2007) 'Measuring and assessing organisational culture in the NHS: Research report', Published, Centre for Health and Public Services Management, University of York.

Mannion, R., Davies, H. and Marshall, M. (2005) 'Cultural attributes of "high" and "low" performing hospitals', *Journal of Health Organisation and Management*, 19 (6), 431–9.

Martin, J. (2002) *Organizational Culture: Mapping the Terrain*. Thousand Oaks, CA: Sage.

Parker, C.P., Baltes, B.B., Young, S.A., Huff, J.W., Altmann, R.A., Lacost, H.A. and Roberts, J.E. (2003) 'Relationship between psychological climate perceptions and work outcomes: A meta-analytic review', *Journal of Organizational Behavior*, 24, 389–416.

Patterson, M.G., West, M.A., Shackleton, V.J., Dawson, J.F., Lawthom, R., Maitlas, S., Robinson, D.L. and Wallace, A.M. (2005) 'Validating the organizational climate measure: Links to managerial practices, productivity and innovation', *Journal of Organizational Behavior*, 26, 379–408.

Payne, R.L. (2000) 'Climate and culture: How close can they get?' in N.M. Ashkanasy, C.P.M Wilderom and M.F. Peterson (eds), *Handbook of Organizational Culture and Climate*. Thousand Oaks, CA: Sage, 163–76.

Quinn, R.E. and Rohrbaugh, J. (1981) 'A competing values approach to organizational effectiveness', *Public Productivity Review*, 5, 122–40.

Quinn, R.E. and Rohrbaugh, J. (1983) 'A spatial model of effectiveness criteria: Toward a competing values approach to organizational analysis', *Management Science*, 29, 363–77.

Schein, E. (2004) *Organizational Culture and Leadership*. San Francisco, CA: Jossey-Bass.

Schneider, B. (1975) 'Organizational climates: An essay', *Personnel Psychology*, 28, 447–79.

Schneider, B., Bowen, D.E., Ehrhart, M.G. and Holcombe, K.M. (2000) 'The climate of service: Evolution of a construct', in N.M. Ashkanasy, C.P.M. Wilderom, and M.F. Peterson (eds), *Handbook of Organizational Culture and Climate*. Thousand Oaks, CA: Sage, 21–36.

Scott, T., Mannion, R., Marshall, M. and Davies, H. (2003) 'Does organisational culture influence health care performance? A review of the evidence', *Journal of Health Services Research and Policy*, 8 (2), 105–17.

Svyantek, D.J. and Bott, J.P. (2004) 'Organizational culture and organizational climate measures: An integrative review', in Thomas, J.C. (ed.), *Comprehensive Handbook of Psychological Assessment: Industrial and Organizational Assessment*. Hoboken, NJ: Wiley, 507–24.

van den Berg, P. and Wilderom, C. (2004) 'Defining, measuring and comparing organisational cultures', *Applied Psychology: An International Review*, 53 (4), 570–82.

Wiley, J.W. and Brooks, S.M. (2000) 'The high performance organizational climate: How workers describe top-performing units', in N.M. Ashkanasy, C.P.M Wilderom and M.F. Peterson (eds), *Handbook of Organizational Culture and Climate*. Thousand Oaks, CA: Sage, 177–91.

2
Changing Management Cultures in the English National Health Service

Russell Mannion, Huw Davies, Stephen Harrison, Frederick Konteh, Rowena Jacobs and Kieran Walshe

Introduction

The language of cultural change is increasingly employed in relation to organizational reforms aimed at improving the efficiency and responsiveness of health systems in many countries. In the wake of high-profile reports documenting gross medical errors in the United States, policy thinking is embracing the notion of culture change as a key element of health system redesign (Institute of Medicine, 1999; Davies et al., 2000) and there is evidence to suggest that many other OECD countries are focusing on cultural renewal and change as a potential lever for health care improvement (Smith, 2002).

In England, the latest pro-market reforms in the National Health Service (NHS) are associated with the premise that a major cultural transformation of the organization must be secured if new values and beliefs are to underpin new ways of working in the organization (Kennedy, 2001), although the precise conceptualization of the term and its supposed relationships to organizational performance are less often specified by policy makers (Davies, 2002; Mannion et al., 2005a). Indeed, organizational analysis and behaviour have been described as perhaps the most difficult of organizational concepts to define. Nevertheless, current interest in this topic by managers, policy makers and academic researchers has spawned a growing literature devoted to ideas and practical approaches to implementing purposeful culture change as a means to levering quality and performance improvement (Mannion et al., 2005b; Scott et al., 2003a; 2003b).

In broad terms, the study of organizational culture focuses on that which is shared between people within organizations, for example:

- beliefs, values, attitudes and norms of behaviour;
- routines, traditions, ceremonies and rewards;
- meanings, narratives and sense-making.

Such shared ways of thinking and behaving help define what is legitimate and acceptable within any given organization; they are the social and normative glue that holds an organization together, and in colloquial terms *'the way things are done around here'*. Culture is thus a lens through which an organization can be understood or interpreted both by its members and by interested external parties through an appreciation of an organization's symbolic codes of behaviour, rituals, myths, stories, beliefs, shared ideology and unspoken assumptions. Organizational culture can be described both qualitatively and quantitatively (for a review concepts and instruments, see Scott et al., 2003a). In this chapter, we focus on changes in senior management team cultures in English NHS hospital trusts between 2001 and 2007, using quantitative data based on the Competing Values Framework (Cameron and Freeman, 1991; see below for a description of the framework). Our chosen period is of particular interest because it spans the implementation of successive pro-market system reforms in the NHS. The study sought to:

- examine senior management cultures in acute care hospitals in the English NHS; and
- explore how senior management team cultures have changed over time, and in particular whether the introduction of pro-market reforms has been associated with such changes.

Organizational culture in the NHS: An overview

No quantitative data on NHS organizational culture exist for the period prior to 2000, and few studies of NHS management and organization prior to that date explicitly employed the term (Pettigrew et al., 1992; Harrison et al., 1992). Nevertheless, much of the pre-2000 qualitative empirical literature can be interpreted as providing a basis for some general remarks about the earlier period. The following brief account is based on literature comprehensively reviewed by Harrison (1988), Harrison et al. (1992), and (less comprehensively) Harrison and Lim (2003).

From the mid-1960s (the date of the earliest research), until the mid-1980s, the literature indicates a consonance between formal organization structures and organizational practice that matches Mintzberg's (1991) description of 'professional bureaucracy'. In relation to the clinical activities of hospitals, individual physicians enjoyed considerable influence and autonomy, though non-clinical activities were governed by administrators in a more bureaucratic manner. In modern jargon, NHS hospitals at this time can be regarded as an amalgam of professional 'clan' culture and administrative 'hierarchical' culture. In overall terms, physicians collectively were more influential than senior managers, whose roles in relation to physicians centred upon facilitation, obtaining resources, handling the government bureaucracy, and smoothing out inter-professional conflict.

As a consequence, organizational change tended to occur reactively and incrementally. This pattern of managerial practice has been summed up by Harrison (1988) as 'diplomatic management'. As noted above, such practice was generally consistent with contemporary organizational formalities, which included the consensus of multidisciplinary decision-making teams, the insulation of physicians' employment contracts from local managerial discretion, and official support for the principle of 'clinical autonomy'.

From the mid-1980s, the reforms inspired by the Griffiths (NHS Management Inquiry, 1983) report led to the abolition of consensus teams and the development of 'general management' (that is, chief executives, though not so termed until later) in hospitals, along with attempts to promote the greater involvement of physicians in budgeting and financial matters (DHSS, 1984; Mannion, 2008). Subsequent research indicated that, although the new general managers (in acute care hospitals) were initially only marginally more influential than their administrative predecessors, the *office* of general manager was widely regarded as legitimate by other staff, including physicians. At the same time, central government had decided upon a more interventionist approach to NHS performance management, manifest in such developments as national performance indicators and fixed-term managers' contracts. In consequence, the new general managers also became more responsive to central government demands than their predecessors had needed to be. In modern jargon, this can perhaps be seen as a modest shift in prevailing organizational culture from 'clan' to 'hierarchy'. Whilst it is important not to overstate the degree of change, it is worth noting that such matters as the perceived legitimacy of general managers is likely to have been a necessary, though not sufficient condition for later organizational reforms.

In the early 1990s, much of the logic underpinning these changes was extended by attempts to develop an internal (quasi-) market (Le Grand, 1998), in which hospitals were supposed to compete for contracts to treat NHS patients. Central to these reforms were attempts to strengthen managerial control and accountability in the NHS and to nurture a competitive 'business culture' throughout the organization (Davies and Mannion, 2000). However, the reforms gave rise to potential political embarrassment (for instance, if an NHS hospital were to be driven out of business), professional resistance and resilience to these changes was more evident than a wholesale transformation of values and behaviour (Jones and Dewing, 1997; Broadbent et al., 1992), and research is more suggestive of collusion than competition (Flynn and Williams, 1997). In modern jargon, this period probably represents only the most modest of cultural adjustment towards a 'rational' or 'market' culture, and notions of NHS competition were initially abandoned by the incoming Labour government of 1997. Again, however, it seems likely that the emergence of a *language* of markets and competition during the mid-1990s helped to legitimate subsequent changes.

In 2001, the highly influential report published by the public inquiry into unacceptable mortality from children's heart surgery at the Bristol Royal Infirmary (Kennedy, 2001) concluded that the culture of healthcare in the NHS *'which so critically affects all other aspects of the service which patients receive, must develop and change'*. It described the prevailing culture at the Bristol Royal Infirmary at the time of the tragic events as a 'club culture', a term previously employed in organizational contexts by Handy (1985) and as a description of the style of UK government by Marquand (1988). In both cases, the 'club' notion implies excessive power and influence amongst a core group elite, whose members are mutually uncritical of each other. The Kennedy Report concluded *'the inadequacies in management were an underlying factor which adversely affected the quality and adequacy of care which children received'* (Kennedy, 2001: 203). Kennedy argued that while some problems were specific to Bristol, other aspects were more typical of the NHS. In particular, he suggested that the cultural characteristics of the NHS that had colluded to fostering a climate where dysfunctional professional behaviour and malpractice were not effectively challenged. As a consequence, a number of cultural shifts were seen as necessary to transform the NHS into a high quality, safety-focused institution, that would be sensitive and responsive to the needs of patients.

The government largely accepted the findings and recommendations of the Bristol Inquiry, and in its published response the Department of Health announced a range of new measures and supporting tactics aimed at tackling the systemic problems identified in the report (Department of Health, 2001). These included the establishment of a National Patient Safety Agency; a new Council for Healthcare Regulatory Excellence to strengthen and co-ordinate the piecemeal system of professional self-regulation; and further release to the public of clinical outcome data (aggregate outcomes data were already publicly available, but this was now extended to individual level data, starting with risk-adjusted mortality rates for all cardiac surgeons in England).

Since the early 2000s, health policy in England (though not other parts of the UK) has seen a return to market incentives and an espousal of 'earned autonomy', under which the highest performing hospitals are subject to less central control and regulatory scrutiny. One product of this approach has been the introduction of a new type of organization – NHS Foundation Trusts – that have a number of operating freedoms not available to other hospitals (Mannion et al., 2007). It is clear from supporting policy documents that the government expects behavioural and cultural changes – especially in relation to innovation, service redesign and customer care – to result from such innovations. Moreover, since 2002 the government has pressed much further than any of its predecessors in introducing pro market reforms. Key structural changes on the demand side include the extension of patient choice of service provider, intended to empower patients to put pressure on hospital providers to improve the quality of elective services; and the development of practice based commissioning with the aim of providing GPs with incentives to reduce inappropriate hospital referrals. These changes have been matched by reforms on the supply side, including an expanded role for independent and voluntary sector providers.

Underpinning and binding these structural reforms is a new prospective funding system termed Payment by Results (PbR) under which hospitals are paid on the basis of the type and amount of work they undertake (conceptualized in case-mix measures similar to Diagnosis Related Groups). PbR replaces block contracting arrangements, according to which hospitals receive a fixed annual sum in order to provide a pre-specified level of activity. The stated aims of PbR are to stimulate hospital activity (thereby reducing waiting lists), reward efficiency, facilitate patient choice and encourage a mixed economy of provision by allowing 'money to follow the patient'. By design, the new financial arrangements will create strong incentives for NHS organizations to behave differently and have the potential to drive major changes in the management cultures of NHS organizations. However, the extent to which NHS organizations will conform to expectations and respond in ways desired by policy makers is as yet unclear and hard to predict given the complexity of concurrent reforms (Mannion and Street, 2009).

Methods

Assessing management cultures

Culture assessment was accomplished through two national surveys using an established tool – the Competing Values Framework (CVF, see e.g. Cameron and Freeman, 1991; Gerowitz et al., 1996; Gerowitz, 1998; Shortell et al., 2000) to assess senior management team cultures in NHS hospitals.

Using two main dimensions – the first describing how processes are carried out within the organization, and the second describing the orientation of the organization to the outside world – the CVF thus articulates four basic organizational cultural 'types' (see Box 2.1). Crucially, organizations (or subgroups within them) are not deemed to be simply one or other of these four types; instead, they are seen to have competing values while nonetheless having a more or less stronger pull to one particular quadrant.

Data gathering

Assessment of the dominant culture orientation for any particular hospital organization was accomplished through use of a postal questionnaire comprising the Competing Values Framework (adapted to be relevant to the UK NHS) and background questions. The CVF questionnaire offered respondents a series of descriptions of a hospital, arranged in five groups of four (copy available from the authors). Within each group of four descriptions, the respondent was asked to 'share 100 points' between them 'according to which description best fits your current organization'. The five groups represent descriptions of hospital characteristics, leadership, emphasis, cohesion and rewards. Collating these 'points allocations' provides a score

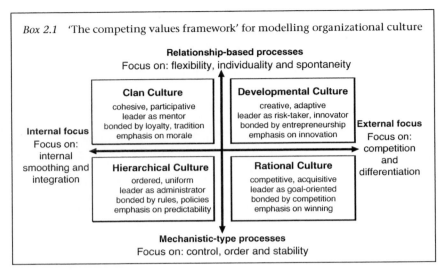

Box 2.1   'The competing values framework' for modelling organizational culture

Relationship-based processes
Focus on: flexibility, individuality and spontaneity

Clan Culture
cohesive, participative
leader as mentor
bonded by loyalty, tradition
emphasis on morale

Developmental Culture
creative, adaptive
leader as risk-taker, innovator
bonded by entrepreneurship
emphasis on innovation

Internal focus
Focus on:
internal
smoothing and
integration

External focus
Focus on:
competition
and
differentiation

Hierarchical Culture
ordered, uniform
leader as administrator
bonded by rules, policies
emphasis on predictability

Rational Culture
competitive, acquisitive
leader as goal-oriented
bonded by competition
emphasis on winning

Mechanistic-type processes
Focus on: control, order and stability

(in the range 0–100) for each individual on each of four cultural subtypes: clan, developmental, hierarchical, or rational (see Box).

The largest score on each cultural subtype defines that individual's dominant culture type; the actual value of this score represents the 'strength' of that dominant cultural type. The dominant culture type, strength, focus and orientation for an organization are calculated by aggregating across the individual scores of the senior management team.

In 2001 the CVF questionnaire was sent to the senior management team (i.e. members of the Executive Board) for all NHS acute hospital Trusts in England (197 organizations; 1,508 senior managers). This was repeated in 2006/07 and yielded culture data from 146 organizations; 1,214 individual respondents at executive board level.

Data analysis

Using data generated from the national survey, we compared changes in hospital culture over two periods – 2001/02 and 2006/07. Individual culture scores using the Competing Values Framework instrument were aggregated to team scores for each hospital. We tested for the appropriateness of aggregation using interclass-correlations and ANOVA and found acceptable levels of agreement. Results were weighted by the number of respondents per organization, though this made little difference.

Results

Changes in dominant culture types

Clan was the most dominant type of senior management team culture in both periods 2001 (53%) and 2007 (42%). (Figure 2.1). Followed by Rational

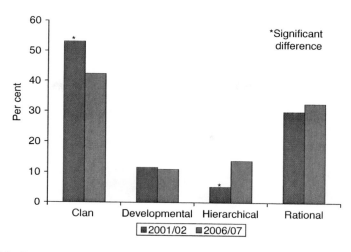

Figure 2.1 Dominant culture types for NHS hospital trusts (N = 187 for 2001/02 and N = 146 for 2006/07)

type cultures in both periods 2001 (30%) and 2007 (33%). The most significant change over the period is a reduction in clan-type cultures and a rise in Hierarchical cultures 2001 (4%) 2007 (13%).

In terms of distinguishing Internal *versus* External focus, and Mechanistic *versus* Relational orientation, the scores are shown in Figure 2.2. These simply add together the relevant average culture scores to form the new focus/orientation score. There was little change in the balance between Internal and External foci. However, there was a significant reduction in Relational and a significant increase in Mechanistic foci. Thus, between 2001–7, the dominant foci of attention was changed from Relational to Mechanistic for senior hospital managers in the NHS.

Discussion

Analysis of our data suggests that there has been a significant change in the nature of the managerial cultures in English acute care hospitals, with a decline in clan-type cultures accompanied by a concomitant rise in hierarchical and rational cultures, underpinned by a general shift away from organic towards mechanistic organizational processes within hospital Trusts. These changes broadly link with the set of values and behaviours expected in more market-oriented health care economies. While it is obviously very difficult to establish a simple causal link between changes in government policy over this period, not least because of the contradictory nature and sheer number of reforms in the NHS, it does appear that there may be some association between system reform and changes in the values and beliefs underpinning management behaviour in the NHS. Indeed the shift towards

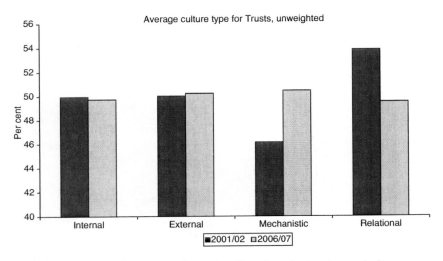

Figure 2.2   Average culture scores for each culture type for trust as a whole

hierarchical cultures may reflect the increased burden of external systems of checking, verification and audit that have grown up within the NHS over recent years, while the shift towards Rational cultures may reflect an increased emphasis on nurturing more competitive values in the organization. Of course, both apparent changes in the values underpinning management behaviour are consistent with a shift towards quasi-market systems in publicly funded services in which providers compete for contracts from publically funded sources and are subject to varying degrees of external regulation and assessment.

While we would in no way assume that the study of senior management team cultures can capture all the relevant dimensions of organizational culture, we feel that we are justified in focusing on this important cultural sub-group given the agenda setting powers and influence of the senior management team.

The rise of pro-market values within an organization that has traditionally been underpinned by a strong public service ethos raises a number of important issues for the future of health care delivery in England. For example, turning to recent work within the Institutional economics literature it is possible to speculate that a change in senior management culture can affect the behaviour and performance of health care organizations in at least four directions (Throsby, 2001; Kreps, 1990; Hodgson, 1996; Carrillo and Gromb, 1999; Hermalin, 2000; Smith et al., 2003):

- First, management cultures may drive economic *efficiency*, via the promotion of shared values and internalized norms within the organization, which in turn condition the ways in which the group's members engage and co-operate in the processes of production and exchange. Specific cultural values may be more or less conducive to (for example) co-operative and team-based working, competitive strategy, a consumer focus and entrepreneurial behaviour.

- Second, management cultures may affect *equity*, for example by being more or less supportive of inculcating shared moral principles of concern for others, and establishing organizational mechanisms that foster departures from purely efficiency-seeking behaviour.
- Third, management cultures may influence the overall *economic and social objectives* that an organization pursues. Thus, a culture based on public service values may be one of concern for employees and their working conditions and these values may mitigate the importance of surplus seeking, market share or other economic goals in the organization's objective function. Alternatively, more competitive and pro-market management cultures may value achieving externally set performance targets over the quality of the working lives of staff, or value their attainment more highly than areas of organizational performance that are not monitored by external agencies. The latter would appear to be in line with recent changes in management cultures in the NHS.
- Finally, where the interaction between agents is extremely complex – and difficult for either party to monitor the actions of their counterparts – management cultures may encourage *co-operation* and relationship-building among agents (intra- and inter- organizational partnership working). The process works through the creation and maintenance of *reputation*, where both parties signal their commitment to co-operation by articulating and adhering to identifiable sets of values.

Theoretical work within evolutionary and Institutional economics has also explored how the transition from traditional public service delivery to market mechanisms can affect the moral and value base underpinning (health) economic activity. For example Bowles (1998) in his article "Endogenous preferences; The cultural consequences of markets and other economic institutions" identifies five mediating cultural effects of market institutions and explores their influence on the evolution of values, tastes and behaviour:

1. *Framing and situational construal*: economic institutions are 'situations' in a social-psychological sense and can therefore influence the framing and situation construal of preferences; a choice in a market environment may be different from an identical choice framed in a non-market situation.
2. *Intrinsic and extrinsic motivations*: the reward systems of different institutions may affect motivation independently of framing effects. For example, an emphasis on external rewards associated with market competition and pay for performance arrangements may *crowd out* intrinsic

motivation when it is perceived to be controlling but *crowds in* intrinsic motivation when it is perceived to be supporting of self-determination and self-esteem. Indeed controlled experimental work in psychology (Deci and Ryan, 1987) has shown that the *crowding-out* effect (in other words the institution is perceived as controlling) is stronger where:

- The rewards are expected (unexpected rewards have a weaker effect, no effect or even negative effect on intrinsic motivation);
- The rewards are most salient;
- The rewards are contingent on task completion or on performance; and
- Deadlines and threats are used alongside intensive surveillance.

3. *Effects on the evolution of norms*: markets may influence the nature of social interactions and affect the evolution of norms by altering the returns to co-operative relationships. For example, the impersonal and ephemeral nature of market transactions in the delivery of health care may place less demands on individual's 'elevated motivations' and therefore affect the costs and benefits of acquiring cultural traits associated with socially desirable behaviours (e.g. altruism, trustworthiness or compassion).

4. *Task performance effects*: market institutions influence the tasks people face and therefore structure not only their capacities but their values and psychological functioning as well.

5. *Effects of the process of cultural transmission*: markets and other institutions affect enculteration processes and may influence how values and beliefs are absorbed and reproduced from one generation to another. The logic applies equally to the transmission of core cultural traits to new generations of employees within an organization over a period of time.

Concluding remarks

There is increasing international interest in managing organizational culture as a lever for health care improvement. To change the organizational culture along with its structure has become a familiar prescription in health system reform. Nowhere is this more apparent than in the English NHS, where the centralized administration of the organization has allowed opportunities for the national government to experiment with a 'top down' approach to instilling new values, beliefs and working relationships.

The rise of competitive values in the management of NHS hospitals aligns clearly with the implementation of the government's pro-market reform agenda. This apparent shift in management cultures across the NHS is more than a purely academic concern as it may hold profound practical consequences (both good and ill) for the planning, organization and delivery of local health services. The challenge for researchers is to identify and track the changing values that underpin managerial thinking in the NHS and to explore the implications of these changes for patients, health care organizations and local health care communities.

References

Bowles, S. (1998) 'Endogenous preferences: The cultural consequences of markets and other economic institutions', *Journal of Economic Literature*, 36, 75–111.

Broadbent, J. and Laughlin, R. et al. (1992) 'Recent financial and administrative changes in general practice. An unhealthy intrusion into medical autonomy', *Financial Accountability*, 8, 129–48.

Cameron, K. and Freeman, S. (1991) 'Culture, congruence, strength and type: Relationship to effectiveness', *Research in Organizational Change and Development*, 5, 23–58.

Carrillo, J.D. and Gromb, D. (1999) 'On the strength of corporate cultures', *European Economic Review*, 43, 1021–37.

Davies, H.T.O. (2002) 'Understanding organizational culture in reforming the National Health Service', *Journal of the Royal Society of Medicine*, 95, 140–2.

Davies, H.T.O. and Mannion, R. (2000) 'Clinical governance: Striking a balance between checking and trusting', in P.C. Smith (ed.), *Reforming Health Care Markets: An Economic Perspective*. Buckingham: Open University Press.

Davies, H.T.O, Nutley S.M. and Mannion, R. (2000) 'Organisational culture and quality of health care', *Quality in Health Care*, 9, 111–19.

Deci, E.L. and Ryan, R. (1987) 'The support of autonomy and the control of behaviour', *Journal of Personality and Social Psychology*, 53, 1024–37.

Department of Health (2001) *Learning from Bristol: The Department of Health's Response to the Report of the Public Inquiry into Children's Heart Surgery at the Bristol Royal Infirmary 1984–1995*. London: Department of Health.

DHSS (1984) *Health Services Management: Implementation of the NHS Management Inquiry*. London: DHSS.

Flynn, R. and Williams, G. (eds) (1997) *Contracting for Health: Quasi-Markets and the National Health Service*. Oxford: Oxford University Press.

Gerowitz, M.B. (1998) 'Do TQM interventions change management culture? Findings and implications', *Quality Management in Health Care*, 6 (3), 1–11.

Gerowitz, M.B. and Lemieux-Charles, L. et al. (1996) 'Top management culture and performance in Canadian, UK and US hospitals', *Health Services Management Research*, 9, 69–78.

Handy, C.B. (1985) *Understanding Organizations*, 3rd edn. Harmondsworth: Penguin.

Harrison, S. (1988) *Managing the National Health Service: Shifting the Frontier?* London: Chapman and Hall.

Harrison, S., Hunter, D.J., Marnoch, G. and Pollitt, C. (1992) *Just Managing: Power and Culture in the National Health Service*. London: Macmillan.

Harrison, S. and Lim, J. (2003) 'The frontier of control: Doctors and managers in the NHS 1966 to 1997', *Clinical Governance International*, 8 (2), 13–17.

Hermalin, B.E. (2000) *Economics and Corporate Culture*. UC Berkeley, Department of Economics working paper, University of California.

Hodgson, G.M. (1996) 'Corporate culture and the nature of the firm', in Groenewegen (ed.), *Transaction Cost Economics and Beyond*. Boston, MA: Kluwer Academic Press.

Institute of Medicine (1999) *To Err is Human: Building a Safer Health System*. Washington, DC: National Academy Press.

Jones, C. and Dewing, I. (1997) 'The attitudes of NHS clinicians and medical managers towards changes in accounting controls', *Financial Accountability and Management*, 13, 261–80.

Kennedy, I. (2001) *Learning from Bristol: Public Inquiry into Children's Heart Surgery at the Bristol Royal Infirmary 1984–1995*. London: Stationery Office, 2001.

Kreps, D.M. (1990) 'Corporate culture and economic theory', in J.E. Alt and K.A. Shepsle (eds), *Perspectives on Positive Political Economy*. Cambridge: Cambridge University Press.

Le Grand, J. and Mays, N. et al. (eds) (1998) *Learning from the NHS Internal Market: A Review of the Evidence*. London: King's Fund.

Mannion, R., Davies, H.T.O. and Marshall, M.N. (2005a) 'Cultural attributes of "high" and "low" performing hospitals', *Journal of Health Organization and Management*, 1 (6), 431–9.

Mannion, R., Davies, H.T.O. and Marshall, M.N. (2005b), *Cultures for Performance in Health Care*. Milton Keynes: Open University Press.

Mannion, R., Goddard, M. and Bate, A. (2007) 'Aligning incentives and motivations in health care', *Financial Accountability and Management*, 23 (4), 401–20.

Mannion, R. (2008) 'General Practitioner commissioning in the English National Health Service: Continuity, change and future challenges', *International Journal of Health Services*, 38 (4), 717–30.

Mannion, R. and Street, A. (2009) 'Managing activity and expenditure in the new NHS market', *Public Money and Management*, 29 (1), 27–34. Marquand, D. (1988) *The Unprincipled Society: New Demands and Old Politics*. London: Jonathan Cape.

Marquand, D. (1988) *The Unprincipled Society*. London: Fontana Press.

Mintzberg, H. (1991) 'The Professional Organisation', in Mintzberg, H. and Quinn, J.B. (eds), *The Strategy Process: Concepts, Contexts, Cases*. 2nd edn. London: Prentice Hall.

NHS Management Inquiry (1983) *Report* (Chairman Mr ER Griffiths). London: Department of Health.

Pettigrew, A.M., Ferlie, E. and McKee, L. (1992) *Shaping Strategic Change: Making Change in Large Organisations – the Case of the NHS*. London: Sage.

Scott, J.T., Mannion, R. and Marshall, M.N. (2003a) *Healthcare Performance and Organisational Culture*. Oxford: Radcliffe Medical Press.

Scott, T. and Mannion, R., et al. (2003b) 'The quantitative measurement of organizational culture in health care: A review of the available instruments', *Health Services Research*, 38 (3), 923–45.

Shortell, S. and Jones, R. et al. (2000) 'Assessing the impact of total quality management and organizational culture on multiple outcomes of care for coronary artery bypass graft surgery patients', *Medical Care*, 38 (2), 201–17.

Smith, P. (ed.) (2002) Measuring Up: improving health system performance in OECD countries. Paris: OECD.

Smith, P., Mannion, R. and Goddard, M. (2003) Performance Management in Health Care: Information, Incentives and Culture, HM Treasury Public Services Productivity Discussion Papers. London: HM Treasury.

Throsby, D. (2001) *Economics and Culture*. Cambridge: Cambridge University Press.

3
Culture Made Flesh: Discourse, Performativity and Materiality

Tim Freeman and Edward Peck

Introduction

Health care organizational culture(s)

Since the election of a Labour government in 1997, UK health policy has been characterized by a series of change initiatives under the general rubric of modernization. Strategies have included changes to formal governance structures such as joint-commissioning (Glendinning et al., 2002) and foundation hospital status (DH, 2002a); quasi-market and incentives systems such as payment by results (DH, 2002b); and changes to staff roles and tasks under re-design initiatives (IHI, 2003; Ovretveit et al., 2002). It is within this policy context that the concept of organizational culture gained importance – the assumption being that it may provide a binding force helping to secure commitment to, and behaviour congruent with, policy requirements seeking to significantly alter the balance of power between professional and managerial interests. Indeed, calls to change organizational culture alongside structural reforms have become a familiar prescription for health system reform (Donaldson and Gray, 1998). Yet, serious questions may be raised about the nature of organizational culture implied by such prescriptions, most crucially its degree of homogeneity and the extent to which it may be directly 'steered'.

Policy prescriptions for the direct management of organizational culture draw on functionalist accounts (Smircich, 1983; Smircich and Calas, 1987), presenting culture as a unitary collective consciousness that can be discovered, measured and manipulated: a series of internalized norms that may be considered a controllable variable (Deal and Kennedy, 1982; Peters and Waterman, 1982; Schein, 1992). Here, culture is measured by attitudes, values and beliefs: it is something organizations have, carried in individuals' heads. In contrast, interpretivist approaches conceive of organizations as constructed by, and constitutive of, patterns of relationships and meaning; organizational culture is a 'way of life' within a particular setting, a way of thinking about organizational reality (Meek, 1988; Hatch, 1997). Here, culture is measured by examining practices, rituals and accountabilities (Peck et al., 2004): it is something organizations are and do, dynamically and collectively, the emphasis being on a continuous process of organizing (Bate, 1994).

Quantitative empirical studies tend to be broadly functionalist, summarizing culture as a relatively stable, multidimensional and holistic construct shared by groups of organizational members supplying a frame of reference giving meaning to, or revealed in, certain practices (Guldenmund, 2000). Cultures are conceptualized as reciprocal and integrating and consist of various aspects, so that several may be distinguished within an organization such as 'safety climate' (Coyle et al., 1995), 'innovation climate' (Ekval and Ryhammer, 1999) or 'clinical governance climate' (Freeman, 2003). Yet, within this empirical literature there is also a general acceptance that organizations may contain multiple 'cultures' within different divisions/ departments and groups, especially so in the case of complex professional bureaucracies, so that the issue of aggregation becomes an important methodological consideration (Hofstede et al., 1990; Keeton and Mengistu, 1992; Helms and Stern, 2001). It is difficult to overstate the cultural complexity of health care organizations. Indeed, the mix of managerial and professional staff groups in which multiple values co-exist, together with power imbalances among the various stakeholders, has long been presented as a distinctive feature of the UK NHS (Harrison et al., 1992; Pollitt, 1993; Dawson, 1999; Davies et al., 2000; Degeling et al., 2001).

Subtle reviews of managed organizational culture acknowledge the functionalist/interpretivist oppositional framing and purport to offer a middle path that retains the promise of culture management of functionalist accounts while acknowledging some of the complexities identified in the interpretivist literature (Mannion et al., 2003; 2005; Scott et al., 2003). Challenges to assumptions of cultural homogeneity (Martin, 2002; Meyerson and Martin, 2002) are accepted and the emergent property of organizational culture, and therefore a limit to its direction and control, is also acknowledged. However, the approach has been criticized for failing to appreciate the full implications of interpretivism (Ormrod, 2003). In this regard, we believe that Judith Butler's work on performativity (Butler, 1990; 1993; 1997) has much to offer researchers and practitioners interested in organizational culture. Writing within a post-structuralist tradition, her approach explicitly incorporates temporal and inter-subjective dimensions of (dis)continuity, offering a course between determinism and voluntarism in cultural reproduction through notions of performativity, citation and reiteration. In the following sections, we offer an introduction to Butlerian performativity, apply the theoretical lens to material collected as part of an earlier study of partnership governance, and consider the general implications for culture change initiatives.

Performativity and material citation

Within mainstream organizational theory, performativity is generally understood as the ability to produce goods effectively, critically reinterpreted by Lyotard (1984) as those techniques and modes of regulation that mobilize comparisons in performance as a means of influence or control. Judith Butler's approach is rather different, performativity defined as 'the reiterative and citational practice by which discourse produces the effects that it names' (Butler, 1993: 2). Crucial to the development of Butler's analysis is the notion of citationality or iterability, which offers an account of that which mediates between social norms and the individuals performing them. Indeed, the distinctive function of the performative is its *productive* role:

> Performativity is neither free-play nor theatrical self-presentation; nor can it simply be equated with performance. Performativity cannot be understood outside a process of iterability, a regularized and constrained repetition of norms. And this repetition is not performed **by** a subject; this repetition is what enables a subject and constitutes the temporal condition for a subject. (Butler, 1993: 95)

The implication is that possibilities for social action are contextually circumscribed, and that possibilities for agency arise out of institutional constructions (Hasselbladh and Bejerot, 2007), in which individuals embody subject-positions. On this reading, organizational environments serve as contexts for iterations of required behaviours and the citation of norms create and discipline subjectivities and inter-relations, through reiteration over time. Boldly stated, cultural (re)production depends upon the embodied, iterative citation of organizational norms and values, under the gaze of interlocutors.

This might suggest the over-determination of social life – actors doing little other than what is required of them – yet this is not the case. In elaborating her position, Butler draws on Derrida's critical commentary on the metaphysics of presence, replacing the logic of essence (fixity) with that of the supplement, in which citations are open and consist of (and are haunted by) traces of other citations (Derrida, 1984). On this view, no action or speech may be fully present; rather, signification is produced through iteration and citation of prior actions, so that actions acquire meanings relative to other actions (relational) and over time (temporal). Iterability encapsulates both 'repetition' (sameness) and 'alterity' (difference) simultaneously – and any given performance (instantiation) may be characterized as an embodied (and thus material) singularity at the head of a chain of prior iterations. Crucially, the instability and indeterminacy of citation implies scope for interpretation (and thus cultural change) within every single iteration. Thus, while iteration is suggestive of recurrent patterning, there is no assumption that there is a natural state which instances merely reflect.

On the contrary, the need for iteration calls attention to the lack of such a foundation existing prior to instantiation – and it is the very lack of such an essence that demands performative enactment (Borgerson, 2005).

The materiality of discourse considered above is in contrast to those voluntaristic accounts which characterize discourse as principally linguistic/ideational, resulting from subjective mental events (Hindess and Hirst, 1977). Such ideation suggests the possibility of infinite free-play in which transcendent agents construct new discourses at will. While the attraction of voluntarism is obvious to those charged with cultural change (and its congruence with 'transformational change' literature and 'charismatic' theories of leadership all too apparent), Derrida is dismissive of such linguistic/ideational readings (Derrida, 1984). Indeed, while the logic of the supplement considered in the previous paragraph implies that processes of signification will be perpetual – there can be no 'finality' to the overflow of meaning – partial fixations may be generated socially (Laclau and Mouffe, 1985). In other words, the indeterminacy in signification is socially bounded, so that discourses are formed though (unstable) regularities in signification which provide an ensemble of differentiated positions, relationally constituted and reiterated over time. The means of cultural (re)production is thus materially embodied, citational performance.

Given the bounded indeterminacy above, there is considerable scope for performative misfire – for instantiations which do not 'bring off' the required enactment and which open the door to challenge. In a recent paper, the authors presented a new institutionalist analysis of a joint commissioning partnership board [JCPB] (Freeman and Peck, 2007), charged with the governance of mental health provision within a UK county. Our approach drew on a dramaturgical framework (Hajer, 2004; 2005), within the tradition of organizational studies as theatre (Goffman, 1959; Mangham and Overington, 1983; 1987; Schreyogg and Hopfl, 2004). We offer below a re-analysis of a seminal event in the life of the partnership board – the rejection of a mental health strategy paper presented for ratification – through the lens of Butlerian performativity, and consider its implications for the study of organizational culture. The national and local contexts of partnership board governance are briefly introduced and the symbolic order of the JCPB outlined, as a prelude to a consideration of the performative misfire that led the board to reject the strategy.

Not quite doing the business – performative misfire at a partnership board

The national (UK) context

In the UK, complex multi-agency partnership arrangements are associated with a managerialist turn in public policy in which complex social problems were recast as requiring the management of cross-system goals, necessitating collaborative action across multiple agencies, professional groups and active citizens, and envisaged as broad, diverse and inclusive partnerships (Clarke and Stewart, 1997). The conjunction between service delivery fragmentation following earlier privatization of public service provision and a political imperative to combat issues cutting across the boundaries of a fragmented organizational landscape required partnership arrangements in order to facilitate negotiation and delivery of public programmes (Skelcher, 2000). Common across multiple UK social policy arenas, partnerships cover a multitude of both mandatory and voluntary arrangements between public, private and voluntary agencies and service users.

The local context

Full details may be found in our earlier paper (Freeman and Peck, 2007). Briefly, The county council and its National Health Service (NHS) partners reached agreement to establish a range of partnerships under Section 31 of the Health Act (1999), relating to mental health, learning disability, drug and alcohol, and child and adolescent mental health services (CAMHS). Arrangements included integrated provision via a local Partnership NHS Trust offering county-wide services; pooled commissioning and provision budgets; and joint-commissioning arrangements. A pooled commissioning budget was formed for each of the care groups across the county and hosted by the County Council, the partnership agreement delegating decision-making to a quarterly JCPB, whose membership, at inception, included eight county councillors and eight Primary Care Trust (PCT) non-executives, with up to four co-opted members, including the strategic health authority and formal observers from the voluntary sector. PCTs are local NHS bodies with responsibility for commissioning and potentially also providing health care services within a defined geographical area, and the partnership arrangements meant that county-wide services were commissioned jointly by the JCPB. The JCPB was supported by a Joint Commissioning Team (JCT), hosted by the County Council and charged with preparing items and papers.

The symbolic order of the JCPB

JCPB meetings were highly formal events, closely following the expected custom and practice of formal County Council meetings. A written agenda and associated reports and appendices were circulated ahead of the meeting together with a copy of the previous meeting's minutes as recorded by the committee secretary. At the start of each meeting, members were asked to review the circulated minutes as an accurate record and suggest any required changes or clarifications. The formal nature of proceedings was matched by the physical environment – meetings were held in a formal committee room in which committee members were seated at a table that filled the length of the chamber (approximately 15 metres long) and necessitated the use of microphone amplification to allow participants to hear each other speak. The layout was a physical manifestation of the committee's adversarial nature.

While all board members were used to formal meetings, there appeared to be an important dichotomy in participants' style: crudely put, while PCT members were typically used to consensus building, County Council members were used to political/adversarial approaches, the latter model predominating. The formal, political and adversarial operation of the JCPB emphasized the oversight and scrutiny of managers' reports, at officer briefing meetings held a few days before the formal board meeting. While the briefings are clearly concerned with provision of information to members to inform board decision-making, elements of 'performance' inherent in the process are clearly acknowledged by participants – and the particular combination of adversarial and theatrical evident in JCPB decision-making cycles meant that officers challenged at the briefing could anticipate public challenge at the subsequent formal board meeting.

Subject-positions available to JCPB board members

County Council officers and PCT non-executive members typically have rather different assumptions of the proper discharge of their roles – of how business gets done. County Council members are elected representatives charged with representing their constituents, making policy, and controlling the executive. Traditionally, they carry a defined portfolio of responsibilities, over time developing a detailed understanding of a particular policy arena, supported by systems of briefings from council officers, and meetings are typically conducted in a robust and adversarial fashion. In marked contrast, PCT non-executive directors (NED) operate as business-style non-executives; they are generalists, typically without a professional background relating to health care. There is no equivalent officer briefing system within health care trusts, nor do NEDs typically work on a portfolio basis. In addition, PCT boards typically pursue strategy formation in a consensual manner, involving members at early stages in contexts outside of the main board meeting and going through multiple iterations before being placed before the board for a final decision. The very different prior practices and role assumptions of county council and PCT representatives had a profound impact on the partnership forum, the assumption of the County Council model constructing PCT members as incapable of discharging decision-making responsibilities. Many PCT representatives expressed considerable vulnerability, interpreted by their County Council colleagues as inability.

In a previous paper (Freeman and Peck, 2007), we presented these difficulties as indicative of a tension between the representational and technical roles of the PCT members. While such members were clearly identified as important in representing the interests of their various organizations, their 'lay representative' status, in the absence of particular expertise in the subject area, led to difficulties in decision-making. PCT representatives faced an additional tension posed by the dual requirement to represent their organization while simultaneously commissioning services for the whole county – requiring them to support disinvestment in services in their own areas in order to improve county-wide services. We consider below the implications of these various cultural assumptions for the governance of strategy formation at the JCPB, drawing on the rejection of the Adult Mental Health (AMH) strategy for illustrative purposes, a seminal event in the JCPB which we present as a performative misfire.

Performative misfire – the case of the Adult Mental Health Strategy

Very different fates befell two strategy documents presented before the JCPB for consideration. While the Child and Adolescent Mental Health Services strategy was passed with no amendment, the Adult Mental Health strategy was rejected. Both were developed without the substantive involvement of the JCPB, which rules out non-involvement as an explanation. One plausible explanation is their different degree of conformance to expectations of content and presentation. Significant cultural transgressions in the AMH strategy included failure to anticipate officers' questions within the text, to conform to expected content style, and (possibly fatally) a presumption of acceptance without attending to expected levels of detail, and thus failing to defend against adversarial exchange. This last was particularly significant as it directly challenged the JCPB's scrutiny role. The formal rejection of the mental health strategy, occasioned by the transgression of expected aspects of presentation outlined above, was enacted through a highly ritualized encounter within the symbolic arena of the board meeting. Qualitative field notes show that the officer's presentation drew combative non-verbal behaviour (drawing attention to watches; shaking of watches and 'listening' to check if they had stopped) followed by 15 exchanges from eight board members rejecting the strategy and raising the need for 'away days' to inform future strategy development, after which the officer simply apologized when asked to comment. The mental health strategy was rejected due to a failure to conduct the required symbolic work or to instantiate the required subject-position (i.e. a robust defence of the paper in adversarial exchange), drawing a negative response from the board due to the failure to comply with the discursive demands of the context.

Discussion

While conceptual distinctions may seem rarefied, they have important policy implications with import well beyond the academy. Culture as attribute holds the possibility of its manipulation in line with particular corporate objectives; an attractive proposition to managers charged with implementing mandated policy reforms. In contrast, organizations conceptualized as cultural systems have considerably reduced potential for the direct management of culture. The mechanistic metaphor breaks down; it is not that the levers are difficult to identify, but in an indeterminate world, they do not have consistent effects when pulled.

The Butlerian approach to organizational culture(s) explored above, drawing on performativity as material citation, may be uncomfortable for those charged with the implementation of broad-based cultural change initiatives. Yet, its implications are clear. Principally, these relate to limitations on the extent to which clear visions for organization change may be articulated, and the degree of scope for agentic behaviour on the part of putative leaders of organizational change.

It is a commonplace that leaders of cultural change initiatives are exhorted to articulate a clear vision of the future. Yet, this is radically problematized if we accept Butler's critique, a la Derrida, of the metaphysics of presence. If text and embodied performance(s) are indeterminate citations of prior text and performance, then any attempt to articulate a future vision is open to the possibility of alternative interpretation. We do not mean to suggest that it is futile to envision alternatives; rather, that account needs to be taken of the indeterminate nature of signification. On this view, prescriptions and visions of change are not fully present but remain haunted by chains of signification that remain elusive – less an ontology than a 'hauntology', in which presence/absence are mutually constitutive. Any attempt to envision an alternative state will thus require continuous (re)statement and is likely to be challenged by alternative possibilities. Vision cannot be 'fixed'; that is, its articulation is an elusive, citational process not simply the first stage in a linear sequence of events, culminating in a stable change in culture from state x to state y. In contrast to accounts of planned cultural change presented as unfreezing, changing and re-freezing (Lewin, 1958), the implication is that cultures are in a constant state of re-enactment. Change is a precondition of organization.

Further, those charged with leading cultural change initiatives need to consider and attend to the interpretations of proposed changes which are likely to be made from alternative subject-positions. By this, we mean those rival (unstable) regularities in signification providing an ensemble of differentiated positions. While ideational/voluntaristic readings of discourse formation may encourage leaders to believe that they may simply generate new ways of thinking/working, these ideas will themselves be interpreted from the perspectives of available alternative subject-positions (Peck *et al* in press). Challenges to any new cultural vision will themselves be instantiations at the head of a chain of citations, drawn from available discourses. In our case study example, the mental health strategy was rejected due to the failure to embody the required institutional norms associated with adversarial governance – failure to observe institutional conventions led to rejection of the strategy document.

Conclusion

Policy prescriptions for organizational culture change are typically functionalist, and assume that cultures are attributes of organizations which may be influenced with a degree of predictability. In contrast, interpretivist approaches suggest that the task is not to influence a pre-existent entity (the organization), but to attend to broad processes of organizing. We offer Butlerian performativity as a potentially useful approach to the study of organizational culture(s), calling attention to the citational and embodied character of processes of organizing, and capable of exploring continuity and change in complex social arenas. Our intention is not to provide a counsel of despair. Rather, in challenging a number of assumptions associated with functionalist-based culture change initiatives, we seek to encourage more subtle readings of organizational culture(s), and their processes of organizing.

References

Bate, P. (1994) *Strategies for Cultural Change*. Oxford: Butterworth-Heinemann.

Borgerson, J. (2005) 'On organizing subjectivities', *The Sociological Review*, 53, 63–79.

Butler, J. (1990) *Gender Trouble: Feminism and the Subversion of Identity*. London: Routledge.

Butler, J. (1993) *Bodies That Matter: On the Discursive Limits of "Sex"*. London: Routledge.

Butler, J. (1997) *Excitable Speech: A Politics of the Performative*. London: Routledge.

Clarke, M. and Stewart, J.S. (1997) *Partnership and the Management of Co-operation*. Birmingham: Institute of Local Government Studies, University of Birmingham.

Coyle, I.R., Sleeman, S.D. and Adams, N. (1995) 'Safety climate', *Journal of Safety Research*, 26 (4), 247–54.

Davies, H.T.O., Nutley, S. and Mannion, R. (2000) 'Organisational culture and quality of health care', *Quality in Health Care*, 9, 111–19.

Dawson, S. (1999) 'Managing, organising and performing in health care: What do we know and how can we learn?' in Mark A. and Dopson S. (eds), *Organisational Behaviour in Health Care*. London: Macmillan.

Deal, T.E. and Kennedy, A.A. (1982) *Corporate cultures*. Reading, MA: Addison-Wesley.

Degeling, P., Kennedy, J. and Hill, M. (2001) 'Mediating the cultural boundaries between medicine, nursing and management – the central challenge in hospital reform', *Health Services Management Research*, 14, 36–48.

Department of Health (2002a) *NHS Foundation Trusts*. London: DoH.

Department of Health (2002b) *Reforming NHS Financial Flows. Introducing Payment by Results*. London: DoH.

Derrida, J. (1984) 'Deconstruction and the other: Interview with Richard Kearney', in R. Kearney (ed.), *Dialogues with Contemporary Continental Thinkers*, Manchester: Manchester University Press, 107–25.

Donaldson, L.J. and Gray, J.A.M. (1998) 'Clinical governance: A quality duty for health organisations', *Quality in Health* Care, 7 Suppl.: S37–44.

Ekval, G. and Ryhammer, L. (1999) 'The creative climate: Its determinants and effects at a Swedish university', *Creativity Research Journal*, 12 (4), 303–10.

Freeman, T. (2003) 'Measuring progress in clinical governance: Assessing the reliability and validity of the Clinical Governance Climate Questionnaire', *Health Services Management Research*, 16, 234–50.

Freeman, T. and Peck, E. (2007) 'Performing governance: A partnership board dramaturgy', *Public Administration*, 85 (4), 907–29.

Glendinning, C., Hudson, B., Hardy, B. and Young, R. (2002) *National Evaluation of Notifications for Use of the Section 31 Partnership Flexibilities in the Health Act 1999. Final Project Report*. Manchester: NPCRDC.

Goffman, E. (1959) *The Presentation of Self in Everyday Life*. New York: Anchor-Doubleday.

Guldenmund, F.W. (2000) 'The nature of safety culture: A review of theory and research', *Safety Science*, 34, 215–57.

Hajer, M. (2004) *Setting the Stage: A Dramaturgy of Policy Implementation*. Amsterdam School for Social Science Research Working Paper 04/06. Amsterdam: University of Amsterdam.

Hajer, M. (2005) 'Setting the Stage: A Dramaturgy of Policy Deliberation', *Administration and Society*, 36 (6), 24–47.

Harrison, S., Hunter, D., Marnoch, G. and Pollitt, C. (1992) *Just Managing: Power and Culture in the National Health Service*. London: Macmillan.

Hasselbladh, H. and Bejerot, E. (2007) 'Webs of knowledge and Circuits of Communication: Constructing Rationalized Agency in Swedish Health Care'. *Organization* 14 (2), 175–200.

Hatch, M. (1997) *Organisation Theory: Modern, Symbolic and Post-Modern Perspectives*. Oxford: Oxford University Press.

Hindess, B. and Hirst, P. (1997) *Mode of Production and Social Formation*. London: Macmillan

Hofstede, G.R., Neuijen, B., Ohayv, D.D. and Sanders, G. (1990) 'Measuring organisational cultures: A quantitative and qualitative study across twenty sites', *Administrative Science Quarterly*, 35, 286–316.

Helms, M. and Stern, R. (2001) 'Exploring the factors that influence employees' perceptions of their organisation's culture', *Journal of Management in Medicine*, 15 (6), 415–29.

Institute for Health Improvement (2003) *The Breakthrough Series: IHI's Collaborative Model for Achieving Breakthrough Improvement*. Boston, MA: IHI.

Keeton, K. and Mengistu, B. (1992) 'The perception of organisational culture by management level: Implications for training and development', *Public Productivity and Management Review*, 16 (2), 205–13.

Laclau, E. and Mouffe, C. (1985) *Hegemony and Socialist Strategies: Towards a Radical Democratic Politics*. London: Verso.

Lewin, K. (1958) 'Group decisions and social change', in G.E. Swanson, T.M. Newcomb and E.L. Hartley (eds), *Readings in Social Psychology*. New York: Holt Reinhart and Winston.

Lyotard, J.F. (1984) *The Postmodern Condition: A Report on Knowledge*, vol. 10. Manchester: Manchester University Press.

Mangham, I. and Overington, M. (1983) 'Dramatism and the theatrical metaphor', in G. Morgan (ed.), *Beyond Method*. London: Sage.

Mangham, I. and Overington, M. (1987) *Organisations as Theatre: A Sociology of Dramatic Appearances*. Chichester: Wiley.

Mannion, R., Davies, H.T.O. and Marshall, M.N. (2003) *Cultures for Performance in Health Care: Evidence on the Relationship Between Organisational Culture and Organisational Performance in the NHS*. York: University of York.

Mannion, R., Davies, H.T.O. and Marshall, M. (2005) *Cultures for Performance in Health Care.* Maidenhead: Open University Press.

Martin, J. (2002) *Organizational Culture: Mapping the Terrain.* Thousand Oaks, CA: Sage.

Meek, L. (1988) 'Organisational culture: Origins and weaknesses', *Organization Studies*, 9 (4), 453–73.

Meyerson, D. and Martin, J. (1987) 'Cultural change: An integration of three different views', *Journal of Management Studies*, 24 (6), 623–43.

Ormrod, S. (2003) 'Organisational culture in health service policy and research: 'Third way' political fad or policy development', *Policy and Politics*, 31, 227–37.

Øvretveit, J., Bate, P., Cleary, P., Cretin, S., Gustafson, D., McInnes, K., McLeod, H., Molfenter, T., Plsek, P., Robert, G., Shortell, S. and Wilson, T. (2002) 'Quality collaboratives: Lessons from research', *Quality and Safety in Health Care*, 11, 345–51.

Peck, E., 6, P., Gulliver, P. and Towell, D. (2004) 'Why do we keep meeting like this? The board as ritual in health and social care', *Health Services management Research*, 17, 100–9.

Peck, E., Freeman, T., 6, P. and Dickinson, H. (2009) "Performing leadership: Towards a new research agenda in leadership studies", *Leadership*, 5(1): 25–40.

Peters, T. and Waterman, R. (1982) *In Search of Excellence: Lessons from America's Best Run Companies.* New York: Harper Row.

Pollitt, C. (1993) 'The struggle for quality: The case of the NHS', *Policy and Politics*, 21 (3), 161–70.

Schein, E.H. (1992) *Organisational Culture and Leadership.* San Francisco, CA: Jossey-Bass.

Scott, J.T., Mannion, R., Davies, H.T.O. and Marshall, M.N. (2003) 'The quantitative measurement of organisational culture in health care: What instruments are available?' *Health Services Research*, 38 (3), 923–45.

Skelcher, C. (2000) 'Changing Images of the State: Overloaded, Hollowed-out, Congested', *Public Policy and Administration*, 15 (2), 3–19.

Smircich, L. (1983) 'Concepts of culture and organizational analysis', *Administrative Science Quarterly*, 28, 339–58.

Smircich, L. and Calas, M. (1987) 'Organisational culture: A critical assessment', in F. Jablin, L. Putnam, K. Roberts and L. Porter (eds), *Handbook of Organisational Communication: An Interdisciplinary Perspective.* Newbury Park, CA: Sage.

Schreyogg, G. and Hopfl, H. (2004) 'Theatre and organization: Editorial introduction', *Organization Studies*, 25, 691–704.

Part II
Relationships and Collaboration

4
Organizational-Professional Conflict in Medicine

Anneke Fitzgerald and Ann Dadich

Introduction

Since the 1980s, the political landscape of many western nations has reformed the public service and associated agencies, with the aim of making the national economy internationally competitive (Van Gramberg and Bassett, 2005). Despite its focus on and interest in the market sector, the neo-liberalist agenda has permeated health care (Martinez and Garcia, 1997). It has altered perceptions of effective management from the health of the patient to the health of the organization – a change that has been witnessed in the United Kingdom, the United States, Canada, New Zealand, and Australia (Harden, 2000; Terris, 1999; Donelan et al., 1999).

To improve the efficiency of Australian public health care services, new strategies have been introduced, including the introduction of clinician-managers (NSW Health, 2000). This hybrid role is thought to have the capacity to reconcile medical priorities with organizational concerns. However, clinicians have a strong professional identity (Freidson, 1994; Illich, 1984) and it might not be easily swayed by organizational concerns.

The aim of this chapter is to examine the role of clinician-managers in uniting two distinct occupational cultures, and thus help to achieve efficiency in the hospital setting. Informed by the work of others (Holt and Kabanoff, 1995; O'Reilly and Chatman, 1986; Meyer and Allan, 1984; Degeling et al., 1998), the chapter explores three constructs of professional identity – professional experience, sense of belonging to place of employment, and professional value systems. This is achieved through a survey of hospital personnel, including managers, clinicians and clinician-managers. The research findings demonstrate that government efforts to align organizational and professional ideologies might have severe consequences. However, before details of this study are presented, it is important to understand the relationship between neo-liberalism, health care and professional identity. This is presented in the following section.

Neo-liberalism and Health Care

Akin to other western nations (McGregor, 2001), neo-liberalism has made a sizeable mark on the Australian health care sector. Reduced government funding to public hospitals has translated into increasing competition, not only with each other, but also with profitable health care enterprises. Additionally, government bodies are paying closer attention to hospital activities, demanding greater accountability from public hospitals (Hamilton and Maddison, 2007). Furthermore, the Australian public service has lost its independence and become increasingly dominated by government interests (Keating, 1999).

For a public hospital, neo-liberalism can be difficult to negotiate. To improve the efficiency of limited health care funds, a number of public hospitals in New South Wales (NSW), Australia have appointed clinicians as managers (NSW Health, 2000). These appointments have the potential to narrow rifts that divide management, professional subordinates, and the wider community. Armed with clinical credibility and management muscle, the clinician-manager can serve as a nexus between those interested in patient health and those interested in hospital health. It thus appears that the hybrid role can benefit both the professional and the organization (Lorsch and Mathias, 1988; Raelin, 1986).

However, sociological literature has long recognized the domination and autonomy of the medical profession, acknowledging that much of the health care sector is directed, either explicitly or implicitly, by the medical profession (Illich, 1977; Freidson, 1994; Illich, 1984). A well-defined professional identity decreases *organisational-professional conflict* (Sorensen, 1967). With a strong affiliation to a given profession, an individual is unlikely to be lured into a conflicting value system that is espoused by an organization.

Organizational-professional conflict

According to Parry and Murphy (2005), organizational-professional conflict is:

> the term used to describe the situation that occurs when an organization's values are incompatible with the professional values of its professional employees

Organizational-professional conflict can be problematic for both the professional and the organization (Gunz and Gunz, 1994). Torn between a sense of loyalty to the profession and a sense of loyalty to the organization, the professional is vulnerable to emotional torment (Aranya and Ferris, 1984). He or she might be required to juggle professional ethics with the organization's bottom line (Brierley and Cowton, 2000). The development of new or different skills may challenge the professional and cause original professional capacities to wane – that is, the individual becomes *deprofessionalized* when the organization requires him or her to give preference to organizational goals, rather than professional goals (Parry and Murphy, 2005). The individual might also be faced with rejection from professional peers for having joined the *dark side*. These challenges, individually or collectively, have the potential to increase job-related stress, reduce job-satisfaction, diminish quality performance, and increase staff turnover (Gouldner, 1957; Wilensky, 1956; Senatra, 1980) – all of which are unwelcome news for most organizations.

Literature on organizational-professional conflict suggests that a clear distinction between organizational and professional values is preferable – this is verified by the use of the value-laden term *conflict*.

However, there are also arguments to suggest that congruence between these two value systems is advantageous (Hefner, 1994). By aligning the professional with the organization – for instance, through the appointment of professionals as managers, both the professional and the organization benefit from the consequent synergy (Lorsch and Mathias, 1988; Raelin, 1986).

From the professional's perspective, some argue that non-professional managers who supervise them cannot give meaningful direction as they lack substantive expertise (Lea and Brostrom, 1988; Rosenbaum, 1991). However, the professional-*cum*-manager role has the ability to overcome this rift; those appointed to this hybrid role can connect with professional subordinates and provide valuable supervision. Furthermore, the hybrid role provides professionals with insight into the governance, management and operation of the environment in which they work; it also enables them to engage in dialogue with other managers and bureaucrats, and in turn, influence policy development within the organization (Kippist and Fitzgerald, 2006; Iedema et al., 2003).

The professional-*cum*-manager role can also benefit the organization (Harrison, 1976). The hybrid role allows the organization to utilize professional expertise in policy development, which in turn, helps to ensure that policies are well-informed (Iedema et al., 2003). It expands the professional networks available to other managers and bureaucrats. It also helps the organization implement reform (NSW Health, 2000) – the professional-*cum*-manager can serve as a conduit between bureaucrats and professional subordinates, helping to make organizational change more palatable at the coalface. The professional-*cum*-manager can also help to rally public support for reform – as a professional committed to the service of the public, above and beyond material incentives (Larson, 1977; Vollmer and Mills, 1966; Moore, 1970), the professional-*cum*-manager is well-positioned to present organizational change that might concern the wider community.

Collectively, these advantages suggest that the hybrid role of professional-*cum*-manager has the potential to enhance congruence between organizational and professional values and redress the *us-versus-them* mentality.

Clinician-managers

Some government bodies have attempted to harness these benefits. Pressured by neo-liberalism, they have implemented strategies to improve the efficiency of government services.

The NSW state government is cognizant of two key issues that its health department must reconcile – 'the growing interference of non-medical (mostly financial) administrators into the clinical domain of hospitals ... [and the availability of] finite health care resources to meet a growing demand, [especially] when there is continuing evidence that the efficiency and quality of health care can be improved' (NSW Health, 2000). The answer is alleged to be found in 'a change in the relationship between managers and clinicians to create a collegiate, accountable and patient-centred culture for the State's health care system'. This translates to a recommendation that the health department 'expand its training programs for clinicians in the areas of health care financing, management and information technology, [which includes] ... sponsoring selected senior clinicians to participate in leading executive management programs'. Evidently, this change has involved the appointment of doctors into salaried (rather than contracted) managerial roles within the hospital setting. In fact, each NSW public hospital now has several clinician-managers.

Among the benefits associated with the hybrid roles, government rhetoric highlights an ability to work more effectively with clinicians and engage them in hospital management – this in turn, is assumed to 'improve health outcomes and/or improve the cost-effectiveness of health care.'

But *how does the hybrid role assumed by clinician-managers influence their professional identity – that is, the way they view themselves, their perception of others*, and *the perception others have of them*? Does it amplify the inherent conflict between organizational values and professional values; or does it dilute a professional identity that is alleged to be robust?

Ostensibly, the hospital setting appears to be a fertile ground for organizational-professional conflict. In accordance with existing literature (Gunz and Gunz, 1994; Aranya and Ferris, 1984), it appears that current government policy (NSW Health, 2000) may inadvertently be encouraging organizational-professional conflict. While managers characteristically want to demonstrate performance as quickly as possible (Raelin, 1986), doctors, like most professionals, appreciate the need for protracted thought and action (Hayes and Fitzgerald, 2007; Hefner, 1994).

To date, no empirical investigation has explored this question. Consequently, government efforts that aspire to achieve congruence between organizational and professional ideologies remain ill-informed.

Heeding the call for further research from Parry and Murphy (2005), this chapter begins to fill this void by examining the professional identities and working alliances of hospital personnel within the NSW public hospital system. This is achieved through an exploration of three constructs of professional identity; namely, *professional experience*, *sense of belonging to place of employment*, and *professional value systems*.

For the purpose of this study, *professional experience* was determined by examining principal area of practice, area of clinical specialty, managerial responsibilities, level and length of employment, as well as educational credentials. *Sense of belonging to place of employment* pertained to respondents' sense of affiliation and commitment to the hospital in which they worked. And *professional value systems* are understood to represent consistent ethical principles that guide ideological integrity (Wenstøp and Myrmel, 2006).

Methodology

Research tools

Informed by the research of others (Holt and Kabanoff, 1995; O'Reilly and Chatman, 1986; Meyer and Allan, 1984; Degeling et al., 1998), a self-completed, close-ended survey was designed to explore the professional identities of managers, clinicians, and clinician-managers. Given the multi-faceted nature of professional identity (Goffman, 1959; Gouldner, 1957; Marshall, 1998), the survey aimed to gather empirical evidence on key constructs through a series of questions that employed closed responses, Likert scales and ranking systems to indicate preferred response. The survey examined respondents' (1) professional experience (for example, *qualifications* and *principal area of practice*); (2) sense of affiliation with the hospital in which they worked (for example, *what the hospital stands for is important to me*); and (3) value systems that guided workplace practice (for example, *status and recognition*). Approval to use the survey was sought from relevant ethics bodies; following this, the survey was piloted and refined accordingly.

Sample

The survey was distributed to 180 respondents from six categories of hospital personnel of a metropolitan referral hospital. These include 30 medical-clinicians, 30 medical-clinician-managers, 30 nurse-clinicians, 30 nurse-managers, 30 lay managers (who were not clinicians or nurses), and 30 lay personnel. The respondents were selected using a systematic sampling method, whereby every fifth person on a randomly-ordered employee list was chosen. Using this process, the response rate was 71.1 per cent (n=128), which adds to the external validity of the research findings. The 128 respondents included at least 20 individuals from each of the six categories of hospital personnel.

Data collection and analysis

Participants were provided with information and a survey, which they completed and returned. The survey was self-administered, un-timed and completed by respondents individually. Survey responses were collated and systematically analysed using appropriate computer software. More specifically, the analytical techniques included descriptive statistics, correlation analysis, Principal Component Analysis (PCA) and Analysis of Variance (ANOVA).

The data were analysed to test four null hypotheses, all of which were informed by extant research in this field. These include:

Null Hypothesis 1: There is no difference between the six categories of hospital personnel with regard to intrinsic or extrinsic affiliation with the hospital;

Null Hypothesis 2: There is no difference between the medical, nursing and other personnel with regard to intrinsic or extrinsic affiliation with the hospital;

Null Hypothesis 3: There is no difference between managerial and non-managerial personnel with regard to intrinsic or extrinsic affiliation with the hospital; and

Null Hypothesis 4: There is no difference between managerial and non-managerial personnel with regard to the ranking assigned to the organizational goals.

Findings

Professional experience

Respondents were asked to indicate their professional experiences. Findings indicated that the medical-clinician-managers were not as likely to hold higher qualifications in management, relative to their nursing counterparts. While it was not the purpose of this study to explore the underlying reasons for this discrepancy, literature on professional identity might suggest that it is partly attributable to the complex parameters that define the medical professions (Freidson, 1994; Illich, 1984).

Given the relationship between professional identity and perceived occupational role (Fitzgerald, 2002; Degeling et al., 1998; Freidson, 1994; Illich, 1984), cross-tabulations were prepared between the six categories of hospital personnel and the principal areas of practice. The findings indicate that, although largely employed as middle and senior managers, a number of medical-clinician-managers professed their principal area to be *patient care* (29 per cent), while none of the nurse-managers perceived this to be the case. These findings are suggestive of a robust professional identity among medical-clinicians. While appointed to positions that strive to improve governance and organizational operation, they ultimately perceived themselves as clinicians first and managers second. This reflects earlier research (Kippist and Fitzgerald, 2006; Iedema et al., 2003; Degeling et al., 1998).

The bond that ties medical-clinician-managers to *patient care* as their principal area of practice, has significant implications. Increased accountability demands, especially with regard to resource allocation, may rouse ethical dilemmas for the professional who assumes two disparate roles. While he or she may want to trial new treatment in the interests of patient care, organizational push toward economic rationalism might constrain. This might widen the divide between the individual (the professional) and the collective (the organization), causing incompatibility between organizational and professional values, that is, organizational-professional conflict (Parry and Murphy, 2005). For this reason, organizational affiliation among the respondents was examined.

Organizational affiliation

Through two factors – *intrinsic* and *extrinsic*, the survey measured respondents' sense of affiliation with the hospital in which they worked. Once homogeneity within the sample had been verified using Levene's test, a one-way ANOVA was used to test the following null hypothesis:

> Null Hypothesis 1: There is no difference between the six categories of hospital personnel with regard to intrinsic or extrinsic affiliation with the hospital.

Table 4.1 indicates an F-statistic of 2.79 for the intrinsic factor. As this exceeds the theoretical F-distribution of 2.21 (Polit and Hungler, 1999), the null hypothesis is *rejected*. The ANOVA indicates a difference between the six categories for intrinsic factors. However, the null-hypothesis for extrinsic factors is *accepted*, with the F-statistic 1.59 not exceeding the theoretical F-distribution.

To investigate the differences between hospital personnel with regard to the intrinsic factor, the means on a scale of 0 to 5 were compared. This factor most strongly discriminates between medical-clinicians and nurse-clinicians, whereby nurse-clinicians have a stronger intrinsic affiliation with the hospital than their medical counterparts (see Table 4.2). Furthermore, medical personnel demonstrated a weaker intrinsic affiliation with the hospital than nurses and other personnel.

The intrinsic and extrinsic factor items were analysed to compare responses between medical, nursing and other personnel. Once homogeneity

Table 4.1   One-Way ANOVA between hospital personnel for intrinsic and extrinsic factors

		Sum of squares	df	Mean square	F	Significance
Intrinsic factor	Between groups	7.26	5	1.45	2.79	0.02
	Within groups	61.89	119	0.52		
	Total	69.14	124			
Extrinsic factor	Between groups	9.89	5	1.98	1.59	0.17
	Within groups	133.34	107	1.25		
	Total	143.24	112			

Table 4.2   Intrinsic affiliation with the hospital by hospital personnel

	Mean	N[a]	SD	Variance
Medicos				
Medical-clinicians	3.23	20	0.79	0.62
Medical-clinician-managers	2.86	21	0.70	0.49
Nurses				
Nurse clinicians	2.52	22	0.63	0.39
Nurse-managers	3.06	20	0.78	0.61
Other				
Lay managers	2.98	22	0.63	0.40
Lay personnel	2.63	20	0.80	0.64
Total	2.87	125	0.75	0.56

[a]N = respondents who responded to the relevant statements

had been verified, a one-way ANOVA was used to test the following null hypothesis:

Null Hypothesis 2: There is no difference between the medical, nursing and other personnel with regard to intrinsic or extrinsic affiliation with the hospital.

Because the F-statistics do not exceed the theoretical F-distribution of 2.99 (Polit and Hungler, 1999), the null hypothesis is *accepted*. There are no significant differences between doctors, nurses and other personnel in their intrinsic or extrinsic affiliation with the hospital.

To compare intrinsic and extrinsic affiliation between those who held a managerial position and those who did not, a similar analytical process was used. Once homogeneity had been verified, a one-way ANOVA was used to test the following null hypothesis:

> Null Hypothesis 3: There is no difference between managerial and non-managerial personnel with regard to intrinsic or extrinsic affiliation with the hospital.

Table 4.3 indicates an F-statistic of 1.71 for the intrinsic factor of affiliation. As this does not exceed the theoretical F-distribution of 3.84 (Polit and Hungler, 1999), the null hypothesis is *accepted*. The ANOVA here indicates that managers and non-managers experience similar intrinsic affiliation with the hospital. In contrast, the null hypothesis for extrinsic factors is *rejected*, as the F-statistic 4.68 exceeds the theoretical F-distribution. Thus, managers and non-managers experience different extrinsic affiliation with the hospital. To further understand this difference, response means were compared. Relative to their non-manager counterparts, managers had a lower sense of choice and a higher sense of necessity to remain employed at the hospital (see Table 4.4).

The findings suggest some significant differences between hospital personnel in their sense of affiliation to the hospital in which they work. Sense of intrinsic affiliation was particularly apparent in nurse-clinicians, relative to their medical counterparts. Furthermore, compared with those in non-managerial positions, managers generally perceived a greater need to

Table 4.3 One-Way ANOVA between managerial and non-managerial personnel for intrinsic and extrinsic factors

		Sum of squares	df	Mean square	F	Significance
Intrinsic factor	Between groups	0.95	1	0.95	1.71	0.19
	Within groups	68.20	123	0.55		
	Total	69.15	124			
Extrinsic factor	Between groups	5.79	1	5.79	4.68	0.03
	Within groups	137.44	111	1.24		
	Total	143.24	112			

Table 4.4 Extrinsic organisation affiliation between managerial and non-managerial personnel

	Mean	N[a]	SD	Variance
Managers	2.64	58	1.05	1.11
Clinicians	3.09	55	1.17	1.37
Total	2.86	113	1.13	1.28

[a]N = respondents who responded to the relevant statements

remain employed at the hospital. The intrinsic feelings are of most interest in the context of organizational-professional conflict, because intrinsic feelings of affiliation might help to explain the incongruity between organizational and professional values.

The findings suggest that when professionals maintain focus on their vocation, clear boundaries are maintained. This was suggested by the acceptance of null hypothesis two. However, when professionals are assigned a role that places them in a dual or hybrid position, their feelings of affiliation to intrinsic factors are affected to the point of significance. This was suggested by the rejection of null hypothesis one. While the literature indicates that strong professional boundaries prevent occupational-professional conflict (Parry and Murphy, 2005; Sorensen, 1967; Gunz and Gunz, 1994) these findings suggest that placing clinicians in a managerial position weakens professional boundaries, potentially increasing occupational-professional conflict. It would therefore be interesting to examine professional value systems in relation to the organization in which they work.

Professional value systems

Respondents ranked eight goals currently pursued by the hospital in which they work. There is little variation in the way the six categories of hospital personnel positioned the organizational goals. In descending order, the goals thought to be pursued by the hospital were (1) *financial viability*; (2) *improved productivity*; (3) *service quality*; (4) *equal access for all patients from the local community*; (5) *organizational stability*; (6) *teaching and research reputation*; (7) *reputation for service innovation and for being an industry leader*; and (8) *staff welfare*.

All personnel, bar the medical-clinicians, awarded *staff welfare* the lowest ranking and all personnel, bar the lay personnel, awarded *financial viability* the highest ranking. This suggests that most respondents consider economic concerns to be driving the hospital system.

Responses between managerial and non-managerial personnel were further analysed. Using Levene's test, *staff welfare, equal access for all patients,* and *financial viability* were found to violate the homogeneity assumption ($p=<0.05$); an ANOVA could not be performed on these items. However, the remaining items did not violate the homogeneity assumption. It was therefore possible to use a one-way ANOVA on the remaining items to test the following null hypothesis:

Null Hypothesis 4: There is no difference between managerial and non-managerial personnel with regard to the ranking assigned to the organizational goals.

Managerial and non-managerial personnel differed significantly in the way ranking was assigned to organizational goals. Differences were demonstrated in the rank assigned to *reputation for service innovation and industry leader, service quality, improved productivity,* as well as *teaching and research reputation.* Thus, the null hypothesis is rejected. This suggests that managers, including medical-clinician-managers and nurse-managers, have different views about the organizational goals pursued by the hospital in which they work, relative to their clinical, non-managerial colleagues. In the scope of this study, the *disparity* between managerial and non-managerial personnel is of key interest, as it confirms the tension that lies between clinical and managerial roles. Assigning a hybrid role to the medical-clinician-manager will not only dilute professional boundaries, but might also increase conflict between professional and superordinate goals.

Discussion

This study has demonstrated that within health care, hybrid roles can benefit both the professional and the organization (Lorsch and Mathias, 1988; Raelin, 1986). However, the dual role assumed by clinician-managers may also influence their professional identity. This chapter explored how the dual role assumed by clinician-managers influence their professional identity through an examination of three constructs of professional identity; namely, *professional experience, sense of belonging to place of employment,* and *professional value systems.*

A self-completed, close-ended survey was developed to investigate the professional identities of 128 hospital personnel, including managers, clinicians, and clinicians-managers. Using a range of analytical techniques, four key findings emerged; namely:

1. Relative to their fellow respondents, particularly their nurse-managers counterpart, the medical-clinician-managers maintained a strong connection to their clinician role;
2. Among the medical-clinician-managers, the intrinsic feelings of affiliation with the organization were weaker than fellow respondents;

3. There was no significant difference between the professions surveyed with regard to intrinsic or extrinsic affiliation with the organization in which they worked; and

4. Those appointed to managerial positions, including medical-clinician-managers and nurse-managers, perceived a greater need to remain employed at the hospital, when compared to those in non-managerial roles.

These findings provide valuable insights into the influence of government health care policy on professional identity. While the aim of such policy might be to 'enhance [health care] management and information systems' (NSW Health, 2000), the research indicates that strategies like the appointment of professionals as managers may in fact amplify organizational-professional conflict. This is in concordance with the sentiments of Parry and Murphy (2005).

Given the fundamental differences in value orientations between managers and professionals (Harrison, 1976), the key finding here presented might hardly be surprising. However, the value of this research is its ability to bridge policy and practice in the context of health care management. More specifically, it sheds light on the implications associated with government efforts that aim to align organizational and professional ideologies by appointing professionals-managers. These include:

1. The (ethical) dilemmas of balancing patient care with organizational interests;
2. A deterioration of professional boundaries;
3. An increase in occupational-professional conflict; and
4. The potential for the consequences associated with such conflict, including increased job-related stress, reduced job-satisfaction, diminished quality performance, and increased staff turnover (Gouldner, 1957; Senatra, 1980; Wilensky, 1956).

Despite the significance of the present findings, a number of methodological limitations must be considered. For example, the cross-sectional nature of this project indicates that the respondents merely provide a snapshot of the ways in which hybrid roles influence professional identity. Although cross-sectional studies have demonstrated relationships between the constructs here explored (Brierley and Cowton, 2000; Bamber and Iyer, 2002; Shafer et al., 2001; Shafer, 2002), the findings are limited by time, context and the nature of individual perspectives. Thus, longitudinal research is needed to confirm the identified relationships (Parry and Murphy, 2005; Shafer, 2002; Lee et al., 2000). Furthermore, in the words of Aranya and Ferris (1984), 'the effects of other possible factors...should not be overlooked. These may include differences in central life interests, as well as regional, ethnic, and social class subculture'. Additionally, Aranya and Ferris advise that ' "affective responses" ... may be influenced by other variables, both endogenous and exogenous, not examined here'. These might include job satisfaction, employment expectations and values, alternative employment opportunities, as well as economic and market conditions.

Notwithstanding these considerations, the present findings are consistent with those in the existing literature (Kippist and Fitzgerald, 2006; Iedema et al., 2003; Degeling et al., 1998). However, most of this research is limited in scope, making this study the first empirical investigation into the influence of the hybrid role assumed by doctors-managers on their professional identity.

The present findings pave the way for future research, particularly on the changing nature of professional jurisdictions in a climate where collaborative decision-making between and within professions is expected (NSW Health, 2000). More specifically, empirical research is required to examine whether the hybrid role is a career or a function, and whether changes in professional identity are related to organizational-professional conflict, the hierarchical division of labour, and the business model of health care. Only through such research will the ramifications of relevant government policy be better understood.

This chapter indicates that the appointment of professionals as managers in health care has the potential to amplify organizational-professional conflict. By implication, this suggests that government efforts to align organizational and professional ideologies might in fact have dire consequences for both the professional and the organization. There is thus a need to reconsider these efforts if better health care management is considered desirable.

References

Aranya, N. and Ferris, K.R. (1984) 'A reexamination of accountants' organizational-professional conflict', *Accounting Review*, 59 (1), 1–15.

Bamber, E.M. and Iyer, V.M. (2002) 'Big 5 auditors' professional and organizational identification: Consistency or conflict?' *Auditing*, 21 (2), 21.

Brierley, J.A. and Cowton, C.J. (2000) 'Putting meta-analysis to work: Accountants' organizational-professional conflict', *Journal of Business Ethics*, 24 (4), 343–53.

Degeling, P., Kennedy, J., Hill, M., Carnegie, M. and Holt, J. (1998) 'Professional subcultures and hospital reform'. Sydney, NSW: Centre for Hospital Management and Information Systems Research, University of NSW.

Donelan, K., Blendon, R.J., Schoen, C., David, K. and Binns, K. (1999) 'The cost of health system change: Public discontent in five nations', *Health Affairs*, 18 (3), 206–16.

Fitzgerald, J.A. (2002) 'Doctors and nurses working together: A mixed method study into the construction and changing of professional identities'. Unpublished Doctoral dissertation, University of Western Sydney, Sydney, NSW.

Freidson, E. (1994) *Professionalism Reborn: Theory, Prophecy, and Policy*. Chicago: Polity Press.

Goffman, E. (1959) *The Presentation of Self in Everyday Life*. Garden City, NY: Doubleday.

Gouldner, A.W. (1957) 'Cosmopolitans and locals: Toward an analysis of latent social roles – I', *Administrative Science Quarterly*, 2 (3), 281–307.

Gunz, H.P. and Gunz, S.P. (1994) 'Professional/organizational commitment and job satisfaction for employed lawyers', *Human Relations*, 47 (7), 801.

Hamilton, C. and Maddison, S. (eds) (2007) *'Silencing Dissent: How the Australian Government is Controlling Pubic Opinion and Stifling Debate'*, Crows Nest, NSW: Allen & Unwin.

Harden, J.D. (2000) 'Making the links: Neoliberalism, medicare and local control in the age of globalization', in Broad, D. and Antony, W. (eds), *Citizens or Consumers? Social Policy in a Market Society*, Halifax, NS: Fernwood Publications, 169–83.

Harrison, F. (1976) 'Synergy in professional organizations', *Business and Society*, 17 (1), 15–23.

Hayes, K. and Fitzgerald, J.A. (2007) 'Business and research forms of debate: Argumentation and dissent as barriers to commercialisation of innovations of hybrid industry-research organisations', *International Journal of Technology, Policy and Management*, 7 (3), 280–91.

Hefner, L.L. (1994) 'Resolving conflicts between records professionals and managers: An elusive organizational goal', *Records Management Quarterly*, 28 (4), 14–55.

Holt, P. and Kabanoff, B. (1995) 'Organisational value systems and HRM systems: A configurational study'. Sydney, NSW: School of Industrial Relations and Organisational Behaviour, University of New South Wales.

Iedema, R., Degeling, P., Braithwaite, J. and White, L. (2003) ''It's an interesting conversation I'm hearing': The doctor as manager', *Organization Studies*, 25, 15–33.

Illich, I. (1977) 'Disabling professions', in Illich, I., Zola, I. K., Mcknight, J., Caplan, J. and Shaiken, H. (eds), *Disabling Professions*. London, England: Marion Boyars Publishers, 11–39.

Illich, I. (1984) *Limits to Medicine: Medical Nemesis: The Expropriation of Health*. Middlesex, England: Penguin.

Keating, M. (1999) 'Accountability in Australian Government symposium: The public service: Independence, responsibility and responsiveness', *Australian Journal of Public Administration*, 58 (1), 39–47.

Kippist, L. and Fitzgerald, J. A. (2006) 'The value of management education for hybrid clinician managers', *'ANZAM (Australian and New Zealand Academy of Management) Conference'*, Yeppoon, QLD.

Larson, M. S. (1977) *The Rise of Professionalism: A Sociological Analysis*. Berkeley, CA: University of California Press.

Lea, D. and Brostrom, R. (1988) 'Managinging the high-tech professional', *Personnel*, 65, 12–22.

Lee, K., Carswell, J.J. and Allen, N.J. (2000) 'A meta-analytic review of occupational commitment: Relations with person- and work-related variables', *Journal of Applied Psychology*, 85 (5), 799–811.

Lorsch, J.W. and Mathias, P.F. (1988) 'When professionals have to manage', *Legal Economics*, 14, 51–8.

Marshall, G. (1998) ' *"Identity": A Dictionary of Sociology'*, http://www.oxfordreference.com/views/ENTRY.html?subview=Main&entry=t88.e1061, 15 December.

Martinez, E. and Garcia, A. (1997) *'What is "Neo-Liberalism"? A Brief Definition for Activists'*, http://www.CorpWatch.org, 28 May.

McGregor, S. (2001) 'Neoliberalism and health care', *International Journal of Consumer Studies*, 25 (2), 82–9.

Meyer, J.P. and Allan, N.J. (1984) 'Testing the "sidebet theory" of organisational commitment: Reexamination of commitment', *Administration Science Quarterly*, 17, 555–73.

Moore, W.E. (ed.) (1970) '*The Professions: Roles and Rules*'. Thousand Oaks, CA: Sage.

NSW Health (2000) 'Report of the NSW Health Council: A better health system for NSW 03/2000'. Sydney, NSW: NSW Health.

O'Reilly, C. and Chatman, J. (1986) 'Organisational commitment and organisational attachment: The effects of compliance, identification and internalisation on prosociual behaviour', *Journal of Applied Psychology*, 71, 492–99.

Parry, J. and Murphy, C. (2005) 'Deprofessionalisation: Striking at the heart of professionalism', in Shehadie, E. (ed.), '*ABBSA (Australasian Business and Behavioural Sciences Association) Conference*', Cairns, QLD.

Polit, D.F. and Hungler, B.P. (1999) *Nursing Research: Principles and Methods*. Philadelphia, PA: Lippincott Williams & Wilkins.

Raelin, J.A. (1986) *The Clash of Cultures*. Boston, MA: Harvard Business School Press.

Rosenbaum, B.L. (1991) 'Leading today's professional', *Research-Technology Management*, 34, 30–5.

Senatra, P. T. (1980) 'Role conflict, role ambiguity, and organizational climate in a public accounting firm', *Accounting Review*, 55 (4), 594–603.

Shafer, W.E. (2002) 'Ethical pressure, organizational-professional conflict, and related work outcomes among management accountants', *Journal of Business Ethics*, 38 (3), 263–75.

Shafer, W.E., Park, L.J. and Liao, W.M. (2001) 'Professionalism, organizational-professional conflict and work outcomes', *Accounting, Auditing & Accountability Journal*, 15 (1), 46–68.

Sorensen, J.E. (1967) 'Professional and bureaucratic organization in the public accounting firm', *Accounting Review*, 42 (3), 553–65.

Terris, M. (1999) 'The neoliberal triad of anti-health reforms: Government budget cutting, deregulation and privatization', *Journal of Public Health Policy*, 20 (2), 149–67.

Van Gramberg, B. and Bassett, P. (2005) 'Neoliberalism and the third sector in Australia (No.5)'. Melbourne, VIC: Victoria University of Technology.

Vollmer, H.M. and Mills, D.L. (eds) (1966) *Professionalization*. Prentice-Hall, NJ: Englewood Cliffs.

Wenstøp, F. and Myrmel, A. (2006) 'Structuring organizational value statements', *Management Research News*, 29 (11), 673–83.

Wilensky, H.L. (1956) *Intellectuals in Labor Unions*. New York, NY: Free Press.

5
People, Place and Innovation: How Organizational Culture and Physical Environment Shaped the Implementation of the NHS TC Programme

Catherine Pope, Andrée Le May and John Gabbay

Introduction

This chapter describes the experience of an organizational change in the English National Health Service (NHS) by focusing on the interconnections between culture and place in shaping that change. We use the term 'place' to mean space in the sense of the physical environment, architecture and layout, rather than location or setting. The idea that culture structures change is familiar, but perhaps the influence of physical environments, architecture and spatial configuration is less well examined. Organizational culture and negotiated order theories have been successfully employed to understand organizational change, and while these perspectives sometimes acknowledge the importance of physical context, few empirical studies have examined the interplay of culture and place in the change process. This chapter therefore focuses on the interaction between people and place in shaping organizational change. It looks at the intersection of culture and place in the context of an ethnography of the development of an innovative form of health care delivery, namely NHS Treatment Centres. Of particular interest are the stories participants in this study told us about the physical environment and the ways in which place influenced their sense-making and decisions around the implementation of this change programme. The chapter considers the possibilities and limitations to organizational change that arise from the powerful structuring effects and interplay of culture, physical and geographical environment, by exploring how Treatment Centres were adapted to the particular local configurations of people and place and then by reflecting on the impact of place on understanding organizational change.

The research

Treatment Centres (hereafter 'TCs') were a top-down organizational innovation introduced as part of wider NHS modernization by the Labour government which came into power in 1997. Originally labelled in *The NHS Plan* (2000) as Diagnosis and Treatment Centres, this new mode of health care delivery was designed partly to streamline patient care and reduce excessive waiting times for routine, planned (elective) surgery and partly to transform traditional professional practices and roles. The core features of TCs were (i) the separation of elective from emergency and unplanned treatment, and, (ii) the 'modernization' of treatment delivery by introducing more patient-focused processes. TCs were seen as embracing a whole new philosophy of care, one that necessitated deep-seated changes in how people worked *and* the culture in which they worked. The Government's original aim was that by 2004, at least eight TCs would be fully operational, treating approximately 200,000 patients a year. By the end of 2006 there were 46 NHS TCs plus 17 private sector TCs. While the TC programme was not primarily intended to be about new buildings many of the new centres involved major renovation or the construction of new facilities.

We conducted a multi-method case study (Yin, 2002) of eight TCs between 2003–6 to provide a longitudinal analysis of the development and early implementation of this organizational change. The project combined a technical evaluation using mathematical modelling with an ethnographic investigation of the organizational and social factors associated with the development of TCs. This chapter draws on the qualitative component of the study which consisted of some 200 organizationally-focused interviews with key informants associated with the TCs, direct observation and documentary analysis (of architectural drawings, photographs, formal business plans, Board minutes and reports). To contextualize the case studies we followed wider policy development and literature during the study (see Bate et al., 2007 for more details). We thematically analysed the data, building theory from the case studies along the lines described by Eisenhardt (1989).

The eight cases provide a broad representation of the range of English TCs existing or in development at March 2003 when the research began. They embody differences in scale, type and geographical location and range from relatively small ward-based initiatives to 'mini-hospitals'. Four were new extensions to existing hospital facilities ('Robbleswade', 'Stanwick', 'Northendon', 'Pollhaven'), two were major refurbishments ('Brindlesham' and 'St Urban's'). The remaining two sites ('Ruckworth' and 'Lakenfield') used existing health care facilities that did not undergo major refurbishment, one a newly acquired ex-private hospital and the other a converted ward.

We have argued elsewhere that the TCs studied were influenced by local history, milieu, and the types of players involved in the implementation of this organizational innovation (Bate et al., 2007; Pope et al., 2006). Here, we suggest that place was not an independent, nor indeed insignificant variable, but was closely entwined with the change process. In making change happen, the participants in the TC programme were affected by, drew on, and shaped the environment and spatial configurations around them. In this chapter, we present data to show how the physical environment shaped the evolution of the TCs. Before we do that however, we briefly consider a TC – not part of our study – which can be considered as the model for the TC policy proposed by *The NHS Plan* (2000).

A prototype treatment centre

The Ambulatory Care and Diagnostic Centre (ACAD) is a purpose-built facility based at a London hospital. The building, which opened in 1999, won high praise from those involved with construction and health care facilities provision. It was awarded the Millennium Product Design Award, and the 'Design category' in the NHS Estates 'Building Better Healthcare' awards in 2000 and was described by its architects as 'one of the most seminal health care buildings of the last decade' (http://www.avantiarchitects. co.uk/ACAD.html. viewed 06/05/04). The then Prime Minister, Tony Blair, described the ACAD as 'a marvelous concept and a vision that has been transformed into quite a stunning reality. [It] is the future for the Health Service.' (Booth et al., 2000).

The building comprises a carefully thought-through sequence of working spaces set around a vast and imposing glass and concrete atrium. The design was created to enable patients to move around the building in a logical sequence in accordance with a 'radical' vision of service delivery, described in the following two quotes from websites:

> Radical ideas underpin the design of this facility. These include the idea that elective health care and emergency care should be separate entities; that flexible design is essential to accommodate future innovation in both equipment and procedures and quality of space is important; and that a hospital does not need traditional wards. The building structure and services systems have to provide for future flexibility of operational planning, as well as a high level of environmental comfort for both staff and patients. (http://www.arup.com/healthcare/project.cfm?pageid=9590 viewed 14/1/2008)

> The main aims were to achieve a flexible, efficient, and economic space that could easily respond to changes in healthcare. Arup [the structural contractors] proposed a clearly defined vertical and horizontal strategy, a structured wiring system, and regular column grids with secondary

services distribution on grid lines. The overall layout of the building, with 'high technology spaces' on one side of a mall and the 'low' technology on the other, was a response to the servicing needs. This allowed separation of spaces needing full air-conditioning and little daylight from those requiring minimal ventilation and maximum daylight. The strategy was developed considering both architectural and engineering needs. The building design therefore emphasises the importance of public spaces in a hospital where patients are mobile and conscious, as well as the need for flexibility as technology develops and healthcare demands change. (Booth et al., 2000).

The ACAD has a novel triangular footprint designed to ensure that '[t]he patient can travel though the building without ever having to re-trace their steps' (ibid.). This layout contrasts with more typical NHS facilities where patients and staff often travel back and forth, and where floor plans and maps are ubiquitous, and often essential, for those unfamiliar with the territory.

The ACAD was a key referent for the nascent TCs. Many of those involved in implementing the TC programme visited it for inspiration (although interestingly policy makers and planners did not, as an NHS Estates report had recommended [NHS Estates, 2001], 'await the incontrovertible evidence that this is the most effective model of care for future generations' before rolling out the TC innovation). Several of our interviewees referred directly to the ACAD as encompassing their vision of what a TC could and should be. The physical environment was central to this vision. At Northendon the team charged with implementing the TC was impressed with the physical patient pathway idea. At this site, the TC was to occupy part of an extension to the existing hospital and the early key players visited other hospitals, and came back and worked with local architects to create a layout that, within the limitations of the external shell, replicated the ACAD footprint. Such influences were felt also by others among our case-study sites, including one where a senior manager had once worked at the ACAD and was therefore a major influence on the layout of the new TC.

The ACAD provided a physical blueprint for the emerging TCs and was an exemplar for new modes of service delivery, but there were a number of other ways in which place shaped (and was in turn shaped by) the way the TC innovation was implemented, which we discuss below.

The possibilities of place

Although, as we have noted, the intent of the TC programme was not to create new buildings, there were often sufficient funds made available to do so and the senior managers in all our case study sites grasped this as an opportunity to alter the physical environments surrounding service delivery. The foresight of these managers in turn enabled staff in the TCs to recognize the importance of place. These staff valued certain kinds of space. The ACAD was modern, light and airy; by contrast many NHS buildings were old institutions, some dating from the 1800s or 1900s, or 1960s 'functional modernist' constructions. Typical NHS facilities were worn, offered limited natural light, and were ill-suited to modern patient care. By contrast TCs were 'huge' and 'airy':

> I'm really pleased and the designers are pleased with how outpatients are going and how we're not griping and moaning about everything because they have given us a total different outpatients remit to ones I've ever been to before. It's so airy. The rooms are huge. Some of the rooms are really huge...and it's a way of valuing outpatients now. It's not that it's somewhere that you stick in the basement somewhere because it's just an outpatients' area. It feels there's value and ownership, I think, from the staff, not just from myself. So, that's good. They all feel happy to be here. (Brindlesham senior manager)

Refurbishments, or better still new buildings, provided a chance to introduce space into care delivery and an opportunity to be modern, 'clean' and 'new'. At Stanwick and Northendon, for example, patients found themselves being treated in modern new buildings. At Robbleswade staff were consulted about colours for the walls, and were influential in getting one architectural feature – a curved interior wall made of glass briquettes – added to a main waiting area. These decorative touches were regarded as integral to *patient-focused* (or as this quote shows, *consumer-oriented*) care:

> Space is one [important feature], patient environment. As you walk round you've got a feel that they thought about colour, they thought about local control, consumerism has been built in, they've got bedside TVs. It's not a bad place to be. One of the markers I use is I wouldn't mind being treated here. I feel quite comfortable; it's an excellent patient environment. (Robbleswade senior manager)

Nowhere was this more obvious that at Brindlesham TC. Here leather sofas and low tables furnished the burnt orange waiting areas, pale limestone tiles clad the toilet walls and floors and light streamed through a glass ceiling, creating a calm and airy atmosphere:

> Every time I go round there there's a feel of plenty of space and not many people and yet they are pushing through much more activity these days. ... It's more like walking into a modern library or modern building than a hospital which is great. All the clinical type areas are hidden

behind that façade and it's great. The waiting areas for outpatients are very nice, very comfortable and very modern with the seating. It's not typical NHS and I think that's a good thing. We need to break the mould really of what the NHS currently looks like – fuddy-duddy. (Senior manager, Brindlesham commissioners)

New TC spaces provided a clear break with the 'typical' NHS, but this could also be achieved without new construction. One TC was located in a former private hospital dating from the 1930s. Some original features, such as dark wood panelling and marble tiles, remained and – this décor had a very significant impact on the staff:

It's really quite different. When you walk through the door, you notice that because there's a huge, marble atrium ... we're very much advantaged here ... we're opposite a big park, beautiful grounds ... you see people out in the gardens alongside the fountain ... And there are quite a few people who work here who could probably go and work somewhere else but I think they enjoy it so much that they just stay within the place. I think those sort of things come across to the patients as well. And I think when you're working in a place that is as aesthetically better looking, you can tell that the patients ... we get letters all the time from patients saying, this is such a wonderful place. And it's probably because it looks ... it's an NHS hospital but it's very private-looking ... and it's got a very private feel about it. So that sort of thing comes through, probably from both staff and patients. (Ruckworth IT manager)

You often hear people walking through the door and they go 'ooh, it's just like a private hospital'. A lot of that is due to the matron because she was the matron when it was a private hospital; the values she holds dear, she's very much fed them down ... I have never worked in a cleaner hospital and it's beautiful and the domestic staff take great pride. And the place is always spotless and we have no infection and that makes a big difference. (Ruckworth therapy manager)

Here we see the interplay of aesthetic and culture: place impacted on these staff by engendering pride, heightening job satisfaction and ensuring staff retention, and this in turn created a better patient experience:

[Patients] want comfort, they want pleasant surroundings, they want clean lavatories, they want decent food. And that's what they get here without having to pay for it. (Ruckworth clinician)

Ruckworth provided clear evidence for the importance of place. The surroundings influenced behaviour and attitudes. By adopting a private sector ethos in keeping with the décor, the staff enacted their environment and the innovation. In dealing with patients, they tried to emulate a stereo-typical private hospital staff. The interconnectedness of place and practice, and these possibilities of place, were recognized in all the TCs. They sought to put patients at the centre of things, and so developed environments in which patient-centredness was possible, even inevitable: tasteful environ-ments induced staff to treat patients as people who had dignity and taste. Staff engaged with the TC environments and attempted to make place *work*, even if this was by comparatively small adjustments to décor. At St. Urban's, this culture change included personal efforts to brighten up the clinic:

> I bring in plants as well and make it friendly for patients. And I'm busy doing the reception area as well. I've puts some plants in there, and I'm going to get paintings and hang paintings. So it doesn't look like a clinic, it looks more like a living room. What we try to do is play classical music as well because it makes people calm. (St. Urban's clinical manager)

> at least you've got a decent, clean, fairly new ward that can work as a [ ] unit. That's something; it's better than nothing at all. (St. Urban's senior clinical manager)

The limitations of architecture

We have described how place positively contributed to the organizational change, but it was not always so positive. The first phase of Lakenfield TC was a refurbished ward in an existing hospital. It was doubtful whether patients were aware of being in a different unit, let alone a TC. Nothing distinguished this space from the rest of the hospital; it retained an old-fashioned, worn appearance. Yet even here, place was in keeping with function, since the ward was used not only for TC patients but also as a flexible space for patients who no longer needed to be on the main wards (known colloquially as 'end of stays'). Interestingly, this place was not part of the original TC vision, but instead was conceived as a small-scale pilot for some new working practices. This space was temporary and as such did not matter, but the plans for the second phase of development were driven by a different vision. Here the aspir-ation was for a complete change in the patient experience, and in the mind's eye of the managers who wanted to achieve that, it was intimately linked to changing the physical environment. They believed Phase 2 would:

> [deal] with the quality issue around 'I'm a patient who's getting an excel-lent pathway in a not so excellent facility'. And it moves to 'I'm a patient who's getting an excellent pathway in an excellent facility' and that's my goal, really, in terms of that redesign. So, it's not just the efficiency gain with modernisation, it's the efficiency gain with modernisation plus 'God, isn't this a nice place' as well. That's what patients are interested in. (Lakenfield senior manager)

Interestingly even in new buildings, physical spaces set limits to innovation. At Robbleswade the structure of the soil and landscape of the proposed site determined the size and configuration of the extension. On completion there were hiccups; one clinician took delight in showing us a sluice room which, despite the months of meticulous planning, was constructed in an impossible space so that a sterilizer (rather like a domestic dishwasher) opened across the width of the room effectively blocking the exit. Yet against these 'glitches' there were other examples of staff imaginatively 'working' the space to achieve their goals. A superb example was at Northendon where staff wanted to ensure that their TC was used only for day-cases. Previous attempts to establish a day care unit had always floundered when frequent bed crises (caused by longer than expected stays or extra emergency admissions) meant that patients were 'temporarily' housed overnight. Staff developing this TC carefully measured the width of the day-case patient trolleys against the standard hospital beds. Discovering that the trolleys were slightly narrower they deliberately chose doors for the TC that were wide enough to admit a trolley, but not a bed. In this way they harnessed the limitations of space to their advantage.

Putting place back in to understanding organizational innovation

This chapter has described how each of the TCs was adapted and shaped by particular local configurations of people and place. People doing the innovating worked with and around the physical environments they were given, and they altered the spaces to fit the TC vision. Conversely, the structure and form of each TC had an impact on the way the staff and patients behaved.

Recent research on work and organizations has begun to engage with ideas about place and space. Sociologists Halford and Leonard, for example, have been influential in drawing attention to how space, place (and time) are negotiated by individuals in constructing and performing gender identities at work. Drawing on the work of Lefebvre they point out that 'space both creates *and* is created by human agency' (Halford and Leonard, 2006: 13). Elsewhere, social geographers have voiced criticisms of how place has been conceived in their discipline, calling attention to the ways in which space structures social life, and arguing for 'a more profound appreciation of geography as constitutive of social praxis, as something with which social actors must actively engage' (Herod et al., 2007: 248). Those studying innovation and organizational change have tended to draw heavily on cultural and interactionist theories that primarily focus on actors/people and not on place. Elsewhere we have argued (Pope et al., 2006) that people create, adapt and enact organizational innovation. Certainly the cultures of our eight sites were all very different from each other and people enacted the TC innovation in different ways. But, as we have shown, alongside this cultural determinant, place also affected the TC innovation. Kornberger and Clegg posit that 'space is both the medium and outcome of actions it recursively organises' (Kornberger and Clegg, 2004: 1096) and we wish to extend this to argue that in order to understand organizational innovation we must account for place. In particular, we need to capture the dynamic interplay of people 'acting back' and enacting their own environment in the Weickian sense (Daft and Weick, 1984; Weick, 1995). By enacting new places (spaces, physical environments and locales) the TCs created a cultural response that reinforced the purpose of that environment. The new culture became an inevitable consequence of the environment that was itself enacted by that culture.

Innovation is about changing cultural mindsets and behaviours so that people 'think and do' in different ways. We concluded our research suggesting that many of the TCs did not achieve, in the long term, the radical transformation envisaged in the original policy. We argued that this was often because of the pull of wider organizational cultures and external contingencies. What we failed to see was how important place was in the process of making change, even the less radical change undertaken in some of these TCs. The people enacting the TC innovation did recognize this, although often not explicitly so. Part of the hook for engaging with the TC programme was the money that came with it which allowed them to change the spaces in which care was delivered and thus to influence how people practised. Reviewing the importance of place in the enactment of this innovation, we suggest that place could be considered as central to organizational change, and possibly as a way of 'freezing' (Lewin, 1947) change so that people cannot drift back into old ways of practising so easily. In thinking about future organizational innovations we would do well to note Kornberger and Clegg's point that:

> It is not strategy that determines structure; rather functions evolve from form...the capacity to fly emerged out of a whole range of formal settings that first made it possible. In fact function (flying) followed form.... Thus, we can conclude that we should not look for solutions within a pre-given frame, but concentrate on forms and new spatial arrangements from where new functions emerge. (2004: 1102)

In short, when thinking about organizational innovation, we should creatively recognize the importance of harnessing the interactions of people *and* place.

References

Ambulatory care and diagnostic centre (ACAD) Central Middlesex Hospital. http://www.arup.com/healthcare/project.cfm?pageid=9590 accessed 14/1/08.

Bate, P., Gabbay, J., Gallivan, S., Jit, M., le May, A., Pope, C., Robert, G., Utley, M. (2007) *The Development and Implementation of NHS Treatment Centres as an Organisational Innovation. A Report to the NHS Service Delivery and Organisation Research and Development Programme.* http://www.sdo.lshtm.ac.uk/files/project/45-final-report.pdf

Booth, M., Iles, A., Kinson, P. and Minson, A. (2000) *The ACAD Project.* http://www.arup.com/_assets/_download/download45.pdf accessed 14/1/08.

Daft, R. and Weick, K. (1984) 'Toward a model of organizations as interpretation systems', *Academy of Management Review*, 9 (2), 284–95.

Department of Health (2000) *The NHS Plan: A Plan for Investment, a Plan for Reform.* CM 4818-I London: The Stationery Office.

Eisenhardt, K. (1989) 'Building theories from case study research', *Academy of Management Review*, 14, 532–50.

Halford, S. and Leonard, P. (2006) *Negotiating Gendered Identities at Work: Place, Space and Time.* Basingstoke: Palgrave.

Herod, A., Rainnie, A. and McGrath-Champ, S. (2007) 'Working space: Why incorporating the geographical is central to theorising work and employment practices', *Work, Employment and Society*, 21 (2), 247–64.

Kornberger, M. and Clegg, S. (2004) 'Bringing space back in: Organizing the generative building', *Organisation Studies*, 25 (7), 1095–115.

Lewin, K. (1947) 'Frontiers in group dynamics 1', *Human Relations*, 1, 5–41.

NHS Estates (2001) *Diagnostic and Treatment Centres: ACAD, Central Middlesex Hospital. An Evaluation.* London: The Stationery Office.

Pope, C., Robert, G., Bate, S.P., le May, A. and Gabbay, J. (2006) 'Lost in translation: A multi-level case study of the metamorphosis of meanings and action in public sector organisational innovation', *Public Administration*, 84 (1), 59–79.

Weick, K. (1995) *Sensemaking in Organizations.* Thousand Oaks, CA: Sage.

Yin, R. (2002) *Case Study Research: Design and Methods* (3rd edn). Newbury Park, CA: Sage.

6

Interpersonal Relationships and Decision-Making about Patient Flow: What and Who Really Matters?

Kathy Eljiz, Anneke Fitzgerald and Terrence Sloan

Introduction

The aim of this research is to give insights into how interpersonal relationships influence managerial decision-making about resource allocation in the health context.

The organizational culture literature suggests that an organization's culture is *unique* (Louis, 1985; Schein, 1985; Van Maanen and Barley, 1985; Smircich, 1983) and *shared* (Schein, 1996; Kunda, 1992; Hofstede et al., 1990; Kroeber and Kluckhohn, 1952), but exactly what is unique and what is shared varies depending on the context. This paper investigates stakeholder saliency in a medium tertiary hospital. The majority of the staff have worked at the institution for more than seven years, live in the local area and interact with one another outside of the institution's boundaries. Initial observations revealed that what was shared in this hospital is the sense of 'community'. Most staff not only knew each other by name, but also new family details of their colleagues, including birthdays and other events.

Interactions between various stakeholders, and relationships with persons who are classified as possessing 'deep smarts' are used to exemplify the shared and unique attributes of the organization's culture, as well as the different decision-making approaches by stakeholders within the hospital. Leonard and Swap (2005: 2) define deep smarts as 'the knowledge that provides a distinctive advantage, both for organizations and for managers as individuals'. In addition, organizational cultural literature has not yet been linked to stakeholder theory and the notion of 'deep smarts'. We begin to address this gap in the literature.

An organization's culture can be made up of several subcultures. Fitzgerald (2002: 30) argues that there are 'special factors that encourage their development' and include 'differential interaction, similar personal characteristics, social cohesion and other bases for subculture formation, such as diversity in educational background and professional identity'. Employees may feel drawn to one another because of similar experiences due to the positions they hold or may have held in the past. The sharedness here is about sharing common understandings of a specific aspect in life, using language that is familiar to those who have worked in similar contexts.

Where researchers have examined organizations with multiple subcultures, it has been found that 'relationships among subcultures may be mutually reinforcing, conflicting, or independent' (Louis, 1985 in Martin, 2002: 103). The degree to which a subgroup is considered *central* by other subgroups is important, as is the degree to which they are seen as *incomparable* by other subgroups (Van Maanen and Barley, 1985; Hickson et al., 1971; Crozier, 1964). Indeed, access to resources may be different depending on the power/importance of a subgroup (Alvesson and Berg, 1992; Turner, 1990; Van Maanen and Barley, 1985). This may be because the subgroup is central to the organization and is thus able to shape the overall culture. This is evident from the power of the Australian Nursing Federation (ANF) in the health system. Although nurses individually have little power, many changes have been implemented in the health system due to the campaigning of the nurses union, expressing power by numbers (the nursing group having the largest number of health care workers). However, while the subgroup of doctors is much smaller, doctors have considerably more power to be authoritative in decision-making about individual patient cases than nurses, both as individual doctors and as a collective. Harrison and Pollitt (1994) also argue that 'contrary to the usual assumptions of textbook management, managers are not the most influential actors in the organization, doctors are' (1994: 35). In examining how different stakeholders create alliances and the role of individuals possessing 'deep smarts', this paper investigates the interactions between professionals when making decisions about patient flow.

Stakeholder theory

Freeman (1994) defines stakeholders as 'any group of individuals who can affect or are affected by the firm' (Freeman, 1994 in Barringer and Harrison, 2000: 376). Mitchell et al. (1997) developed a stakeholder model in which three factors were used to determine salience (Figure 6.1). The first factor, stakeholder power, is the ability to influence decisions. The second factor, authority, is legitimacy or verification to use their ability to influence decisions. The third factor, urgency, includes time sensitivity and criticality of the decisions. Mitchell et al. (1997: 865–6) claim that 'power by itself does not guarantee high salience in a stakeholder-manager relationship.

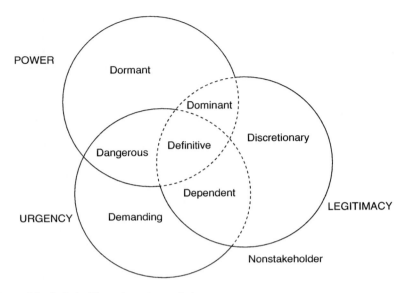

Figure 6.1   Stakeholder categories and classes

Source: Adapted from 'Toward a theory of stakeholder identification and salience: Defining the principle of who and what really counts.' 22(4) by Mitchell, R.K., Agle, B.R. and Wood, D.J. Copyright (1997) by Academy of Management. The Academy of Management Review (Reproduced with permission of Academy of Management. The Academy of Management Review via Copyright Clearance Center).

Stakeholder power gains authority through legitimacy, and it gains exercise through urgency'. Mitchell et al. further claim that when all three attributes can be found in a stakeholder class, managers will take their opinions more seriously.

However, Mitchell's model is limited in that it does not deal with the multitude and magnitude (strength/thickness) of the combined attributes. We argue that in addition to the components in Mitchell's model, the saliency of the definitive stakeholders is largely dependent on a capacity to network formally and informally.

Our research shows that in a conducive hospital context (where the organizational culture allows), decisions about patient flow are mostly influenced by definitive decision-making stakeholders who have highly developed skills and know-how essential to the organization, who can see the bigger picture as well as the details, and focus on relevant data. In addition, these pivotal staff members can make swift, wise decisions taking into account the context, including how networks really work. Further, these managers recognize patterns and make use of heuristics for decision-making (Bazerman, 2002). These skills and knowledge are attributes that Leonard and Swap (2005) call 'deep smarts', complement the stakeholder roles set out by Mitchell et al., and fill a pivotal, central, role. Deep Smarts are the attributes that 'really matter'.

Methodology

This paper reports on the exploratory phase of a larger research project. Research material collected through semi-structured face-to-face interviews was combined with observational notes used to capture events and thoughts created by the interactions between staff.

The interviews focused on socialization between professionals, specifically exploring collaboration in decision-making between doctors, managers, clinicians and nurses. The questions centred on the following themes: organizational culture; decision-making and bed allocation; social networks; formal policies and procedures; and relationships between and across occupational groups. Observations were made in the emergency and other departments in the hospital, where the researcher followed individual key stakeholders during their duty shifts.

Approval to conduct the research was gained from the relevant Area Health Service ethics committee, and endorsement subsequently given by the university ethics committee. Convenience sampling methods were initially used to select informants, with snowball sampling subsequently used to identify key informants.

Analysis of research material

The strategy used for integrating the research material was comparative analysis (Lambert and McKevitt, 2002). This approach involved interrogating the material to identify similarities and differences to develop and test theory, as illustrated by narratives from the field (Blaikie, 2000).

The researchers recognize that individual perceptions of the issues under investigation cannot claim exclusive privilege in the representation of those issues. To address this problem, on most occasions two interviewers were present to diversify the interpretation of the research material. Furthermore, the researchers met regularly to discuss the research material and compare their interpretations.

Findings/Discussion

Several key themes emerged, surrounding the social construction of decision-making centered on what Leonard and Swap (2005) term 'deep smarts'. Four characteristics of deeps smarts include organizational know-how, seeing the bigger picture, focus on relevant data, and understanding how networks really work. These key themes revealed that maintaining relationships is important. The conduciveness of the organizational culture influences relationship building and maintenance. Hence, 'keeping it in the family' and a bounded environment for relationship growth implicates organizational decision-making efficiency. In the following section, field illustrations are used to exemplify the use of some 'deep smart' attributes and cultural conduciveness for relationship maintenance.

Organizational skills and know-how

Knowing the reputation of managers of wards and staff within those wards helps senior management know how to 'deal' with them. Each ward has its own reputation/personality which also varies from day to night. Some staff commented that they had been offered better positions in other hospitals on the basis of their performance in their current role. However, they had turned down the positions because they argued that they would not be able to do the same job at another hospital because they did not have the relationships that helped them do their job in the first place. One Nurse Manager commented:

> I was offered a better job at (another) Hospital but turned it down. ... because I don't have the networks, people don't know me there, and it would take me too long to establish those networks and relationships ... That's what's important – is that people know who you are.

Therefore, it is important not only for managers to understand their environment, but also their staff to know who they are and that they are able to approach their managers. The building of trust networks by managers is important especially when staff are distressed. This distress may filter into the ward and may affect the work outcomes of the staff member in distress, as well as the other members of staff. A nurse manager highlighted the importance of personal-ability as part of her ability to manage her staff.

> I'll have a cigarette with a nurse if they're in distress. I quit smoking years ago but it's about that person-ability.

Face-to-face contact with staff, regarding issues that are deemed private, is an important strategy used by managers to help them foster a productive working environment. One might argue that keeping family and work lives separate is the essence of professionalism; however people bring their problems to work, and having that understanding of staff and what issues they may be having helps managers comprehend how best to deal with the problem.

Seeing the bigger picture (systems thinking)

Another dimension of 'deep smarts' is systems thinking, or knowledge of both the big picture and the details. Working in the same groups and departments may lead staff to look at the organization with a silo mentality. However, having regular contact with staff from other departments provides an opportunity for those staff to understand the problems that their colleagues face. A doctor manager spoke extensively about the chats that he had with doctor managers in other departments and how they helped him understand the big picture of the organization:

> If there's a problem, we always talk it over at lunch, or a coffee, or something like that. ... in my experience, nothing has gone up to, say, for the General Manager, to intervene. Always we have tried to work it out ourselves and it always works... You know someone, you can short-circuit things.

Understanding the big picture is essential, particularly in organizations such as hospitals where one department, such as the Emergency Department, cannot effectively treat a patient without the cooperation of another department, such as the Imaging Department. Therefore, by bypassing the formal rules for reporting incidences that are not life or death, staff are able to build their relationships and levels of trust with not only people in their own departments, but also staff from other departments. For example, if a manager of one department lets a manager know they are busy and asks if they can transfer a patient to their ward, there is a level of trust and understanding which would allow a transfer to occur more quickly.

Focussing on relevant data (separation of signal from noise)

Understanding how networks really work is difficult. In this hospital, the researchers observed that the majority of staff have informal chats. However, informal chats in this context should not be seen as a negative thing (although there may have been negative outcomes). It appeared to be the quickest way of disseminating information in the hospital, where the formal avenues of communicating information were not available to a large portion of the employees. For example, nurses with non-managerial duties did not have access to email and often relied on chats with other groups in the hospital to exchange information. Moreover, chatting was different depending on the level of employees involved. Staff in the wards chat at the nurses' station between patients. Higher level management chat takes place in corridors. Chatting is not only important for information sharing but also for relationship building. For example, managers come across different groups in corridors and are able to have chats about a range of issues from staff rostering to conversations about family circumstances. One manager spoke about the difficulty of getting staff to take on extra shifts. Her tactic was to ask how the family situation was, whilst trying to remember when a nurse's child's birthday was approaching.

> Having those chats, it's a means to an ends – you need to tell people what they will get out of it. For example, if you find out if someone has

a birthday for a child coming up and get them to do an extra shift. You win, they win.

Rather than using the formal rules to ask staff to take on an extra shift, the manager was able to keep the staff on side by fostering and maintaining the relationships while fulfilling an essential key performance indicator (KPI) of the hospital to reduce the likelihood of bed block. This may be the essence of how to get things done in a medium-sized hospital, where having a personal relationship allows for improvement of organizational performance.

It may thus be argued that Mitchell et al.'s stakeholder theory falls short in that it assumes the strength of relational ties (saliency) is similar each time. However, it is evident that magnitude or thickness of relationship is important. For example, when comparing two different shifts with two different managers, different groups of staff within the same wards had preferences as to which manager they preferred to work with, as well as who could provide the most information.

A doctor commented that within his department he had preferences for certain managers over others:

You have your own preferences, because some bed managers actually go and see, physically walk around…and they are going around, helping, OK, let's get this patient out…

Therefore, the differences in the magnitude of relationships is deterministic in that when one manager asks staff to do something, they can get an entirely different response to the same request if asked by another manager who does not have the same relationship with the staff. Therefore, it is not just being able to put a face to name; it is also *whose* face that matters. Having a good reputation with staff is important as it can mean that tasks, such as bed allocation, can happen more promptly.

Understanding how networks really work

The development of relationships is inconsistent at best. Whilst formal educational and professional roles delineate certain groupings, other points of commonality challenge professional boundaries and causes boundary crossing. For example one nurse manager stated:

Its funny – you know I used to watch the old smoking area up the back of the cafeteria. Everyone sits together – doctors, nurses, admin. And then they all go back into their little groups in the hospital.

This inconsistency of relational developments is consistent with Martin's (2002: 103–4) ambiguity perspective of culture where tribal groupings are temporarily ungrouped for the purpose of smoking a cigarette, and then reformed when the activity is finished. This is not to say the one type of relationship is more important or stronger than another, but that having commonalities draws people together who may not have otherwise interacted. This is because informal sharing of organizational knowledge, such as informal chats, is important not just for information sharing, but also for relationship building.

Keeping it all in the family (relationship maintenance)

This particular hospital had grown from a small community hospital and a large proportion of the staff trained and continue to work in the hospital. Consequently, the hospital is not only a professional working environment but also a place where they are familiar with a large amount of other staff and their families. A doctor manager spoke about the sense of belonging:

> It's run by dedicated people who live within the community. No one comes from outside. 95% of people live within the area. And in that, you are part of the community.

The sense of community and belonging is important because strong personal relationships based on commonalities of understanding helps staff look at the bigger picture rather than focusing on the differences. The issue of mentoring of newer organizational members by more experienced organizational members is also important, and is facilitated by being a member of a community. For example, a middle level manager spoke about mentoring junior managers:

> You have to groom them because you want to make sure they're team players. You have to, otherwise you're behind the eight ball... It's in our best interest to get in managers we can work with and groom, cause it makes our job easier.

Giving advice to staff who are coming through the ranks is an important element of attempting to integrate staff members into the way that things are done within the organization. It is also in the best interest of those more senior managers to have staff that will toe the company line and understand the way that things are done within the organization. Fostering relationships between staff is important, especially when senior staff encourage other staff to get involved in the organization and 'play the game'.

Limitations of the study

One medium-sized hospital has been analysed in this project so far. Therefore, caution should be exercised in accepting the knowledge as being appropriate to other systems/organizations within the health systems in

NSW and Australia. However, early indications of subsequent research seem to confirm these findings. Moreover, other hospitals are being examined and the researchers will use the analysis of those hospitals to triangulate the knowledge generated from this study.

Further, the focus of the research was on managerial saliency and involved interviewing mainly clinical staff along with managers. More support staff, such as wards people and cleaners, could have been consulted to generate a richer and more detailed data set. This also is an area for future research. Additionally, further research may be conducted in similar health systems internationally, to compare and contrast findings.

Implications and conclusions

Mitchell et al.'s (1997) stakeholder class theory resonates well within the health context. Individual relevance, when making decisions, is subject to the organizational cultural environment, as well as the degree- or extent- of urgency, legitimacy and power attached to the individual's decision-making capabilities. It was found that saliency is affected by individuals' (formal and informal) social interactions utilizing 'deep smarts' from both within and outside the workplace. Implicitly or explicitly, co-workers formed strategic alliances with those possessing 'deep smarts' to 'get things done'.

Professional groups in hospitals often behave like tribes. However, in some circumstances, tribal boundaries disappear and mixing between and within professions is possible. Meeting and spending time with co-workers from different tribes means that employees are developing and maintaining relationships. This is important for the organization's performance.

Engaging in informal chats is an essential element of organizational members' information sharing. When the formal avenues for communication are not readily available, employees look to using other means to share knowledge. Even in circumstances where a formal communication medium is available, it is often easier to have corridor conversations that help members within and across groups build their relationships. Relationship building is important as staff respond better to those peers and managers they have formed close relationships with, and are then more likely to take on additional duties.

Because of the importance of forming close relationships with other organizational members, it is also imperative for staff to know one another's reputation and be able to put a name to a face. Reputation is important in bureaucracies where staff may feel jaded and unrecognized. Being able to approach peers and managers and touching base is essential in building networks with others within an organization. Having an informal chat over a coffee or during a cigarette break can mean the difference between escalating a simple misunderstanding using the formal avenues for complaints, or picking up the phone and smoothing over the situation within a few minutes.

Moreover, working in an organization where staff members feel a sense of belonging is important when attempting to communicate the organization's bigger picture. Encouraging team players is made easier when staff members have an understanding of their external environment, and understand that the majority of the organization's members share a common understanding, despite substantial differences in personalities and priorities. Investing time and effort in junior staff who are part of the organization's community is commonsensical intelligent as it means there is a greater likelihood that the staff will want to continue to improve the community around them. This mentoring allows the development of 'deep smarts'.

Therefore, it is important to look at not only the formal power, legitimacy and urgency, but also the need to consider the relationships/networks that people form/are part of when trying to class stakeholders into groups, and understand those groups. Informal social networks were found to be powerful classes of stakeholders, something that has not been considered by those advocating the importance of stakeholder theory in determining stakeholder classes. Networks were found to exist within and across occupational groups. It was found that these networks were used to influence decision-making about resource allocation. The magnitude/strength of such networks varied from one network to another. Furthermore, the stronger the relationships between the people within the networks, the more likely it became that the network members could influence decision-making about bed allocation, regardless of position and formal decision-making privileges.

Mitchell et al. (1997) state that *'power gains authority through legitimacy'* (869). We find this somewhat limited. It does not consider those people who give information to the decision-makers, which is a form of power that is unrecognized. Furthermore, the statement follows on with *'and it (power) gains exercise through urgency'* (869). This may be the case, but Mitchell et al. (1997) do not take into consideration those people who use other methods to create that urgency. In fact, those people may not necessarily be the formal decision-makers.

In conclusion, there are three main findings arising from this exploratory study. First, despite its limitations, Mitchell's stakeholder theory is useful to understand how decisions are made within a health organization. The researchers propose that adding a fourth dimension to Mitchell's stakeholder model is compelling. This fourth dimension, the *magnitude* of relationships, may be considered to be the glue that holds the other three dimensions together.

Second, decision-makers who really matter have highly developed 'deep smarts'. Leonard and Swap (2005) profess that rules of thumb – or heuristics as per Bazerman (2002) – are best and quickest applied by people with deep smart attributes to come to a judgement. These judgements are an interplay of personal and organizational values, beliefs and experiences, and are linked to the organizational conduciveness for informal network and alliance building. Hence, our third finding is that the organization's culture in this hospital heavily influences who and what really matters when making health services management decisions. Hospital managers, who encourage, maintain and nurture informal social networking, extending friendships, trust and loyalty, will benefit from such networks by creating an organizational culture that allows the development and use of 'deep smarts', maximizing efficiency when making decisions.

References

Alvesson, M. and Berg, P.O. (1992) *Corporate Culture and Organizational Symbolism*. Berlin, New York: de Gruyter.

Barringer, B.R. and Harrison, J.S. (2002) 'Walking a tightrope: Creating value through interorganizational relationships', *Journal of Management*, 26 (3), 367.

Bazerman, M.H. (2002) *Judgment in Managerial Decision Making* (5th edn). Hoboken, NJ: Wiley.

Blaikie, N. (2000) Using triangulation and comparative analysis to advance knowledge in the social sciences: The role of four research strategies. Paper presented at the 5th International Conference for Methodologists in Social Sciences. Cologne, Germany.

Crozier, M. (1964) *The Bureaucratic Phenomenon*. Chicago, IL: University of Chicago.

Fitzgerald, J.A. (2002) Doctors and nurses working together: A mixed method study into the construction and changing of professional identities. PhD thesis, School of Management. University of Western Sydney, Sydney.

Freeman, R. (1994) 'The politics of stakeholder theory: some future directions', *Business Ethics Quarterly*, 4 (4), 409–21.

Harrison, S. and Pollitt, C. (1994) *Controlling Health Professionals: The Future of Work and Organization in the National Health Service*. Buckingham: Open University Press.

Hickson, D.J., Hinings, C.R., Lee, C.A., Schneck, R.E. and Pennings, J.M. (1971) 'A strategic contingencies' theory of intraorganizational power', *Administrative Science Quarterly*, 16 (2), 216.

Hofstede, G., Neuijen, B., Ohayv, D.D. and Sanders, G. (1990) 'Measuring organizational cultures: A qualitative and quantitative study across twenty cases', *Administrative Science Quarterly*, 35, 286–316.

Kroeber, A.L. and Kluckhohn, C. (1952) *Culture: A Critical Review of Concepts and Definitions*. Cambridge, MA: Harvard University Press.

Kunda, G. (1992) *Engineering Culture*. Philadelphia, PA: Temple University Press.

Lambert, H. and McKevitt, C. (2002) 'Anthropology in health research: From qualitative methods to multidisciplinarity', *British Medical Journal*, 325 (7357), 210–13.

Leonard, D. and Swap, W. (2005) *Deep Smarts: How to Cultivate and Transfer Enduring Business Wisdom*. Boston, MA: Harvard Business School Press.

Louis, M.R. (1985) 'An investigator's guide to workplace culture', in P. Frost, L. Moore, M.R. Louis, C. Lundberg and J. Martin, *Organizational Culture*. Beverly Hills, CA: Sage, 73–94.

Martin, J. (2002) *Organizational Culture: Mapping the Terrain*. Thousand Oaks, CA: Sage.

Mitchell, R.K., Agle, B.R. and Wood, D.J. (1997) 'Toward a theory of stakeholder identification and salience: Defining the principle of who and what really counts',
Academy of Management. The Academy of Management Review, 22 (4), 853.

Schein, E.H. (1985) *Organizational Culture and Leadership*. San Francisco, CA: Jossey-
Bass.

Schein, E.H. (1996) 'Culture: The missing concept in organization studies',
Administrative Science Quarterly, 41 (2), 229–40.

Smircich, L. (1983) 'Concepts of culture and organizational analysis', *Administrative
Science Quarterly*, 28 (3), 339.

Turner, B.A. (1990) 'The rise of organizational symbolism', in J. Hassard and D. Pym
(eds), *The Theory and Philosophy of Organizations*. Routledge: London, 83–96.

Van Maanen, J. and Barley, S. (1985) 'Cultural organization: Fragments of theory', in
P. Frost (ed.), *Organizational Culture*. Newbury Park, CA: Sage.

7

Bullying, Culture, and Climate in Health care Organizations: A theoretical Framework

Juliet MacMahon, Sarah MacCurtain and Michelle O'Sullivan

Introduction

Culture and climate – two distinct but inexorably linked terms, as many of the chapters in this book illustrate. In this chapter we focus on a compelling topic – bullying. In keeping with the theme of the book, we explore bullying in health care in terms of its links to culture and its relationship to climate and ultimately implications for patient and service user outcomes. This chapter arises from theoretical analyses, and studies relating to climate carried out by the authors in two large public health care organizations in Ireland where the issue of bullying arose not only in terms of its effect on individuals who experienced bullying, but also the effect of bullying on the collective perception of the organization and variables that are associated with climate. We are aiming in this chapter therefore to – perhaps tentatively – explore the culture-bullying-climate nexus and to provide a conceptual framework for further research. To this end the chapter examines first the 'meaning' of bullying and the incidence and extent of bullying. A conceptual model is then presented which links antecedents of a bullying culture to both individual outcomes and organization climate. This is followed by a discussion of the key variables presented in the model.

Bullying

The term 'bullying' is one which in itself poses difficulty, as interpretations of what constitutes bullying can be very subjectively based (Quine, 2001). Nonetheless, there appears to be international consensus among many researchers on certain dimensions of bullying from a definitional point of view. Key accepted definitional aspects are that the behaviour must be continuous and frequent and have negative outcomes for the victim (Agervold, 2007; Lewis, 2006a; Salin, 2008; O'Connell et al., 2007; Einarsen et al., 2003; Quine, 2001). Other features highlighted by the research include an imbalance of power between the parties (Lewis, 2006; Zapf and Gross, 2001; Einarsen et al., 2003; Vandekerckhove and Commers, 2003) and intent of the perpetrator (Agervold, 2007; Rayner Hoel and Cooper, 2002). This last condition poses difficulties as conflict can often arise between an individual's perception that behaviour towards them constitutes bullying whereas the alleged perpetrator(s) may argue that no harm was intended (Agervold, 2007).

For the purposes of this chapter, we utilize the definition provided by the Irish Labour Relations Commission (2006: 2), and the Irish Health and Safety Authority (2007) which seem to encapsulate much of the conditions above

> repeated inappropriate behaviour, direct or indirect, whether verbal, physical or otherwise, conducted by one or more persons against another or others, at the place of work and/or in the course of employment, which could reasonably be regarded as undermining the individual's right to dignity at work. An isolated incident of the behaviour described in this definition may be an affront to dignity at work but, as a once off incident, is not considered to be bullying.

Bullying manifests itself in many ways and is not limited to the manager/subordinate relationship. Research has highlighted instances of collective and individual bullying, peer bullying (Salin, 2003; Edwards and O'Connell, 2007), upward bullying (Branch et al., 2007) and bullying by clients/customers of organizations. Cited examples of workplace bullying (Zapf, 1999; O'Connell et al., 2007; Hansen et al., 2006) tend to fall into two categories – the first being more explicit forms of bullying such as: being subjected to physically aggressive behaviour, teasing, threatening, verbally abuse and being humiliated in front of others. The second category contains more subtle forms of bullying such as being subjected to unreasonable work demands, being excluded or isolated, being undermined or having necessary work information withheld.

Bullying in health care – the extent of the problem

Bullying in the workplace is a problem which transcends national boundaries (cf. Parent-Thirion et al., 2007). This is particularly true of the health care sector as evidenced in the range of studies and findings from different countries such as Ireland (O'Connell et al., 2007; O'Moore et al., 1998), UK (Quine, 2001; Randle, 2007; Hume et al., 2006; Lewis, 2001; 2006b), US (Lutgen-Sandvik et al., 2007), India (Bairy et al., 2007), Scandinavian countries (Leymann and Gustavson, 1996; Salin 2003; 2008) and Australia (Mayhew and Chappell, 2001; 2003; Rutherford and Rissell, 2004). Studies also reveal that bullying is widespread at all levels of health care, including amongst junior doctors (Cheema, 2005; Quine, 2002), nurses (McMillan, 1995; Yildirim and Yildirim, 2007; Duffy, 1995; Quine, 1999; Farrell, 2001; Lewis, 2001), social care workers, supervisors and managers, (Salin, 2005) and across all facets whether it be hospitals, smaller clinical practices or social care settings. The vulnerability of workers in the sector is further exacerbated by bullying/aggressive behaviour from a wider range of people than may be the case in other workplaces. Identified sources of bullying in health care can include patients/clients/service users and their families (De Martino, 2003) as well as colleagues and managers (Ferrinho et al., 2003; Rutherford and Rissel, 2004).

Bullying causes – the link with organization culture

One research approach to investigating the reasons for bullying behaviour has been to focus on personality – the personality of the victim and the bully. Certain characteristics of the victim have been noted as making them susceptible to bullying. Victims have been identified as being 'different'; overachievers, naïve, oversensitive, suspicious, angry and having low self-esteem (Brodsky, 1976; Einarsen, 1999; Einarsen et al., 1994; Felson, 1992; Gandolfo, 1995). Conversely, bullies have been described as having diffi-cult personalities and of being envious and uncertain about themselves (BjoÈrkqvist et al., 1994; Einarsen et al., 1994; Seigne, 1998; Vartia, 1996). However, caution must be exercised when linking personality traits to bully-ing. Rayner and Hoel (1997) note the tendency for people to attribute nega-tive behaviour to personality traits rather than the environment. Going further, Leymann (1996) and Lewis (2006) maintain that personality traits are irrelevant when studying the causes of bullying. Lewis (2006: 55) argues that the personality of the bully is "predominantly contextually workplace mediated" and that

> what becomes particularly intriguing from an interactionist's perspec-tive is the socializing effect of the organization, the reinforcement of the dominant definition of the situation, and so-called norms of behaviour and acceptance of the same by so many.

More recently, more holistic frameworks of investigation such as that developed by Einarsen and Skogstad (1996) argue that bullying may be understood to be the outcome of interrelated factors, such as interpersonal, intrapersonal, organizational, and social dimensions. In much of the cur-rent research the nexus or mix of variables expressed as the 'culture' of the organization are often cited as being positively related to the existence and persistence of bullying.

Figure 7.1 below graphically represents the link between culture, bully-ing, and climate. In presenting this conceptual framework, we argue that a

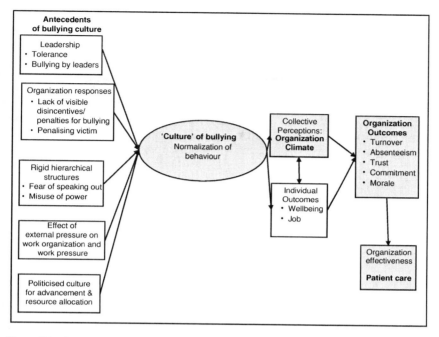

Figure 7.1 Conceptual framework linking culture, bullying and climate

culture of bullying within organizations is strongly influenced by certain antecedents. This in turn has consequences not only for individuals but also for climate and ultimately for patient care.

Applying a cultural paradigm to bullying

There is some evidence that certain organizational cultures (e.g. power cultures based on rank and position) can lead to the normalizing of bullying behaviours (Archer, 1999). A deeper understanding of cultural issues can help understand why bullying is pervasive in certain organizations and sectors. Schein (2006) defines culture as a collection of traditions, values, policies, beliefs and attitudes that constitute a pervasive context for everything we do and think in an organization, or more simply 'how we do things around here' (Deal and Kennedy, 2000). Indicators of organizational culture include socialization and initiation rites, group norms, language, ceremonies and rituals and stories that convey to employees what is valued in the organization. 'Bullying cultures' can be affected or caused by alienating socialization and initiation rites (Archer, 1999), exclusionary language and norms and a management style that is hierarchical and authoritarian.

Furthermore, bullying in the workplace can be reinforced by health care professionals' education. It has been found that bullying practices have transferred from the hospital/clinical setting into higher education institutes. This occurs mainly through the employment of people directly from health care as teaching/administrative staff into health/medical education schools who bring with them 'cultural baggage' reflecting cultures of the workplace (Edwards and O'Connell, 2007; Stevenson et al., 2006). Thus medical, nursing and other health care students are vulnerable to bullying and an informal component of their learning experience is the 'normalizing' of such behaviour (Wood, 2006; Bairy et al., 2007). As these students transfer into the workplace, they can perpetuate the problem, reinforcing the cycle and culture of bullying (Wood, 2006).

Delving further into the role of management, a frequent issue identified by bullying literature is the part played by leadership (Schein, 2004; Sims and Brinkman, 2003). Schein and others argue that leaders are the main shapers of organizational culture. Recent studies have found that aspects of 'destructive' leadership (Skogstad et al., 2007; Salin, 2008) contribute to the prevalence of bullying in organizations whereby managers effectively condone bullying through *laissez faire* approaches of non intervention. Einarsen et al. (1996) find that the highest incidences of workplace bullying are found where senior management are perceived as tolerating/ignoring such behaviour and allowing such a culture to develop (cf. Lewis, 2006; Brennan, 2001; and Mayhew and Chappell, 2003). Not only can senior colleagues tolerate the behaviour, but they can be the sources of bullying (Einarsen and Skogstad, 1996; Salin, 2008; Lewis, 2006; Kelly, 2006; McMillan, 1995; Paterson et al., 1997; Quine, 1999). Hutchinson et al. (2008: 65) hypothesize that the misuse of legitimate authority for the purpose of bullying may explain the frequent reports that the perpetrators are more commonly managers. Harassment can be institutionalized as part of leadership and managerial practice (Ashforth, 1994; Brodsky, 1976).

Organizations with rigid hierarchical structures and marked management/staff boundaries foster 'them and us' cultures with opportunities for bullying to be accepted as normal behaviour which increases the risk of bullying (Mayhew and Chappell, 2001; Randle, 2007). For instance, nurses have reported that violence and aggression are part of nursing workplace culture (Erikson and Williams-Evans, 2000). Another serious issue for managers in health care organizations is the consistent findings of research that incidences of bullying are rarely reported on a formal basis (Mayhew and Chapell, 2001; Birman, 1999; Kelly, 2006; Field, 2003) often due to a fear of no longer fitting with the accepted norms of the organization. McAvoy and Murtagh (2003: 776) refer to the 'toxic workplace', which 'perpetuates dysfunction, fear, shame, and embarrassment, intimidating those who dare to speak out and nurturing a silent epidemic'.

A very recent perspective focuses on the power contexts within health care organizations whereby work environments create 'circuits of power' (Hutchinson et al., 2006) that facilitate and, in a sense, act to condone bullying behaviour. The power bestowed on individuals or groups due to organizational structure or culture can be used to engage in bullying behaviour in order to maintain the status quo or get desired results or resources. Salin (2003: 1218) argues that the imbalance of power between the possible victim and perpetrator is an example of an enabling structure which can 'provide fertile soil for bullying'. In addition, engaging in bullying behaviour can be a rational decision on the part of the perpetrator when they believe it can lead to benefits for them, for example, in a politicized culture, where high internal competition exists or when there is competition for a superior's approval (Salin, 2003; BjoÈrkqvist et al., 1994; Vartia, 1996). Salin (2003) found evidence of possible increased engagement in bullying as a micropolitical strategy for eliminating unwanted persons or improving ones' own position through such behaviour as deliberate withholding of information. This self-interested approach by perpetrators can be fostered in egoistic organizational cultures, because their self-interest is supported by the organization (Hutchinson et al., 2008). Hutchinson et al. (2008) identify that informal organizational alliances within workplaces provide the mechanism through which bullying becomes a learned organizational behaviour and they draw links between such alliances and the tolerance and reward of bullying (cf. Brodsky, 1976; Einarsen, 1999). Thus, organizations develop 'cultures' whereby bullying is part of the fabric of the organization.

High levels of support at work have been linked to reducing the likelihood of workers being subjected to bullying and to protecting individuals from some of the harmful effects of bullying (Quine, 2001; Hansen et al., 2006) However, the research would seem to indicate that many organizations struggle with the issue of bullying and their response is often to remove the victim from the workplace rather than the perpetrator(s) (Leymann, 1996). Salin (2008) highlights that very often there seems to be no visible disincentive cost to perpetrators to discourage them from bullying, that is, the risk of being discovered and reprimanded. Thus, negative cultures which are perceived to support bullying behaviour are perpetuated through lack of action by management.

External pressures

Cultural and organizational factors which affect bullying can be exacerbated by external pressures. In many countries health services are under strain due to increasing pressure to improve efficiency and cost effectiveness whilst at the same time improving quality of service (Barman, 2007; Quinn, 2006; Passey et al., 2000; Sparks et al., 2001; Kellock et al., 2001; Brito et al.,

2001; Ledwith, 1999). There are inherent tensions in these aims and indeed changes in working conditions and work pressures in organizations can act as precipitating triggers for bullying (Hickling, 2006; Leymann, 1990; Salin, 2003). These can include high levels of stress, role ambiguity, job cuts, precarious employment, reorganization, top-down targets, organizational change and work intensification (Brodsky, 1976; Nabb, 2000; Kenny, 2002; Randle, 2007). Vandererckhove and Commers (2003) argue that it is not the organization shifts as a result of external pressures that are to blame – rather it is inadequate transformation of leadership and power in reaction to those shifts, which leaves certain organizational members isolated and vulnerable.

Health care organizations have been characterized as being/becoming transactional in nature, where a focus on productivity and scant regard for the means used to achieve the outcome can engender tolerance and reward of bullying (Hutchinson et al., 2008). Organizational restructuring or changes may create opportunities for employees to misuse legitimate authority and processes to further self-interest (Hutchinson et al., 2008). In public sector bureaucracies, where there can be difficulties in laying off employees with permanent status or where colleagues may be competing for scarce promotional opportunities in more competitive work environments, the potential exists for individuals to attempt to undermine each other (Salin, 2003: 435).

Outcomes of bullying and effects on climate

The direct impact of bullying on individual well-being and on the organization is extensively reported. For the victim, research confirms an association between bullying and a range of psychosocial and physiological symptoms such as sleeping problems, stomach ache, anxiety and irritability (Parent-Thirion et al., 2007). Health care staff subjected to bullying have reported burn out, psychological and somatic complaints, dissatisfaction, anxiety, depression, job dissatisfaction, job stress, perceptions of injustice, low trust, propensity to leave, suicidal behaviour, sleeplessness, self-hatred, stress, lowered confidence and self-esteem, anger, powerlessness, drug and alcohol abuse and an increase in absence or sickness (Randle, 2003; O'Connell et al., 2007; Kivimäki et al., 2000). In addition, victims can become bullies themselves (Randle, 2003). From the organizations' perspective, bullying has been associated with absenteeism, turnover, replacement costs, deterioration in productivity and performance, patient care, possible compensation and litigation and loss of public goodwill and reputation (Hoel et al., 2003; Kauppinen et al., 1997; Kivimäki et al., 2000; Parent-Thirion et al., 2007; Zapf and Gross, 2001). Whilst these are extremely serious issues for management, recognition also needs to be given to the fact that the effects of bullying can go beyond individual consequences and outcomes and affect the *collective* perception of the organization – even among those employees who have not experienced bullying themselves. Thus, bullying can have a serious impact on climate and can have major further implications for management of health care organizations in terms of collective staff morale, retention/turnover trust and ultimately of patient/service user care.

The issue of climate and, more particularly, the climate/patient outcome nexus is one which has attracted significant attention and there is recognition that these issues are linked (Hatton et al., 2001; Hatton, C., Rivers, M., Mason, H., Mason, L., Kiernan, C. et al., 1999a; Patterson et al., 2005; Stone et al., 2004; Gershon et al., 2004). Climate can be generally understood as a 'surface' manifestation of culture which reflects employees' perceptions of organization culture (Schneider 1990; Gershon et al. 2004). It refers to the day-to-day practices in the organization, its policies and reward procedures, the 'encapsulation of the organization's true priorities' (Ahmed, 1998: 31). A more comprehensive definition may be that of Moran and Volkswein (1992: 20) when they describe climate as:

A relatively enduring characteristic of an organisation which distinguishes it from other organisations: and (a) embodies members' collective perceptions about their organisation with respect to such dimensions as autonomy, trust, cohesiveness, support, recognition, innovation and fairness; (b) is produced by member interaction (c) serves as a basis for interpreting the situation; (d) reflects the prevalent norms values and attitudes of the organizational culture; and (e) acts as a source of influence for shaping behaviour.

The link between bullying and climate becomes clear when we examine literature on the antecedents to climate and climate measures. Many of the individual outcomes of bullying listed above have been identified as elements of organizational climate; for example perceptions of support/isolation, negative management style, job overload, low trust, general distress, absenteeism and turnover (Rose and Rose, 2005; Michie and Williams, 2003; Hatton et al., 2001; Hatton, C., Rivers, M., Mason, H., Mason, L., Emerson, C. et al., 1999b; Borrill et al., 1996; Carter and West, 1999). Bullying therefore can be held to directly affect climate or could contribute along with other factors to fuelling a 'toxic' climate. In the authors' own study, significant correlations were found between bullying and outcomes such as employee morale, commitment, perceptions of organizational justice and tenure intent.

Empirical findings have found climate in turn exerts a significant influence on organizational performance which for health care organizations is ultimately the quality of care given to patients/service users (Baer and Frese, 2003; Mudrack, 1989; Moss-Kanter, 1983). Anderson et al. (1992) found climate to be associated with innovation in their case study of the National Health Service (NHS) in the UK. A study conducted by Borrill et al. (2000)

of more than 500 NHS teams found climate to be linked to effectiveness in delivering patient care and Carter and West (1999) found that organizational climate was related to levels of stress in primary care teams (see also Rose et al., 2000). Another 'reverse' dimension is the perception of potential employees of particular health care workplaces. If a workplace is perceived as having a negative climate or evidence of bullying and unfair treatment of staff, then this will serve to dissuade people from entering employment in such an organization where they have any element of choice.

Conclusion

In this chapter we presented a conceptual framework linking cultural antecedents, bullying and organizational climate which requires further empirical testing. The chapter contends that bullying is a serious, damaging and pervasive issue in health care organizations, the causes of which are firmly rooted in the mix of variables commonly associated with the 'culture' of the organization. Whilst acknowledging the seriousness of the impact of bullying in terms of individual outcomes, we argue that bullying has wider consequences in that it can affect the collective perception of the organization – that is the climate. Thus, the effects of bullying have serious consequences for all employees, for patients/service users and for the ability of the organization to provide a service and attract employees. Public health care organizations differ from other organizations; rather than producing an inanimate product, they are ultimately responsible for the wellbeing/health and welfare of their customers. Quality of patient care is the ultimate goal and *raison d'etre* of all public health care providers and therefore any organizational factors which hinder this outcome must be viewed seriously in this context. Factors leading to poor climate such as bullying can have serious implications in organizations which care for particularly vulnerable groups (like those with intellectual disabilities) in the sense that demoralized/stressed staff may not be able to provide the level of care required for enhancing quality of life of service users (Hatton et al., 2001; Felce et al., 1993; Fisher, 2004).

References

Agervold, M. (2007) 'Bullying at work: A discussion of definitions and prevalence, based on an empirical study', *Scandinavian Journal of Psychology*, 48, 161–72.

Ahmed, P.K. (1998) 'Culture and climate for innovation', *European Journal of Innovation Management*, 1 (1), 30–43.

Anderson, N.R., Hardy and West, M.A. (1992) *Team Climates for Innovation*, MRC/ESRC, Social and Applied Psychology Unit, University of Sheffield, Memo 1430.

Archer, D. (1999) 'Exploring "bullying" culture in the para-military organisation', *International Journal of Manpower*, 20 (1/2), 94–105.

Ashforth, B. (1994) 'Petty tyranny in organizations', *Human Relations*, 47, 755–78.

Baer, M. and Frese, M. (2003) 'Innovation is not enough: Climates for initiative and psychological safety, process innovations, and firm performance', *Journal of Organisational Behaviour*, 24, 45–69.

Bairy K.L., Thirumalaikolundusubramanian, P., Sivagnanam, G., Saraswathi, S., Sachidananda, A. and Shalini, A. (2007) 'Bullying among trainee doctors in Southern India: A questionnaire study', *Journal of Postgraduate Medicine*, 53, 87–90.

Barman, E. (2007) 'What is the bottom line for nonprofit organizations? A history of measurement in the British Voluntary Sector', *Voluntas-Iinternational Journal for Voluntary and Non Profit Organisations*, 18 (2), June, 101–15.

Birman, J. (1999) 'Covert violence in nursing', *Australian National Safety Journal*, 7, 17–21.

BjoÈrkqvist, K., Esterman, K. and Hjelt-Back, M. (1994) 'Aggression among university employees', *Aggressive Behavior*, 20, 173–84.

Borrill, C., West, M.A., Shapiro, D. and Rees, A. (2000) 'Team working and effectiveness in health care', *British Journal of Health Care*, 6 (8), 364–71.

Branch, S., Ramsay, S. and Barker, M. (2007) 'Contributing factors to workplace bullying by staff – an interview study', *Journal of Management and Organisation*, 13 (3), 264–81.

Brennan, W. (2001) 'Bully off', *Health and Safety at Work*, 23 (96), 17.

Brito, P., Galin, P. and Novick, M. (2001) *Labour Relations, Employment Conditions and Participation in the Health Sector*, Workshop on Global Health Workforce Strategy, Annecy, France, 9–12 December.

Brodsky, C.M. (1976) *The Harassed Worker*. Toronto: Lexington Books, DC Heath and Company.

Carter, A. and West, M. (1999) 'Sharing the burden: Team work in health care settings', in J. Firth-Cozens and R. Payne (eds), *Stress in Health Professionals: Psychological and Organisational Causes and Interventions*. Chicester: John Wiley & Sons, 191–202.

Cheema, S., Ahmad, K., Giri, S.K., Kaliaperumal, V.K. and Naqvi, S.A. (2005) 'Bullying of junior doctors prevails in irish health system: A bitter reality', *Irish Medical Journal*, 98 (9), October, 274–5.

Deal, T.E. and Kennedy, A.A. (2000) *Corporate Culture: The Rites and Rituals of Corporate Life*. Boston, MA: Perseus.

De Martino, V. (2003) *Relationship of Work Stress and Workplace Violence in the Health Sector*. Geneva: ILO.

Duffy, E. (1995) 'Horizontal violence: A conundrum for nursing', *Collegian*, 2, 5–17.

Edwards, S. and O'Connell, C.F. (2007) 'Exploring bullying: Implications for nurse educators', *Nurse Education in Practice*, 7, 26–35.

Einarsen, S. (1999) 'The nature and causes of bullying at work', *International Journal of Manpower*, 20, 16–27.

Einarsen, S., Hoel, H., Zapf, D. and Cooper, C.L. (2003) 'The concept of bullying at work: The European tradition', in S. Einarsen, H. Hoel, D. Zapf and C.L. Cooper (eds), *Bullying and Emotional Abuse in the Workplace: International Perspectives in Research and Practice*. London: Taylor and Francis, 3–30.

Einarsen, S., Raknes, B.I. and Matthiesen, S.B. (1994) 'Bullying and its relationship to work and employment: An exploratory study', *European Journal of Organisational Psychology*, 4, 381–401.

Einarsen, S., Raknes, B.I. and Matthiesen, S.M. (1994) 'Bullying and harassment at work and their relationships to work environment quality – an exploratory study', *European Journal of Work and Organizational Psychology*, 4, 381–401.

Einarsen, S. and Skogstad, A. (1996) 'Bullying at work: Epidemiological findings in public and private organizations', *European Journal of Work and Organizational Psychology*, 5, 185–202.

Erickson, L. and William-Evans, S.A. (2000) 'Attitudes of emergency nurses regarding patient assaults', *Journal of Emergency Nursing*, 26 (3), 210–15.

Farrell, G.A. (2001) 'From tall poppies to squashed weeds: Why don't nurses pull together more?' *Journal of Advanced Nursing*, 35 (1), 26–33.

Felce D., Lowe K. and Beswick, J. (1993) 'Staff turnover in ordinary housing services for people with severe or profound mental handicaps', *Journal of Intellectual Disability Research*, 37 (Pt 2), April, 143–52.

Felson, R.B. (1992) 'Kick 'em when they're down: Explanations of the relationships between stress and interpersonal aggression and violence', *Sociological Quarterly*, 33 (1), 1–16.

Ferrinho, P., Biscaia, A., Fronteira, I. Antunes, I.C., Conceicao, C., Flores, I. and Santos, O. (2003) 'Patterns of perceptions of workplace violence in the health care sector', *Human Resource Health*, 1, 1–11.

Field, T. (2003) 'Workplace bullying: The silent epidemic', editorial, *BMJ*, 326, April, 776–77.

Fisher, K. (2004) 'Nursing care of special populations: Issues in caring for elderly people with mental retardation', *Nursing Forum*, 39 (1), January–March, 20–31.

Gandolfo, R. (1995) 'MMPI-2 profiles of worker's compensations claimants who present with complaints of harassment', *Journal of Clinical Psychology*, 51, 711–15.

Gershon, R.M., Stone, P.W., Bakken, S. and Larson, E. (2004) 'Measurement of organisation culture and climate in health care', *Journal of Nursing Administration*, 34 (1), January, 33–40.

Hansen, A., Hogh, R., Persson, B., Karlson, A., Garde, P. and Ørbæk (2006) 'Bullying at work, health outcomes, and physiological stress response', *Journal of Psychosomatic Research*, 60 (1), 63–72.

Hatton, C., Emerson, E., Rivers, M., Mason, H., Swarbrick, R, Mason, L., Kiernan, C., Reeves, D., and Alborz, A. (2001) 'Factors associated with intended staff turnover and job search behaviour in services for people with intellectual disability', *Journal of Intellectual Disability Research*, 45 (3), 258–70.

Hatton, C., Rivers, M., Mason, H., Mason, L., Kiernan, C., Emerson, E., Alborz, A. and Reeves, D. (1999a) 'Staff stressors and staff outcomes in services for adults with intellectual disabilities: The staff stressor questionnaire', *Research in Developmental Disabilities*, 20, 269–85.

Hatton, C., Rivers, M., Mason, H., Mason, L., Emerson, E., Kiernan, C., Reeves, D. and Alborz, A. (1999b) 'Organizational culture and staff outcomes in services for people with intellectual disabilities', *Journal of Intellectual Disability Research*, 43, 206–18.

Health and Safety Authority (2007) *Code of Practice for Employers and Employees for the Prevention and Resolution of Bullying at Work*. Dublin: HSA.

Hickling, K. (2006) 'Workplace bullying', in Randle, J. (ed.), *Workplace Bullying in the NHS*. Oxford: Radcliffe Press, 7–24.

Hoel, H., Einarsen, S. and Cooper, C.L. (2003) 'Organisational effects of bullying', in Stale Einarsen, Helge Hoel, Dieter Zapf, Cary L. Cooper (eds), *Bullying and Emotional Abuse in the Workplace*, London: Taylor & Francis, 145–62.

Hume, C., Randle, J. and Stevenson, K. (2006) 'Student nurses' experiences of workplace relationships', in Jacqueline Randl (ed.), *Workplace Bullying in the NHS*, London: Routledge, 63–76.

Hutchinson, M., Jackson, D., Wilkes, L. and Vickers, M.H. (2008) 'A new model of bullying in the nursing workplace organizational characteristics as critical antecedents', *Advances in Nursing Science*, 31(2), 60–71.

Hutchinson, M., Vickers, M., Jackson, D. and Wilkes, L. (2006) 'Workplace bullying in nursing: Towards a more critical organisational perspective', *Nursing Inquiry*, 13 (2), 118–26.

Kauppinen T., Aaltonen, M. and Lehtinen, S. (1997) *Work and Health in Finland 1997*. Helsinki: Finnish Institute of Occupational Health.

Kellock Hay, G., Beattie, R.S., Livingstone, R. and Munro, P. (2001) 'Change, HRM and the voluntary sector', *Employee Relations*, 23 (3), 240–5.

Kelly, D. (2006) 'Workplace bullying – a complex issue needing IR/HRM research?' in Pocock, B., Provis, C. and Willis, E. (eds), *21st Century Work: Proceedings of the 20th Conference of the Association of Industrial Relations Academics of Australia and New Zealand*. University of South Australia, February, 274–84.

Kenny, J. (2002) 'The process of employee violence: The building of a workplace explosion', in M. Gill, B. Fisher and V. Bowie (eds), *Violence at Work Causes Patterns and Preventions*. Devon: Willan.

Kivimäki, M., Elovainio, M. and Vahtera, J. (2000) 'Workplace bullying and sickness absence in hospital staff', *Occupational Environmental Medicine*, 57, 656–60.

Labour Relations Commission (2006) *Procedures For Addressing Bullying in The Workplace*, Code of Practice no. 6. Dublin: Labour Relations Commission.

Ledwith, F. (1999) 'Policy contradictions and collaboration in community mental health services in Britain', *International Journal of Public Sector Management*, 12 (3), 236–48.

Lewis, M. (2001) 'Bullying in nursing', *Nursing Standard*, 15, 39–42.

Lewis, M.A. (2006a) 'Organisational accounts of bullying: An interactive approach', in Jacqueline Randle (ed.), *Workplace Bullying in the NHS*. London: Routledge.

Lewis, M.A. (2006b) 'Nurse bullying: Organizational considerations in the maintenance and perpetuation of health care bullying cultures', *Journal of Nursing Management*, 14, 52–8.

Leymann, H. (1990) 'Mobbing and psychological terror at workplaces', *Violence and Victims*, 5, 119–26.

Leymann, H. (1996) 'The content and development of mobbing at work', *European Journal of Work and Organizational Psychology*, 5, 165–84.

Leymann, H. and Gustafsson, A. (1996) 'Mobbing at work and the development of post-traumatic stress disorder', *European Journal of Work and Organisation Psychology*, 5 (2), 251–75.

Lutgen-Sandvik, P., Tracy, S.J. and Alberts, J.K. (2007) 'Burned by bullying in the American workplace: prevalence, perception, degree and impact', *Journal of Management Studies*, 44 (6), September, 837–62.

Mayhew, C. and Chappell, D. (2003) 'Internal Occupational Violence (or Bullying) in the Health care Industry', *Journal of Occupational Health and Safety*, Australia and New Zealand, 19 (1), 59–71.

Mayhew, C. and Chappell, D. (2001) *Internal Violence (or bullying) and the Health Workforce*. Taskforce on the Prevention and Management of Violence in the Health care Workplace. Discussion paper no. 3. Sydney: University of New South Wales School of Industrial Relations and Organisational Behaviour and Industrial Relations Research Centre.

Michie, S. and Williams, S. (2003) 'Reducing work-related psychological ill health and sickness absence: a systematic literature review', *Occupational and Environmental Medicine*, 60, 3–9.

Moran, E.T. and Volkswein, J.F. (1992) 'The cultural approach to the formation of organisational climate', *Human Relations*, 45, 19–48.

Moss-Kanter, R. (1983) *The Change Masters: Innovation for Productivity in the American Corporation*. New York: Simon & Schuster.

Mudrack, P.E. (1989) 'Group cohesiveness and productivity: A closer Look', *Human Relations*, 42, 771–86.

McAvoy, B. and Murtagh, J. (2003) 'Workplace bullying the silent epidemic', *BMJ*, 326, 776–7.

McMillan, I (1995) 'Losing Control', *Nursing Times*, 91, 40–3.

Nabb, D (2000) 'Visitors' violence: The serious effects of aggression on nurses and others', *Nursing Standard*, 14 (23), 36–8.

O'Connell, P.J., Calvert, E. and Watson, D. (2007) *Bullying in the Workplace, Survey Reports*. Dublin: Department of Enterprise Trade and Employment.

O'Moore, M., Seigne, E., McGuire, L. and Smith, M. (1998) 'Victims of bullying at work in Ireland', *Journal of Occupational Health and Safety: Australia and New Zealand*, 14 (6), 568–74.

Parent-Thirion, A., Macías, E.F., Hurley, J. and Vermeylen, G. (2007) *Fourth European Working Conditions Survey*. Luxembourg: Office for Official Publications of the European Communities.

Passey, A., Hems, L. and Jas, P. (2000) *The Voluntary Sector Almanac 2000*. London: NCVO Publications.

Paterson, B., McComish, A. and Aitken, I. (1997) 'Abuse and bullying', *Nursing Management*, 3 (10), 8–9.

Patterson, M.G., West, M.A., Schackelton, V.J., Dawson, J.F., Lawthom, R., Maitlis, S., Robinson, D.L. and Wallace, A. (2005) 'Validating the organizational climate measure: Links to managerial practices, productivity and innovation', *Journal of Organizational Behavior*, 26, 379–408.

Quine, L. (1999) 'Workplace bullying in NHS Community Trust: Staff Questionnaire Survey', *BMJ*, 318, 228–32.

Quine, L. (2001) 'Workplace Bullying in Nurses', *Journal of Health Psychology*, 6 (73), 73–84.

Quine, L. (2002) 'Workplace Bullying in Junior Doctors, Questionnaire Survey', *British Medical Journal* (BMJ), 324, 878–9.

Quinn, E. (2006) *Managed Migration and the Labour Market: The Health Sector in Ireland*. Report prepared for the European Commission Directorate-General Justice, Freedom and Security and published by the ESRI, Dublin, July.

Randle, J. (2003) 'B'ullying in the nursing profession', *Journal of Advanced Nursing*, 43 (4), 395–401.

Randle, J. (2007) 'Reducing Workplace Bullying in health care organisations', *Nursing Standard*, 21 (22), 7 February, 49–56.

Rayner, C. and Hoel, H. (1997) A Summary Review of Literature Relating to Workplace Bullying. *Journal of Community & Applied Social Psychology*, 7, 181–91.

Rayner, C., Hoel, H. and Cooper, C. L. (2002) *Workplace Bullying*. London: Taylor and Francis.

Rose, J., Jones, C. and Elliott, J.L. (2000) 'Differences in stress levels between managers and direct care staff in group homes', *Journal of Applied Research in Intellectual Disabilities*, 13 (4), December, 276.

Rose, D. and Rose, J. (2005) 'Staff in services for people with intellectual disabilities: The impact of stress on attributions of challenging behaviour', *Journal of Intellectual Disability Research*, 49 (11), November, 827–38.

Rutherford, A. and Rissel, C. (2004) A survey of workplace bullying in a health care organisation, *Australian Health Review*, 28 (1), September, 65–72.

Salin, D. (2003) 'Ways of explaining workplace bullying: A review of enabling, motivating, and precipitating structures and processes in the work environment', *Human Relations*, 56, 1213–32.

Salin, D. (2005) Workplace Bullying among Business Professionals: Prevalence, Gender Differences and the Role of Organizational Politics (PISTES), 7 (3), http://www.pistes.uqam.ca/

Schein, (2004) *Organisational Culture and Leadership*. Wiley: Jossey Bass.

Salin, D. (2008) 'The prevention of workplace bullying as a question of human resource management: Measures adopted and underlying organizational factors', *Scandinavian Journal of Management*, 24 (3), 221–31.

Schneider, B. (1990) *Organizational Climate and Culture*. San Francisco, CA: Jossey Bass.

Seigne, E. (1998) 'Bullying at work in Ireland', in Rayner, C., Sheehan, M. and Barker, M. (eds), *Bullying at Work*, Research Update Conference Proceedings. Stafford: Staffordshire University.

Sims, R.R. and Brinkman, J. (2003) 'Enron ethics: Culture means more than codes', *Journal of Business Ethics*, 45, 243–56.

Skogstad, A., Einarsen, S., Torsheim, T., Aasland, M.S. and Hetland, H. (2007) 'The destructiveness of laissez-faire leadership behavior', *Journal of Occupational Health Psychology*, 12 (1), 80–92.

Sparks, K., Faragher, B., and Cooper, G.L. (2001) 'Well-Being and occupational health in the 21st century workplace', *Journal of Occupational and Organisational Psychology*, 74, 489–509.

Stevenson, K., Randle, J., Grayling, I. (2006) 'Inter-group conflict in health care: UK students' experiences of bullying and the need for organisational solutions', *OJIN: The Online Journal of Issues in Nursing*, 1 (2), Manuscript 5.

Stone, P.W., Harrison, M.I., Feldman, P., Linzer, M., Peng, T., Doblin, D., Scott-Cawiezel J., Warren N., Williams, E.S. (2004) *Organizational Climate of Staff Working Conditions and Safety – An Integrative Model*. New York: Columbia University School of Nursing.

Vandekerckhove, W. and Commers, M.S.R. (2003) 'Downward workplace mobbing: A sign of the times?' *Journal of Business Ethics*, 45 (1), June, 41–50.

Vartia, M. (1996) 'The sources of bullying – psychological work environment and organizational climate', *European Journal of Work and Organizational Psychology*, 5, 203–14.

Wood, D. (2006) 'Bullying and harassment in medical schools', *BMJ*, 333, 664–5.

Yildirim, A. and Yildirim, D. (2007) 'Mobbing in the workplace by peers and managers: Mobbing experienced by nurses working in health care facilities in Turkey and its effect on nurses', *Journal of Clinical Nursing*, 16, 1444–53.

Zapf, D. (1999) 'Organizational, work group related and personal causes of mobbing/bullying at work', *International Journal of Manpower*, 20, 70–84.

Zapf, D. and Gross, C. (2001) 'Conflict escalation and coping with workplace bullying: A replication and extension', *European Journal of Work and Organisational Psychology*, 10 (4), 497–522.

8
Changing Relationships between Health Service Managers: Confrontation, Collusion and Collaboration

Paula Hyde

Introduction

This chapter focuses on relationships between human resource (HR) and clinical managers. It explores the policy and practice implications arising from research into changing human resource management (HRM) arrangements in the English National Health Service (NHS). The empirical data on which the discussion is founded concerns the enactment of HRM in the NHS as health care managers, many of whom are highly qualified clinical professionals, face increasing demands to fulfil HRM functions. Relationships between human resource and line managers have a turbulent history, with line managers generally being identified as vital intermediaries between HRM strategy and frontline workers (Purcell et al., 2003). Recently, attempts to devolve responsibility for HR functions to line managers whilst HR retains responsibility for managerial control have led to a change in relationships, with line managers being alternately cast as either unco-operative or lacking in competence (Whittaker and Marchington, 2003). As a result, the impression of a negative relationship between HR and line managers has been created. This general situation is mirrored in the English NHS where the potential for troubled relationships between HR and clinical managers has been highlighted as important, especially as a result of attempts to change NHS culture (Fitzgerald et al., 2006).

This empirical chapter draws on interviews with 78 health service managers from six NHS organizations undertaken as part of a wider study. Participants included clinical, general, and HR managers. Elaborations of how these relationships work in practice are presented, explaining how changes to HRM arrangements are played out in various ways through interactions with line managers. Three types of exchanges are explored: confrontation (see also Purcell et al., 2003); collusion (Hyde and Davies, 2004); and collaboration. These exchanges suggest several potential problems for health service delivery as gaps in HR provision emerge and responsibility for organizational problems can become dispersed throughout the organization. Over time the HR function has transformed into a strategic function serving organizational goals. The resultant dependency on general and clinical managers to fill the consequent HR gaps, which this strategic move necessitates, often goes unacknowledged. Relationships between clinical and HR managers are important because they can affect the sustainability of large scale changes to culture and climate in the NHS (Fitzgerald et al., 2006).

Business model changes in health care organizations

Mature organizational fields are established through a process of structuration that includes not only suppliers, consumers, regulatory agencies, and other organizations producing similar products and services but also includes interaction between members and the development of connections between them. These relationships and connections lead ultimately to recognition of mutual involvement in a common enterprise (DiMaggio and Powell, 1983: 148). As well as structural changes, institutional logics form an important component of system changes. These institutional logics refer to the organizing principles that guide participants and refer to a set of belief systems and associated practices (Reay and Hinings, 2005; Scott, 2001; Scott et al., 2000).

Models for health care organization and delivery are changing, not least in the English NHS. However, these changes are not limited to England, but are replicated in other national systems. There have been substantial changes in the governance, management and accountability of health services which have been termed 'new public management' (Ferlie et al., 1996). In the HR context, modernization has generally been used in policy documents to describe increased private sector involvement in health services as well as attempts to reform pay, working conditions and work practices (Bach, 2004). These structural changes have been presented as a change in institutional logic and it has been argued that health care systems are making the transition from 'medical professionalism' towards 'business-like' orientations. Reay and Hinings (2005) offered a case study example from the Canadian health system. They identified competing institutional logics contrasting 'medical professionalism' and 'business-like' orientations. These logics differed in the following ways. Medical professionalism involved beliefs that the doctor-patient relationship was the most important component of health care, quality was controlled and services were provided by doctors, and the goal was to provide all medically necessary services. In contrast, business-like health care saw patients as consumers of services, quality was determined by market forces and services were provided by the lowest cost provider, aimed at effective and efficient services. These orientations had contrasting associated practices. Medical professionalism involved physicians as gate keepers of services who held decision-making authority in deciding how services were provided. Physician payments encouraged treatment of medical problems. Whereas business-like health care involved teams of health care providers, including physicians and consumers in choosing providers, physician payments were aimed at health maintenance and commissioners determined available services. Physician decisions were made within this constraint (Reay and Hinings, 2005).

Recent elaborations of public sector reforms in England suggest that similar changes, towards a market orientated model, are taking place in the NHS. In 2006, the Cabinet office summarized public sector reforms describing four main principles driving change (Cabinet Office, 2006). The four principles were: *top down performance management*, including outcome targets, regulation and standard setting, performance assessment including inspections and direct intervention; *market incentives* to increase efficiency and quality of service through increasing competition and contestability and splitting providers and purchasers to separate out commissioning of services; *users shaping services* by giving users choice and personalized services, funding following service user choices and engaging users in service delivery decisions; and investment in *capability and capacity* of the NHS workforce at a national level through leadership, workforce development and reform and organizational development and collaboration. These changes signalled a move towards business-oriented public services and included the NHS.

These systemic changes determine the way that business is done in the NHS and necessitate changing logics throughout the system. Such bureaucratic measures, aimed at changing the system, have the potential to be translated as coercive or enabling (Adler and Borys, 1996). Where new systems seem to encapsulate 'bad' rules they become resented, whereas 'good' rules become taken for granted and may rarely be noticed (Perrow, 1986: 24). Changing the organization of a system disrupts existing patterns of work and can give rise to both positive and negative effects. Gouldner's (1954) contrast of three patterns of bureaucracy suggested a means of understanding how organizational members react to such rules. Representative bureaucracy occurs when rules serve the interests of managers and workers, punishment-centred bureaucracy prevails when rules serve to legitimate one party's rights to sanction another in areas of conflict, and mock bureaucracy involves rules being ignored by both parties (Adler and Borys, 1996). Adler and Borys developed these ideas to describe enabling and coercive phenomena. They suggested that systems are perceived as coercive when there is a mismatch between the level of formalization and the routinization of the task. So employees 'will react positively both when high levels of formalization are associated with routine tasks and when low levels of formalization are associated with

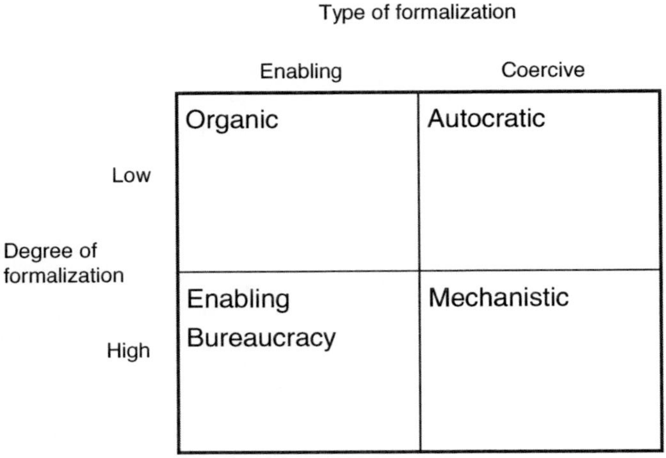

Type of formalization

	Enabling	Coercive
Low	Organic	Autocratic
High	Enabling Bureaucracy	Mechanistic

Degree of formalization

Figure 8.1   A Typology of organizations (Reprinted from 'Two types of bureaucracy: Enabling and coercive' by Paul S. Adler and Bryan Borys published in Vol. 41, pp. 61–89 by permission of Vol. 41 © Johnson Graduate School of Management, Cornell University)

Source: Adler, P. Borys, B. (1996).

nonroutine tasks.' From an enabling perspective the coercive mode appears unduly restrictive, preventing autonomy and worker control and to the coercive viewpoint the enabling mode can appear utopian and unmanaged (Adler and Borys, 1996: 65).

Figure 8.1 shows four organizational types across two axes; enabling/coercive and high/low formalization (source: Adler and Borys, 1996). Adler and Borys argued that enabling organizations could have either high or low levels of formalization depending on the technical requirements of the work. Such enabling types of formalization allows for employees to participate and shape organizational routines based on their learning and expertise. On the other hand coercive formalization gives rise to autocratic institutions (with low degrees of formalization) or mechanistic institutions (with high degrees of formalization), both of which involves low levels of trust of employees and perceived needs for high levels of control. Employees play little part in shaping work procedures. Factors that entrench coercive logics include: power asymmetry between managers and employees that allows responsibility to be deflected downwards more easily than upwards; and the absence of reality checks provided by competitive rivalry or by demanding customers or clients. These organizations have a tendency to become inwardly focused as parochial conflict overtakes other factors. In contrast enabling logics are designed to help users around the system by making it possible for them to have a mental model of the system they are using. If systems break down or mistakes are made users can regain control. If the system can be improved, users are enabled to formulate and evaluate suggestions for improvement. In coercive organizations such mental models are superfluous because employees are only expected to follow explicit instructions (Adler and Borys, 1996).

Current changes to HR provision in the NHS, then, are likely to be viewed positively when there is a match between degree of formalization and routinization of the job at hand. For example, a high degree of formalization for routine tasks and low degree of formalization of non-routine tasks. Alternatively, they are likely to be viewed negatively when there is a mismatch.

Methods

This section provides a brief overview of the research methods and directs the reader to more detailed sources. The empirical data arose from a wider study into HRM and performance in the NHS which included six case study organizations (two each of acute care hospitals, mental health organizations and primary care organizations) and over 200 face-to-face interviews. Each of these organizations had achieved high levels of performance according to national metrics (Boaden et al., 2007; Hyde et al., 2006).

The source of analysis is 78 semi-structured face-to-face interviews with clinical, general and HR managers at the six case study organizations as well as documentary analysis. All interviewees were asked about HRM in their organization. Managers were also asked about their level of involvement in HRM, what helped/hindered them in this role, whether HRM responsibilities were part of their appraisal and to what extent HRM was a priority. Details of the methods for the study as a whole is available elsewhere (Boaden et al., 2008).

The process of synthesis and analysis involved transcribing interviews and reviewing organizational documents. These data were organized using NVivo, a qualitative data analysis software tool. The material was analysed by an iterative process involving several members of the team in identifying themes independently and then reviewing these in discussion meetings. This was followed by reading to improve validation across case studies by multiple members of the research team. For the purposes of this paper, those interviews involving HR, clinical and general managers have been subjected to subsequent analysis, re-reading transcripts to identify aspects of inter-managerial relationships.

Results: Managerial relationships in the NHS

All 78 managers had responsibility for aspects of HRM. The perceived effectiveness of HRM specifically depended to some extent on the local 'micro' context: the relationships that developed, especially between HR and clinical managers (Boaden et al., 2008; Fitzgerald et al., 2008).

Bearing in mind that the case study organizations were all performing well according to national metrics it should not be surprising that many participants described positive working relationships and accommodation to the HR function within the role. Managers suggested that positive relationships between themselves and the HR team, coupled with good HR infrastructure, managerial skill development and role clarity enabled them to engage with HRM more effectively. Conversely, managers struggled to engage with their HR role where HR was being devolved without concurrent training and appraisal for managers, where they experienced role overload and competing demands which meant that patient care was prioritized above staff management.

HR functions have a specific role to play when services are changing. This role involves translating policy and aligning worker expectations with policy requirements. For example, one NHS trust took national targets and translated them into locally meaningful actions. This was important in unfreezing workers' task oriented perceptions of work when services were changing. Employees suggested that supportive relationships and a range of HR practices enabled them to meet changing expectations. HR had an important role to play in translating national targets into outcomes desirable to local patients, that is, meaningful patient related activity.

Three types of relationships were identified. These related to the changing requirements for managers to be more closely involved in delivering HR policies and are presented under the following headings; confrontation, collusion and collaboration.

Confrontation

> HRM is a very low [priority]. I don't see it affects my job...if you took HR out of the health service, the health service would still run. If you took nurses out of the health service, the health service wouldn't run. (General manager)

The first set of accounts described confrontational relationships whereby responsibility for HRM was contested between HR and other managers. Confrontation between clinical and HR managers seemed to arise out of perceptions of competing performance logics – the clinical managers being focused on delivering patient care and HR managers seemingly concerned to meet national and local targets, as the following two extracts illustrate:

> I don't think [HR policies] are a priority to me. They are a very important part of the trust...but as a priority, my priorities lie with my team, my patients, and the relatives. (Clinical manager)

Whilst we try and involve managers in as many different ways and get their views, I am realistic enough to know where the priority is going to lie at the end of the day. (Assistant HR director)

Both groups described the other as being out of touch with modern realities of health care work. These accounts exposed confrontational relationships, whereby both sets of managers actively contested who was or should be responsible for HRM and how policies should or could be better enacted. HR managers wanted control over HR procedures and were trying to hand off responsibility to clinical managers. These relationships were resonant of the coercive mode of formalization described by Adler and Borys (1996) and suggested a mismatch of understanding about how routine the work was and the degree of formalization in place. Each set of managers blamed the other for HR problems and these became overt sites of contested power relationships. Such poor relationships between HR and clinical managers have been reported elsewhere (Fitzgerald et al., 2006; Marchington and Wilkinson, 2005; Purcell et al., 2003; Sparrow and Cooper, 2003).

Collusion

Collusion involved both HR and clinical managers maintaining things the way they were whilst claiming that changes had been made. The most common tangible illustration of collusion was given by the production of many written policies by both clinical and HR managers relating to HRM to which neither expected the other to pay attention to, as the following extracts illustrate:

I think there is a lack of understanding from staff for the reason behind policies ... I suppose that it is partly a managerial shortfall as much as it is a HR one. (Clinical manager)

I could fill this room with policy folders, it's trying to get a handle on it really, key things that have got to be done and that I've really got to know about and what things to some extent you can leave to other people ... it's sheer volume of policies. (Clinical manager)

Look them up if you need them ... I can even write policies and not remember what I've written, there are just so many of them. (Clinical manager)

If there was a choice to read HR policies or do the things that you are going to get kicked up the backside from the chief exec ... I know what I would choose to do. (HR manager)

This collusion is reminiscent of Gouldner's (1954) mock bureaucracy, where neither side pays attention to documented rules. In this case, many HR policies were written but went unused. As a process, writing detailed procedural policies did not seem be what was required for this form of work. Instead, statements of general principles, guidelines or approach to HRM were found to be more useful as guidance for clinical managers. This type of collusion has been reported in the NHS elsewhere (Hyde and Davies, 2004).

Collaboration

Many HR and clinical managers in these successful NHS trusts had developed collaborative, local working relationships. Rather than being an idealized state, there was a degree of trust and agreement between the two parties about what was required of whom and why as illustrated below:

> They have devolved quite a lot of work over the last three years to operational managers, clinical managers and I think we're probably the best people to deal with 90% of the stuff. (Clinical manager)

> ... obviously HR is important because we need to make sure that we've got the resources available to continue to deliver the highest quality of care so we need to make sure staff are in post and there are no vacancies, and that people are managed appropriately and that we look at individual flexibility in roles, and we try to make sure we encourage people to stay within the trust. (Clinical manager)

Clinical managers recognized the expertise of HR managers and HR managers recognized that clinical managers may be in the best position to take day to day decisions even as they might contradict existing procedures. In these instances, mistakes could be used as opportunities for learning. There was also a recognition that all contingencies could not be prescribed in advance.

> We get circulated all the policies and procedures that sit in my office which I share with my colleagues. If you wanted advice on something, yes you pick up the phone to HR. (Nurse consultant)

> They are very approachable [HR department], if you want to speak to them, they will clarify some particular point for you. They are very good at that. (Medical secretary)

> I actually would have probably been quite lost without them, without the [HR]department purely because when I first started it was 'What's this, what's this? What do I here, what do I do there?' So the policy book, the blue book was kind of my bible when I came and their phone number which I will remember for ever. (Ward Manager)

In these accounts of managerial relationships both clinical and HR managers were often involved in face-to-face discussions and telephone conversations to establish general principles and in a small number of cases, HR policies were under continuous review, being seen as an evolutionary process rather than as a one-off production task. These collaborative relationships incorporated aspects of the enabling formalization described by Adler and Borys (1996). Some HR tasks are more routinized than others and so long as the degree of formalization matched the routine nature of the task, staff developed positive working relationships.

Discussion

These findings have illustrated differing relationships between HR and clinical managers in the English NHS during a time of changing institutional arrangements. Three differing types of relationships between HR and clinical managers have been described: confrontation, collusion and collaboration. Relationships ranged from the 'us and them' battling of confrontation, through the denial of any difficulty incorporated into collusion, to the co-operative state of collaboration.

Rather than being features of specific health care organizations, these relationships developed between small groups of people in a 'micro' context, although they could go on to inhibit or develop capacity to provide health care effectively. Whilst this study did not seek to differentiate by clinical profession, Reay and Hinings (2005) showed how a change to the health system in Alberta, Canada, was received differently by different professional groups. They described an 'uneasy truce' developing between physicians and managers (physicians accepted roles on the board of the new structure), whilst some professional groups such as physiotherapists accommodated the new logic more readily. Whilst not differentiated by profession, where managers disputed institutional logic, conflict arose; between clinicians as they claimed devotion to patients versus perceptions that HR managers were only concerned with meeting targets. Here managers were polarized in their views, discounting the opposing standpoint and acting in opposition. Such confrontational relationships have been reported elsewhere as having a negative effect on organizational functioning (Marchington and Wilkinson, 2005). It should not be surprising that clinical and HR managerial relationships form as points of conflict as the NHS moves away from 'medical professionalism towards a more 'business-like' orientation and the professional 'old guard' go to war with the new 'business elite'.

It has been argued that insufficient attention has been paid to the processes that accompany the devolution of particular HR practices and how well these are able to achieve and sustain localized changes (Buchanan et al., 2006). However, the critical role of immediate line managers has been identified (Purcell et al., 2003; Marchington and Wilkinson, 2005). Clinical managers have a significant impact on employee satisfaction, commitment, motivation and discretion. However, the devolution of HRM responsibility to managers has been problematic with the HR function being criticized for being out of touch with commercial realities, attempting to retain too tight a grip on managers, allowing them too little discretion, being unresponsive and slow to act and putting forward impractical ideas. In response, clinical managers have been criticized for lacking skills and knowledge to put HR practices into practice, being dismissive of the HR function and unwilling to learn, being inconsistent in decision-making and for having priorities that supersede HRM. As a result a negative impression of relationships between managers and the HR function emerged. However, this study has illustrated positive co-operative relationships in practice.

In order to devolve responsibility for HRM to managers, there is a need to develop enabling formalizations. This would consist not only of training and skills development in HRM and expert advice from a specialist HR function, but also degrees of formalization that match the routine nature of the task. Where organizations are changing the degrees of routinization, at least for a time, will reduce. Devolution also suggests higher levels of discretion for managers and tailored packages and solutions based on two-way dialogue in order to achieve flexibility, choice and fairness (Sparrow and Cooper, 2003). This exploration of troubled relationships between HR and clinical managers has illustrated the effects of changes to NHS culture generated by changing the business model. It has also highlighted the HR dependency on clinical managers because of the need for clinical managers to extend their HR roles necessitated by this strategic move.

Conclusion

This chapter has illustrated how relationships between clinical and HR managers in changing NHS organizations can become a locus of conflict symptomatic of higher level changes. Specifically, it has demonstrated how recent changes to business models affected intra-organizational relationships. The changing business model of the NHS from medical professionalism towards 'business-like' health care implies necessary changes to NHS culture and climate. Such changes have affected traditional inter-managerial relationships. These relationships are played out in various ways through interactions with clinical managers. Three types of exchanges were explored: confrontation, collusion and collaboration.

Although this research draws on small numbers of interviews in a limited range of organizations, it has indicated that relationships between clinical and human resource managers illuminate several potential problems for health service delivery as gaps in human resource management provision emerge and responsibility for organizational problems are dispersed throughout the organization. As the HR function has changed there has been increasing dependency on clinical managers to implement HR practices. However, clinical managers may lack capacity and motivation for this role which necessitates their collusion in transferring power to general managers. Examination of these relationships illustrated the effects of attempted changes to NHS culture, and the resultant dependency on clinical managers to adopt HR roles, which this strategic move necessitated. As health services continue to change, there is potential for further professional/ HR power struggles. However, moving HR expertise into the system via clinical and general managers can also serve to translate and align policy and employee goals if clinical managers are engaged in an enabling system for HRM. Where this is unsuccessful, HRM can become a locus for conflict.

Sustainability of new forms of HRM is dependent upon individual managers who require training, skills development and involvement in organizational developments. This dependence upon individual managers for the sustainability of changes has also been highlighted elsewhere (Buchanan et al., 2006). Furthermore, the development of bridging roles for people who have skills in both HRM and clinical management will be important and has been identified elsewhere as has the development of HRM systems to reward and support all such roles and careers (Fitzgerald et al., 2008).

These findings have wider implications for health service organizations in other health systems, as similar changes in health organizations are a global phenomenon.

Acknowledgements

We would like to thank the organizations and interviewees for their co-operation in this study. The full research team included Ruth Boaden, Marilyn Carroll, Penny Cortvriend, Claire Harris, Paula Hyde, Mick Marchington, Sarah Pass and Paul Sparrow. This article represents the views of the author and does not necessarily reflect those of the research sponsors (Chartered Institute for Personnel and Development, Department of Health and Health Professional Managers Association).

References

Adler, P. and Borys, B. (1996) 'Two types of bureaucracy: Enabling and coercive', *Administrative Science Quarterly*, 41, 61–89.

Bach, S. (2004) *Employment Relations and the Health Service: The Management of Reforms.* London: Routledge.

Boaden, R., Marchington, M., Hyde, P., Harris, C., Sparrow, P., Pass, S., Carroll, M. and Cortvriend, P. (2008) *Improving Health through HRM: The Process of Engagement and Alignment.* London: CIPD.

Buchanan, D., Fitzgerald, L. and Ketley, D. (eds) (2006) *The Spread and Sustainability of Organizational Change Modernizing Health Care.* London: Routledge.

Cabinet Office (2006) *The UK Government's Approach to Public Service Reform: A Discussion Paper.* London: Cabinet Office.

DiMaggio, P.J. and Powell, W.W. (1983) 'The iron cage revisited: Institutional isomorphism and collective rationality in organizational fields', *American Sociological Review*, 48 (2), 147–60.

Ferlie, E., Ashburner, L., Fitzgerald, L. and Pettigrew, A. (1996) *The New Public Management in Action*. Oxford: Oxford University Press.

Fitzgerald, L., Dopson, S., Ferlie, E. and Locock, L. (2008, forthcoming) '*Knowledge to action? The implications for policy and practice of research on innovation processes*', in McKee, L., Ferlie, E., and Hyde, P. (eds), *Organizing and Reorganizing: Power and Change in Health Care Organizations*. London: Palgrave Macmillan.

Fitzgerald, L., Lilley, C., Ferlie, E., Addicott, R., McGivern, G. and Buchanan, D. (2006) *Managing Change and Role Enactment in the Professionalised Organisation*. London: National Co-ordinating Centre for NHS Service Delivery and Organisation Research and Development.

Gouldner, A.W. (1954) *Patterns of Industrial Bureaucracy*. New York: Free Press.

Hyde, P., Boaden, R., Cortvriend, P., Harris, C., Marchington, M., Pass, S., Sparrow, P. and Sibbald, B. (2006) *Improving Health Through Human Resource Management: Mapping the Territory*. London: CIPD.

Hyde, P. and Davies, H.T.O. (2004) 'Service design, culture and performance in health services: consumers as co-producers', *Human Relations*, 57 (11), 1407–26.

Marchington, M. and Wilkinson, A. (2005) 'Direct participation', in S. Bach and K. Sisson (eds), *Personnel Management: A Comprehensive Guide to Theory and Practice*. Oxford: Blackwell's.

Perrow, C. (1986) *Complex Organizations: A Critical Essay* (3rd edn). New York: Random House.

Purcell, J., Kinnie, N., Hutchinson, S., Rayton, B and Swart, J. (2003) *Understanding the People and Performance Link: Unlocking the Black Box*. London: CIPD.

Reay, T. and Hinings, C.R. (2005) 'The recomposition of an organizational field: health care in Alberta', *Organization Studies*, 26 (3), 351–84.

Scott, W.R. (2001) *Institutions and Organizations* (2nd edn). Thousand Oaks, CA: Sage.

Scott, W.R., Ruef, M., Mendel, P.J. and Caronna, C.A. (2000) *Institutional Change and Health Care Organizations*. Chicago, IL: University of Chicago.

Sparrow, P. and Cooper, C.L. (2003) *The Employment Relationship: Key Challenges for HR*. London: Butterworth Heinemann.

Whittaker, S. and Marchington, M. (2003) 'Devolving HR responsibility to the line: Treat, opportunity or partnership?' *Employment Relations*, 25 (3), 245–61.

9
HRM Practice Systems in Employer-of-Choice Health Care Organizations

Kent V. Rondeau and Terry H. Wagar

Introduction

In the past few years, organizations in a variety of industries have been urged to consider adopting human resource management (HRM) practices that can better capture the full of potential of their human capital (Pfeffer, 1994; 1998). Drawn by the promise for enhanced organizational performance, these HRM practices represent novel and progressive ways of deploying human resources. The rationale for their adoption is to improve employee and customer satisfaction, decrease operating expenses and lower costs, while sharpening organizational effectiveness and financial performance. Although not without controversy, there is a large and rapidly expanding body of evidence which shows a strong relationship between the adoption of certain HRM practices and higher levels of organizational performance (Becker and Gerhart, 1996; Boselie, Dietz and Boon, 2005; Bowen and Ostroff, 2004; Colbert, 2004; Delaney and Huselid, 1996; Guest, 1997; Huselid, 1995; Paauwe and Boselie, 2005; Wood, 1999).

Although the reasons most often advanced for adopting new forms of work arrangement are products of a variety of forces including social, economic, and technical factors, it is not known which specific HRM practices or policies have the ability to affect organizational performance, or even which combinations can enhance the ability of organizations to pursue their valued objectives. Some proponents of the HRM practice–performance linkage predict that any contribution to performance is strongly mediated by the normative culture or workplace climate (Jackson, Schuler and Rivero, 1989), the degree to which its operative strategy 'matches' or 'fits' with its HRM practices (Delery, 1998), the degree of flexibility provided to an organization by its HRM practices (Wright and Snell, 1998), and the overall synergies that are released when certain HRM practices are combined together, or purposefully omitted (MacDuffie, 1995). Nevertheless, researchers have not always been successful in their efforts to elucidate these affects because it is not clear which practices to include or exclude, their impact on performance is often lagged and not observed right away, or the relationship is mediated by any number of unaccounted factors (Ramsay, Scholarios and Harley, 2000).

Most of the work to date has concentrated on identifying which HRM practice elements, when combined together, constitute a distinct 'bundle' or 'system.' The search for an effective HRM practice system implies that no single HRM practice has the potential to significantly impact performance, but rather, a positive influence on organizational performance comes about when a coherent bundle (or system) of practices creates a set of 'powerful connections' or similarly, detracts from performance when 'deadly combinations' of practices are added to the mix (Delaney and Huselid, 1996).

A key discourse among scholars studying the HRM practices – performance linkage is the distinction made between so-called 'best practice' versus 'best fit' approaches. One group of scholars contends that there are certain practices in HRM management (see Pfeffer, 1994) that will always lead to better performance regardless of the situation, while another perspective (see Wood, 1999) holds that there are no inherent ideal practices per se, but only best practices so identified when aligned with other contextual factors. That is to say, HRM practices only improve organizational performance when there is a proper 'internal fit' (i.e. the HRM practices that are adopted are internally coherent or consistent) with the culture and workplace climate, or when these practices produce 'external fit' by aligning with an organization's strategy or to its environment. Drawing upon this distinction, Delery and Doty (1996) expand upon this perspective by identifying three conceptual approaches which they label: (1) the universalist perspective; (2) the contingency perspective; and (3) the configurational perspective.

The *universalist perspective* holds that certain HRM practices are inherently progressive by their nature and that when successfully implemented will lead to higher performance in all types of organizations, regardless of context. For instance, Osterman (2000) has argued that a number of innovative work practices such as self-managing teams, job rotation, and quality improvement teams, result in productivity gains for most organizations across a wide range of industry settings. To date, there is significant empirical evidence in support of the universalist or best practice approach (Delery and Doty, 1996).

The *contingency perspective* argues that the HRM work practices that an organization chooses to adopt must be consistent with other aspects of the organization, such as its strategy, operative culture, or workplace climate. This perspective suggests that the inherent strength of these HRM practices only emerges to impact performance when these practices properly align (or 'fit') with the organization's contextual realities (Jackson, Schuler, and Rivero, 1989).

The third perspective, the *configurational perspective*, is concerned with 'how the pattern [or cluster] of multiple independent variables is related to a dependent variable' (Delery and Doty, 1996: 804). This approach is consistent with the need to conceptualize HRM practices as 'bundles', as 'programs', or as 'systems' acting synergistically on organizational performance. To date, there is modest support for this perspective, yet there is no sharp consensus in the literature as to which specific practice to include (or exclude) from any high performance bundle (Doty and Glick, 1994).

HRM practice systems and employer-of-choice organizations

Being perceived as a great place to work by those inside and outside the organization is an important performance outcome because it has the potential to lead to easier recruitment of human resources, more powerful retention of engaged staff, higher levels of employee creativity and innovation, and is often translated into superior customer satisfaction. This may be of particular benefit for health care organizations in western industrial nations that are facing a critical shortage of professional and technical staff (Brownson and Harriman, 2000). The business press has characterized those organizations which have fostered strong employer-of-choice reputations as having done so through the development and promulgation of an effective employee recruitment and retention culture (see Ashby and Pell, 2001; Herman and Gioia, 2000; Leary-Joyce, 2004). Earning a reputation as an employer-of-choice may produce a significant competitive advantage in attracting and retaining employees over other organizations without such reputations.

The notion of employer-of-choice is not a foreign idea in health care. Employer-of-choice is strongly rooted in early conceptualizations of the magnet hospital – institutions of excellence that have the characteristic of being better able to attract and retain nursing personnel (Kramer, 1990). In magnet health care organizations, positive perceptions of managerial actions, as well as workplace and environmental characteristics improve the job satisfaction or nurses and increase their commitment to the organization (Upenieks, 2002). Magnet hospitals utilize forms of work organization and work practice that promote professional autonomy and accountability strongly preferred by nursing staff.

It is interesting to speculate how the selection of a HRM practice system is associated with perceptions of being an employer-of-choice. A key research question arises from this: *Are health care organizations commonly perceived in their local labour markets as being great places to work (ie. employers-of-choice) able to be distinguished on the basis of the adoption of a particular system of HRM work practice?* To date, there have been few published studies in the health care management literature examining the HRM practice – performance linkage (see Harmon, et. al., 2003; Rondeau and Wagar, 2001; Rondeau, 2007), and none that we are aware that has examined the association between HRM practices (or systems of practice) in health care establishments widely perceived as being a strong employer-of-choice. It seems plausible to suggest that a health care organization's array of human resource policies, practices and programs could potentially strongly influence how that organization is going to be perceived as a great place to work by existing and potential employees. Of course, the assumption that one makes about the employer-of-choice concept, unlike the magnet designation for all US hospitals which is open to all who apply and meet its requirements, is that only a select number of organizations can be judged to be an employer-of-choice. This would imply that the HRM practices adopted need to be significantly novel to afford their adopters this distinction. The degree of novelty would be moot if the HRM practices were not truly valued by existing and potential employees. In addition, organizations which have adopted these practice innovations need to create an awareness of these practices to a wider audience outside of the establishment.

Testing a theoretical model

One can identify and construct three distinct systems of HRM practice: traditional, employee-centered, and employee-involvement. Organizations adopting a *traditional HRM practice system* do so to facilitate the more efficient management of their human capital. Examples of traditional HRM practices include employee performance appraisal, employee selection tests, and workplace drug testing policies. Traditional HRM practice systems are considered non-strategic because their adoption is not predicted to provide their adopters with unique competitive advantage. That is to say, organizations adopting these practices should not expect to receive any distinct advantage from having done so, in part because this type of HRM system can be easily replicated by other organizations and are common HRM practices used across a variety of industries and settings (Huselid, Jackson and Schuler, 1997). This leads one to advance the following research hypothesis:

H1: There is no association between the use of a traditional HRM system and perceptions of being an employer-of-choice.

Organizations adopting an *employee-centered HRM practice system* do so because they are interested in creating a humanistic work environment, one that strongly values employee quality of worklife, both on and off the job. An employee-centered HRM system is composed of practices that most employees prefer and include such things as the availability of on-site childcare, employee assistance programs, and formal career planning and counselling. Some organizations are motivated to adopt employee-centered or high performance HRM practices not out of concern for employee welfare, but rather because they believe that by advancing such policies and practices they will be better able to induce (or compel) otherwise satisfied employees to contribute to higher levels of organizational performance (Godard, 2004). Nevertheless, many existing and potential employees will be attracted to organizations offering such HRM practices and might potentially stay because of them. One can advance the following testable hypothesis:

H2: There will be a positive association between the use of an employee-centered HRM system and perceptions of being an employer-of-choice. This HRM work system will have a stronger association on employer-of-choice when implemented in an organization with a formal HRM function.

An *employee-involvement HRM practice system* is designed to increase employee commitment and engagement to the work enterprise. The objective of implementing this HRM system is to better align the goals pursued by the organization with employee behaviour. High-involvement work practices, such as self-managing work teams and performance-based pay can potentially impact performance by creating a strong employee commitment to the work enterprise, ostensibly because these practices aim to foster higher forms of employee participation, empowerment, engagement, and accountability (Parkes, Scully, West and Dawson, 2006). Although in practice many employees are quite likely to favour this type of HRM work system, its adoption usually requires an appropriate workplace climate and culture, one that re-enforces its application. This leads to the following hypothesis:

H3: There will be a positive association between the use of an employee-involvement HRM system and perceptions of being an employer-of-choice. This HRM work system will have a stronger association on employer-of-choice when implemented in a supportive culture that values participative employee decision-making.

Methods

In late 2005, a survey questionnaire was sent to 2,208 hospitals and long-term care organizations (nursing homes and residential care facilities) operating in all 10 provinces and three territories of Canada. All establishments with 25 or more beds were included in our study population, with identifying information provided by the Canadian Healthcare Association (2001). The study received ethics approval from the University of Alberta Health Research Ethics Board. The survey questionnaire was mailed to the site administrator who was asked to forward the documents to the individual responsible for managing the nursing function at that worksite. After one follow-up mailing, 713 usable surveys were received for a response rate of 32.3%. Early and late responders were compared as a check on non-response bias. No significant difference between the two groups with reference to establishment size and location.

Dependent variable

The major goal in the study is to explore the relationship between systems of human resource management practice and perceptions of being an employer-of-choice for registered nursing staff. Employer-of-choice was measured using a five-item scale developed by Rondeau and Wagar (2006). Each item was assessed using a seven-point agree-disagree scale. Two sample questions are 'This organization really believes that its human resources are its most important asset' and 'In our geographic area, this organization is generally seen as an employer-of-choice by nurses.' The employer-of-choice scale produced a Cronbach alpha of .91 for the sample, indicating an acceptable level of internal reliability.

Human resource management practices

It is interesting to postulate how the adoption of certain workplace HRM practices is associated with perceptions of being an employer-of-choice. This interest is based on the belief that health care organizations that adopt an appropriate HRM system will be more likely perceived as great places to work by both those working in the organization as well as potential employees in the local labour market.

One can identify three broad categories of HRM practice labelled as traditional, employee-centered, and high-involvement. Consistent with the strategic human resource management literature on the use of 'systems' or 'bundles' of HRM practices and their relationship with organizational outcomes (Becker and Gerhart, 1996; MacDuffie, 1995; Paauwe and Boselie, 2005; Wood, 1999), an overall measure of the three HRM practice systems can be produced by averaging responses. The eight discrete practices that comprise each HRM system can be found in Table 9.1.

To construct the traditional HRM practice bundle or system, participants in each establishment were asked to indicate the percentage of their nursing workforce covered by eight specific practices (orientation program [for new hires], written job descriptions, formal performance appraisal system, realistic job previews, employee selection tests, minority recruitment/ retention policy, and drug testing policy). These HRM practices are considered traditional or non-strategic and are selected to constitute a discrete HRM bundle, ostensibly because they reflect contemporary approaches used by organizations for the specific purpose of regulating and managing their human resources. Importantly, none of these practices can be considered to either be sufficiently employee-centered or to have the ability to generate significant employee-involvement, identity and engagement with the work enterprise.

When constructing the employee-centered HRM practice system, nursing leaders in each establishment were asked to indicate the percentage of their nursing workforce that are covered under eight specific practices (employee assistance program, voluntary job sharing, flexible work hours, internal promotion policy, employee career counselling, voluntary job rotation, child care program, no layoff policy). These HRM practices are considered 'employee-centered' and are somewhat progressive because their primary appeal is to promote humanism (quality of worklife) both on and off the job, while having the potential to generate high levels of employee satisfaction. Again, none of these HRM practices will generate significant employee-involvement or engagement.

In creating the employee-involvement HRM practice system, study participants in each establishment were asked to indicate the percentage of their nursing workforce covered by eight specific practices (quality improvement teams, employee recognition system, employee attitude survey, employee suggestion system, shared governance, job enrichment/job enlargement, self-managing teams, incentive-based pay). These HRM practices were chosen to comprise a distinct HRM practice system inasmuch as they are considered to lead to 'high involvement' and produce 'high commitment' with the potential to generate an enhanced level of employee participation, engagement, identification, and empowerment.

To measure the degree of uptake of each HRM practice, respondents were asked (in cases where a practice did exist) to estimate the extent of coverage for each practice using the options, less than 50% of nurses covered, 50–99% coverage, and every nurse (100%) covered by the practice (0 = no nurses covered to 3 = 100% of nurses covered). This measure is a more robust way to view workplace practice adoption because it assesses not only the presence of the practice in an organization but also accounts for the degree to which the specific HRM practice (or policy) has become 'embedded' in the workplace (Cox, Zagelmeyer and Marchington, 2006).

HR system control variables

It is essential to control for confounders that might potentially be associated with one or more of the three HRM practice systems or with perceptions of employer-of-choice. These variables have been separated from the establishment variables because they are suspected of having their influence at the HRM systems level. The presence of a human resource management department (1=yes; 0=no) can be dummy coded. It is suspected that organizations with a formal HRM department would be more likely to have greater expertise necessary to create and advance humanistic, employee-centered practices and policies (by establishing on-site child care programs, employee assistance programs, and no layoff policies), than those establishments without an organized HRM function.

The employee decision-making climate that predominates in the health care establishments was also controlled. Organizations can be differentiated on the basis having a progressive decision-making climate; one that stresses employee participation, autonomy, and accountability in decision-making. It is suspected that organizations with more sophisticated employee-involvement practices may be more likely to have a strongly inculcated progressive decision-making climate. Workplace climate needs to be controlled because it may be that having a participatory (progressive) decision-making workplace climate may be associated with employer-of-choice status while masking the affect of an employee-involvement HRM practice system. It might be expected that neither the traditional HRM practice system nor the employee-centered human resource (HR) practice system would necessarily be associated with the presence of a progressive decision-making culture. Following from the work of Goll (1991), an eight-item measure assessing progressive decision-making climate can be constructed using a seven-point 'agree-disagree' scale. Two sample questions from this scale are: 'This establishment decentralizes decision-making authority to its staff' and 'Nurses at all levels in this establishment actively participate in decisions that affect them.' A single factor solution for this scale produced a Cronbach alpha of .89.

Establishment control variables

Three establishment-level variables can be controlled: establishment size (measured as the natural log of the number of beds), establishment location (coded as 1 = rural to 5 = metropolitan), and establishment type (coded as 1 = hospital and 2 = nursing home). Establishment size is controlled because larger health care organizations have the potential to adopt a greater array of human resource management programs and practices because of access to greater resources. Establishment location is controlled because urban establishments have potentially a greater access to a more highly trained workforce. Establishment type is controlled because of fundamental differences in technological complexity and patient acuity that characterize nursing work in hospitals as compared with nursing activities in long-term care workplaces. This may affect which HRM practices are adopted in the workplace.

Results

The descriptive statistics separated by organization type for the sample of health care workplaces are summarized in Table 9.1. The establishments varied in size (as measured by the number of beds) with about 24% having

50 or fewer beds, 34% with 51 to 100 beds, and 42% with more than 100 beds (not shown). About 85% of the participants report that their nursing staff is unionized. In our sample, approximately 33% are hospitals and 67% are long-term care facilities. With respect to geographic location, 10% of the establishments are located in rural areas (population base of less than 1,000 residents), 32% are in towns (1,000 to 9,999 residents), 26% are in small cities (10,000 to 99,999), 16% in large cities (population of 100,000 to 499,999), and 16% are in large cities (population of 500,000 or greater).

Table 9.1   Health care establishment characteristics

	Hospital Mean value	LTC facility Mean value
Establishment Characteristics		
Number of establishments	232	473
Establishment size (#beds)	219.3	111.0
Establishment location (as valid percentage)		
Rural (<1000 residents)	3.9	13.0
Town (1,000 to 10,000 residents)	35.7	29.0
Small city (10,000 to 100,000 residents)	28.3	24.8
Large city (100,000 to 500,000 residents)	13.0	18.1
Metropolitan (>500,000 residents)	19.1	15.1
Formal Human Resources Department	0.92	0.50
Number of RNs employed	412.3	17.4
Number of non-RN auxiliaries employed	84.5	29.7
Employer-of-choice score for RNs	5.02	5.27
Per cent with Traditional HRM Practice Systems		
Orientation program (for new hires)	99.6	100.0
Written job descriptions	98.7	99.8
Formal performance appraisal system	96.9	93.9
Formal job evaluations	81.1	77.8
Realistic job previews	62.1	56.2
Employee selection tests	44.6	31.6
Minority recruitment/retention policy	29.7	32.9
Drug testing policy	6.8	1.8
Per cent with Employee-Centered HRM Practice Systems		
Employee assistance program	96.8	65.2
Job sharing	66.7	45.8
Flexible work hours	63.8	51.9

Continued

Table 9.1   Continued

	Hospital Mean value	LTC facility Mean value
Internal promotion policy	46.8	54.4
Employee career counselling	43.8	20.5
Job rotation	36.2	36.3
Child care program	15.3	1.6
No layoff policy	11.5	18.1
Per cent with Employee-involvement HRM Practice Systems		
Quality improvement teams	91.2	83.5
Employee recognition program	88.6	83.0
Employee attitude surveys	75.6	68.3
Employee suggestion program	68.2	82.3
Shared governance	46.8	30.2
Job enlargement/enrichment	40.3	33.5
Self-managing teams	33.2	39.5
Incentive based/merit pay	11.7	10.8

Table 9.2 is the correlation matrix for the study variables. Simple bi-variate analysis suggests that establishments perceived as being strong employers-of-choice are much more likely to have implemented all three HRM systems: traditional, employee-centered, and employee-involvement ($p<.001$). These establishments are also more likely to have a strong progressive decision-making climate ($p<.001$). Establishments perceived as being strong employers-of-choice are slightly more likely to be long-term care establishments ($p<.01$). Curiously, strong employer-of-choice establishments are slightly less likely to have an organized HRM department ($p<.01$).

Traditional HRM systems are more likely to be found in establishments which have a progressive decision-making climate ($p<.001$), to be larger establishments ($p<.01$), to be a long-term care organization and located in establishments in more urban locations ($p<.001$). Employee-centered HRM practice systems are more likely to be found in establishments with progressive decision-making climates ($p<.001$), in larger and more urban establishments ($p<.01$). They are more likely to be found in hospitals and in organizations with a formal human resource management department ($p<.001$). Employee-involvement HRM systems are more likely located in establishments with a very strong progressive decision-making climate ($p<.001$), and slightly more likely to be found in long-term care workplaces ($p<.01$). Establishments in the sample with a progressive decision-making climate are more likely to be long-term care organizations, and less likely to be in establishments which have a formalized HRM function ($p<.001$).

Table 9.2 Correlation matrix

Variables	Mean	SD	1	2	3	4	5	6	7	8	9
1. Employer-of-choice score	5.19	1.01	1.00	.16**	.22**	.35**	.67**	.06	.09	.12*	-.12*
2. Traditional HRM system score	1.66	.49		1.00	.30**	.39**	.20**	.12*	.17**	.05	.09
3. Employee-centered HRM system score	.89	.49			1.00	.38**	.20**	.12*	.10*	-.16**	.21**
4. Employee-involvement HRM system score	1.31	.61				1.00	.40**	.06	.06	.11*	.04
5. Progressive decision-making culture	5.20	.89					1.00	-.01	.01	.23**	-.18**
6. Establishment size (ln beds)	4.55	.86						1.00	.58**	-.13**	.19**
7. Establishment location[a]	2.98	1.24							1.00	-.05	.10*
8. Establishment type[b]	1.67	.47								1.00	-.40**
9. Formal human resources department	.64	.49									1.00

* p<.01; ** p<.001
[a] coded as 1= rural to 5 = urban
[b] coded as 1 = hospitals, 2 = nursing homes

Establishment which have a designated HRM department are more likely to be larger and to be located in hospitals (p<.001).

HR Systems and Perceptions of Employer of choice

The objective of this research is to examine if the adoption of 'systems' or 'bundles' of human resource management practices is associated with perceptions of being an employer-of-choice. It is based on the supposition that how an organization deploys its human resources influences the perceptions of that organization as a great place to work by existing as well as potential employees.

Table 9.3 provides OLS regression results for employer-of-choice strength. A four-stage model is used to separate the effects of the HRM practice system on employer-of-choice. Four establishment-level factors and two HRM system-level factors are controlled.

In model A, the establishment control factors are entered into the linear regression. Establishment factors explain only 2.3% of the variance in employer-of-choice strength, with establishment type producing the only significant association. In model B, the three HRM practice system variables are entered. Results suggest strong associations with employer-of-choice are produced with the employee-centered and employee-involvement HRM practice systems, but no significant association is observed with the traditional HRM practice system. Overall, the three HRM practice system variables produce an additional 12% of variance in the dependant variable, employer-of-choice strength.

In order to further assess the potential of HRM practice systems to explain the variance in employer-of-strength, additional confounding influences need to be accounted. In model C, the contribution from having (or not having) a formal HR function is addressed. Organizations with a formalized HRM function could potentially be more able to create or adopt more sophisticated HRM systems. Curiously, the regression result does not support this supposition. When the formal HRM function variable is added it provides only a very modest contribution to the variance observed in employer-of-choice (1.7% of variance explained). Although statistically significant, the inclusion of this variable does not remove (nor add to) the degree of significance made independently by the HRM practice system variables. In other words, the magnitudes and levels of statistical significance in the relationship between two of the HRM practice systems (employee-centered and employee-involvement) and employer-of-choice is not significantly changed when the formal HRM function is controlled.

The effect of workplace climate on the relationship between the HRM practice system and employer-of-choice can be controlled. There is some suggestion that specific HRM practices or systems of practice might matter less to employees than does the existence of a workplace culture or

Table 9.3 OLS regression results for employer-of-choice strength[a]

	Model A	Model B	Model C	Model D
Establishment Factors				
Establishment Size	.049	.006	.033	.061
(ln beds)	(.056)	(.053)	(.054)	(.043)
Establishment Location	.059	.045	.039	.032
	(.038)	(.037)	(.037)	(.029)
Establishment type	.262**	.233**	.107	-.070
	(.083)	(.080)	(.086)	(.069)
Human Resource Practice Systems				
Traditional HRM practice		-.040	-.017	-.065
system		(.085)	(.084)	(.067)
Employee-centered HRM		.313***	.348***	.190**
practice system		(.084)	(.084)	(.067)
Employee-involvement		.466***	.462***	.128*
HRM practice system		(.069)	(.069)	(.058)
HRM Practice System Control Variables				
Formal HRM department			-.326***	-.102
			(.082)	(.066)
Progressive decision				.725***
making culture				(.037)
Constant	4.351***	3.820***	4.067***	1.004***
	(.268)	(.275)	(.282)	(.274)
Adjusted R-square	.023	.143	.160	.472
Δ R-square		.120	.017	.312
F statistic	5.312	27.211	18.364	72.458

[a] (Regression coefficient with standard errors in parenthesis)
* p<.05; ** p<.01; *** p<.001

climate that fully hears, values and utilizes employee voices and input. One aspect of workplace climate that facilitates employee-involvement or commitment to the work enterprise is the degree to which employees are engaged in all aspects of organizational decision-making. In model D, the contribution of progressive decision-making climate in the workplace is added. The results suggest a very large contribution in explained variance to employer-of-choice, adding an additional 31.2%. Indeed, there is a slight diminution in the level of significance for our employee-centered and employee involvement HRM practice systems, yet they remain statistically significant, suggesting that these HRM practice systems continue to play a role in explaining how potential and existing employees view their employers as great places to work.

Discussion

The results provide some support for our research hypotheses. Nevertheless, the implications of these findings should not be understated – how we manage our human resources matters! If health care organizations want to be perceived as great places to work, its managers need to adopt new approaches to managing and deploying human resources, and crafting policies and practices that promote not only the welfare of all employees but also engages them fully in the work enterprise. Health care organizations which adopt an employee-centered HRM practice system, and to a lesser extent an employee-involvement HRM system, will be more likely to be seen as employers-of-choice in their local labour markets.

There are some important limitations in the design of this study that need to be identified. First, the data collected reflects the subjective opinions of nurse managers. As our data are drawn from a single source and subject to the usual biases of respondents, common method variance has the potential to confound results. Second, the measure that assesses the strength of a HRM practice remains subject to further refinement. Although the degree to which a particular practice has become 'embedded' in the organization was addressed by our methodology, one should remember that there is a difference between what managers believe is occurring in their establishments and what is actually happening. For instance, nurse managers may well report that 60% of their nursing staff is organized under self-managing teams, but there are many forms of self-management with some teams having complete autonomy in their decision-making authority, while other teams exercising their autonomy in a much more limited fashion (Cox, Zagelmeyer and Marchington, 2006). Third, the grouping of HRM practices into discrete bundles or systems although perhaps conceptually justified are arbitrarily assigned for the testing of theory and reflect a very inexact placement. There is no consensus in the literature that can provide us with clear direction in this regard. For instance, voluntary job sharing and job rotation are included as employee-centered practices because of they are strongly valued and preferred by many nurses, yet they could also be considered employee-involvement practices because they reflect and extract higher forms of employee autonomy and empowerment. For the sake of being able to empirically test our conceptual models, value judgments have been made by making clear distinctions when categorizing each practice when one may not be so easily made. Fourth, the design of the study is retrospective and reflects merely a snapshot in time. One is not able to establish causality between the variables of interest. That is to say, one is unable to say that adopting a particular HRM practice system will 'cause' health care establishments to become employers-of-choice, merely the choice of a particular HRM practice system appears to be associated with perceptions of being considered an employer-of-choice. Finally, although specific HRM practice systems may be associated with employer-of-choice, we do not know the exact means by which these practices (or systems or practice) actually work. Future research needs to be conducted to more fully elucidate the mechanism by which HRM practice systems impact employer-of-choice. For instance, is the strength of association mediated by such factors as employee satisfaction, workplace human and social capital, leadership styles of behaviour, or pre-existing levels of organizational performance.

In conclusion, although the results reported herein are preliminary and somewhat exploratory, they do strongly suggest that if health care organizations want to be considered strong employers-of-choice, they need to think about adopting employee-centered practices, or employee-involvement practices embedded in a decision-making climate that stresses employee participation, empowerment and accountability. By carefully choosing HRM practices that can forge a coherent system of human resource management; by creating and nurturing a progressive decision-making climate that values the contributions of everyone, leaders can begin to build health care organizations that can more easily attract and retain their staff.

References

Ashby, F.C. and Pell, A.R. (2001) *Embracing Excellence: Becoming an Employer of Choice to Attract and Keep the Best Talent.* Upper Saddle River, NJ: Prentice-Hall.

Becker, B. and Gerhart, B. (1996) 'The impact of human resource management on organizational performance: Progress and prospects', *Academy of Management Journal*, 39 (4), 779–801.

Boselie, P., Dietz, G. and Boon, C. (2005) 'Commonalities and contradictions in HRM and performance research', *Human Resource Management Journal*, 15 (3), 67–94.

Bowen, D.E. and Ostroff, C. (2004) 'Understanding HRM-firm performance linkages: The role of the "strength" of the HRM system', *Academy of Management Review*, 29 (2), 203–21.

Brownson, K. and Harriman, R.L. (2000) 'Recruiting and retaining staff in the twenty-first century', *Hospital Material Management Quarterly*, 22 (2), 34–44.

Canadian Healthcare Association (2001) *Guide to Canadian Healthcare Facilities, 2001–2002.* Ottawa, Canada: CHA Press.

Colbert, B.A. (2004) 'The complex resource-based view: Implications for theory and practice in strategic human resource management', *Academy of Management Review*, 29 (3), 341–58.

Cox, A., Zagelmeyer, S. and Marchington, M. (2006) 'Embedding employee involvement and participation at work', *Human Resource Management Journal*, 16 (3), 250–67.

Delaney, J.T. and Huselid, M.A. (1996) 'The impact of human resource management practices on perceptions of organizational performance', *Academy of Management Journal*, 39 (4), 949–69.

Delery, J.E. (1998) 'Issues of fit in strategic human resource management: Implications for research', *Human Resource Management Review*, 8 (3), 289–309.

Delery, J.E. and Doty, D.H. (1996) 'Modes of theorizing in strategic human resource management: Tests of universalistic, contingency and configurational perform- ance predictions', *Academy of Management Journal*, 39 (4), 802–35.

Doty, D.H. and Glick, W.H. (1994) 'Typologies as a unique form of theory building: Toward improved understanding and modeling', *Academy of Management Review*, 19 (2), 230–51.

Godard, J. (2004) 'A critical assessment of the high-performance paradigm', *British Journal of Industrial Relations*, 42 (2), 349–78.

Goll, I. (1991) 'Environment, corporate ideology, and involvement programs', *Industrial Relations*, 30 (1), 138–49.

Guest, D.E. (1997) 'Human resource management and performance: A review and research agenda', *International Journal of Human Resource Management*, 8 (3), 263–76.

Harmon, J., Sotti, D.J., Behson, S., Farias, G., Petzel, R., Neuman, J.H. and Keashly, L. (2003) 'Effects of high-involvement work systems on employee satisfaction and service', *Journal of Healthcare Management*, 48 (6), 393–406.

Herman, R.E. and Gioia, J.E. (2000) *How to Become an Employer of Choice*. Winchester, VA: Oakhill Press.

Huselid, M.A. (1995) 'The impact of human resource management practices on turn- over, productivity, and corporate financial performance', *Academy of Management Journal*, 38 (3), 635–72.

Huselid, M.A., Jackson, S.E. and Schuler, R.S. (1997) 'Technical and strategic human resource management effectiveness as determinants of firm performance', *Academy of Management Journal*, 40 (1), 171–88.

Jackson, S.E., Schuler, R.S. and Rivero, J.C. (1989) 'Organizational characteristics as predictors of personnel practices', *Personnel Psychology*, 42 (4), 727–86.

Kramer, M. (1990) 'The magnet hospitals: Excellence revisited', *Journal of Nursing Administration*, 20 (9), 35–44.

Leary-Joyce, J. (2004) *Becoming an Employer of Choice. Making Your Organisation a Place Where People Want to Work*. London, UK: Chartered Institute of Personnel and Development.

MacDuffie, J.P. (1995) 'Human resource bundles and manufacturing performance: Organizational logic and flexible production systems in world auto industry', *Industrial & Labor Relations Review*, 48 (2), 197–221.

Osterman, P. (2000) 'Work reorganization in an era of restructuring: Trends in dif- fusion and effects on employee welfare', *Industrial & Labor Relations Review*, 53 (2), 179–96.

Paauwe, J. and Boselie, P. (2005) 'HRM and performance. What next?' *Human Resource Management Journal*, 15 (4), 68–83.

Parkes, C., Scully, J., West, M. and Dawson, J. (2006) ' "High commitment" strategies. It ain't what you do; it's the way that you do it', *Employee Relations*, 29 (3), 306–18.

Pfeffer, J. (1994) *Competitive Advantage Through People: Unleashing the Power of the Workforce*. Boston, MA: Harvard Business School Press.

Pfeffer, J. (1998) *The Human Equation: Building Profits by Putting People First*. Boston, MA: Harvard Business School Press.

Ramsay, H., Scholarios, D. and Harley, B. (2000) 'Employee and high performance work systems: Testing inside the black box', *British Journal of Industrial Relations*, 38 (4), 501–31.

Rondeau, K.V. (2007) 'The adoption of high involvement work practices in Canadian nursing homes', *Leadership in Health Services*, 20 (1), 16–26.

Rondeau, K.V. and Wagar, T.H. (2001) 'Impact of human resource management practices on nursing home performance', *Health Services Management Research*, 14 (3), 192–202.

Rondeau, K.V. and Wagar, T.H. (2006) 'Nurse and resident satisfaction in magnet long-term care organizations: Do high involvement approaches matter?' *Journal of Nursing Management*, 14 (3), 244–50.

Upenieks, V.V. (2002) 'Assessing differences in job satisfaction of nurses in magnet and nonmagnet hospitals', *Journal of Nursing Administration*, 32 (11), 564–76.

Wood, S. (1999) 'Human resource management and performance', *International Journal of Management Reviews*, 1 (4), 367–413.

Wright, P.M. and Snell, S.A. (1998) 'Toward a unifying framework for exploring fit and flexibility in strategic human resource management', *Academy of Management Review*, 23 (4), 756–72.

10
Team Climate and Clinical Information Systems

Joanne L. Callen, Jeffrey Braithwaite and Johanna I. Westbrook

Introduction

West and Wallace (1991) have argued that group or team processes can hinder or facilitate innovations. The climate that the team operates in is an important factor in determining the success of innovations but there are few empirical studies of innovation which have measured climate in health care teams (Williams and Laungani, 1999; Borrill et al., 2000). This chapter presents the results of a study which measured the perceptions of four groups of doctors and nurses about their team climate and related this to their attitudes to, and satisfaction with a single innovation, namely a hospital-wide mandatory computerized provider order entry (CPOE) system.

Background

Work teams provide an enabling structure for organizations to achieve their goals. The key advantages of teams are said to be flexibility; capacity to take advantage of a diverse workforce and utilize interdisciplinary skills; propensity to engage, empower and motivate; and potential to create a sense of belonging amongst team members. Health care delivery increasingly relies on multidisciplinary work teams and several studies have shown that teams can be effective (Borrill et al., 2000; Gerowitz et al., 1996; Hearn and Higginson, 1998; Meterki et al., 2004; Risser et al., 1999; Sommers et al., 2000; Nagi, 1975; Williams and Laungani, 1999). The question this chapter poses, however, is do productive team climates predict effectiveness in the uptake of an innovation (in this instance the CPOE system)?

Method

Research design and settings

A cross-sectional research design was used. Data were collected by administering two survey instruments (Team Climate Inventory and User satisfaction survey) to the population of doctors and nurses (n = 249) in two Emergency

Departments (EDs) and two Haematology/Oncology wards, in two Australian metropolitan public teaching hospitals. The four teams comprised the doctors and nurses from each of the four units. The choice of hospitals was based on their mandatory use of the same computerized test management system to order and view all laboratory and radiology tests. At the time of the study one hospital, Hospital B, only utilized the test viewing or reporting function of the computerized test management system with the ordering of diagnostic tests completed manually using paper-based order forms. We measured satisfaction with viewing test results electronically, and general attitudes towards CPOE. Doctors and nurses were the primary users of the computerized test management system however they had different levels of use.

Survey instruments

Team culture was measured using the Team Climate Inventory (TCI) (Anderson and West, 1999), and satisfaction with computerized viewing of results, and attitudes towards the computerized test management system were collected with a purpose-designed user satisfaction survey. The instruments were administered face-to-face and participants took approximately 7–10 minutes to complete each questionnaire.

The TCI has four climate scales:

- Participative safety is defined as involvement in decision-making in an environment which is non-threatening. It incorporates four sub-scales: *information sharing; safety* (for example, how much they trust each other and are able to try new ideas); *influence* (how much individuals' views are genuinely listened to) and, *interaction frequency* (contact between team members);
- Support for innovation has two elements, namely, *articulated support* (the team professes support for the innovation) and *enacted support* (adequate practical support is given in terms of resources and time);
- Team vision includes *vision clarity* (the degree to which the teams objectives are clear); *perceived value* (the extent to which the objectives have a valued outcome); *sharedness* (the extent to which the vision gains widespread acceptance) and *attainability* (extent to which goals appear realistic), and
- Task orientation is characterized by *excellence* (high levels of performance); *appraisal* (appraisal of team member's potential weaknesses and monitoring of colleagues' performance) and *ideation* (providing useful ideas and help for other team members).

A user satisfaction questionnaire based on previous clinical system evaluation questionnaires (Tierney et al., 1994; Anderson and Aydin, 1994) was developed and piloted on doctors who did not work in the EDs and Haematology wards in hospitals A & B. The final survey contained 22 questions relating to the impact of computerized ordering and viewing of diagnostic tests on work practices and patient care, and the doctors' and nurses' satisfaction with, and attitudes to, the system. Questions were also included on frequency of use of the computerized test ordering system; how ordering and viewing were undertaken when the system was not operational; and doctors' and nurses' self-reported computing skills. Two open-ended questions asked respondents what features they would like to see included and any other general comments on the computerized order management system.

Analysis of data

The TCI data were entered into the TCI software which provided sten profile scores (standardized against a comparison group which in this case were primary health care teams supplied with the software) for each team on each of the four scales and sub-scales of the Inventory (Anderson and West, 1999: 17–20). The sten scores run from 1 (representing a low score) to 10 (high). The TCI software provided a standard set of pole descriptions for each of the scales and sub-scales which assist with the interpretation of the sten scores. Deviations from the pole descriptors require the interpreter to tone-down or modify their interpretation of the teams' climate. Scoring on the fifth sten would indicate an entirely average climate on this factor relative to comparator group (Anderson and West, 1999: 15–16). The TCI data were also entered into SPSS (Version 11.5 for Windows) to enable significance testing by comparing the mean scores on the scales and sub-scales for the four teams. The user satisfaction survey data were analysed using descriptive statistics.

Results

Population and respondents

The overall response rate for the TCI survey was 71% (n = 176) and for the User satisfaction survey was 76% (n = 189).

Perceived team climate by the doctors and nurses in the two Emergency Departments

The ED teams performed well in terms of the *interaction* between team members and support for innovations both voiced (*articulated support*) and practical (*enacted support*) where team members give time, resources and cooperation for the development of new ideas (Table 10.1). These sub-scales are critical for the acceptance and uptake of new innovations. *Ideation* also scored highly which indicates that members of the ED team often share useful ideas and build on the ideas of other team members. The team at Hospital A scored in the high average range on the *safety subscale* and the vision sub-scales of *clarity, perceived value* and *attainability*. ED team members at Hospital A are more likely to play with new and different ideas if they find that the team provides a sense of safety and support in the expression of those ideas. The *clarity* and *ideation* sub-scales were in the high average sten range for the ED team at Hospital B which indicates that team members were clear about the objectives of their group and were more likely to build upon each others' ideas and have a good flow of ideas (Table 10.1).

Perceived team climate by the doctors and nurses in the two Haematology wards

Overall the Haematology team at Hospital A scored high marks on *information sharing, interaction frequency, articulated* and *enacted support, clarity* and *ideation* (Table 10.2), whilst the team at Hospital B recorded high scores on *interaction frequency, articulated and enacted support* (Table 10.2). These are all essential team characteristics for the implementation of new innovations.

There were no significant differences (p>0.05) between the teams on the four scales nor between the teams within the two hospitals (p>0.05).

Results from the user satisfaction survey

ED teams' satisfaction with, and attitudes to, CPOE

The majority of respondents from both ED teams were satisfied with computerized viewing of diagnostic and radiology test results (96%). Both teams agreed that computerized viewing was reliable (90%), improved productivity (84%) and did not hinder communication between health professionals (82%). There was a significant difference between the two hospitals in relation to whether computerized viewing reduces patient care errors ($X^2 = 6.482$, df = 2, p = 0.039) with the majority of Hospital A respondents agreeing (57%) compared to only 42% respondents at Hospital B. There were no significant differences in the perceptions of the doctors and nurses from the two ED teams with both agreeing that work was completed more quickly (83%), was easier (88%) and was completed more accurately (66%).

Most respondents from both EDs did not agree that computerized test viewing depersonalized medicine and alienated the doctor from the patient (Table 10.3). Responses to whether computerized systems helped in the process of deciding which tests to order were similar at both hospitals with approximately half the respondents at each site agreeing (Table 10.3). Responses to whether CPOE resulted in over ordering of tests were also similar with 45% of Hospital A's respondents and 37% of Hospital B's agreeing with this statement. There were significant differences between the ED teams of the two hospitals in their responses regarding whether computerized test management systems resulted in cookbook medicine (p<0.05) with 23% of Hospital A respondents agreeing and only 7% agreeing from Hospital B. There were also significant differences in the responses (p<0.01) to the question about whether computerized test management systems improved the practice of medicine, with 73% of Hospital A respondents agreeing and 51% agreeing from Hospital B.

Table 10.1   Team climate inventory profile for the ED at Hospital A & B (n = 54)

Scale/subscale	STEN profile score[†] (Average 3.5–7.5)									
	1	2	3	4	5	6	7	8	9	10
Participative safety						*•	*	*		
Information sharing						*•				
Safety						*•	*	*		
Influence				•	*•	•				
Interaction frequency						*•	*•	*•	*•	*
Support for innovation						*•	*	*	*	
Articulated support					•	*	*	*	*	
Enacted support						*•	*•	*•	*•	*
Vision						*•				
Clarity						*•	*•	*•		
Perceived value						*•	*	*		
Sharedness				*•	*•	*•				
Attainability						*•	*	*		
Task orientation					•	*				
Excellence					•	*				
Appraisal				*•	*•	*				
Ideation						*•	*•	*•	*	

† Compared to 35 NHS primary health care teams
* Hospital A
• Hospital B

Table 10.2 Team climate inventory in the haematology wards of Hospital A & B (n = 28)

Scale/subscale	STEN profile scores[†] (Average 3.5–7.5)									
	1	2	3	4	5	6	7	8	9	10
Participative safety						* •	*	*	*	
Information sharing						* •	* •	* •	*	
Safety						* •				
Influence				•	•	* •				
Interaction frequency						* •	* •	* •	* •	*
Support for innovation						* •	* •	* •	* •	
Articulated support						* •	* •	* •	* •	
Enacted support						* •	* •	* •	* •	* •
Vision					•	*	*	*		
Clarity						* •	* •	* •	*	
Perceived value				•	•	* •	*	*		
Sharedness				* •	* •	* •				
Attainability						* •	* •	* •		
Task orientation						* •				
Excellence						* •	*	*		
Appraisal					•	*				
Ideation						* •	* •	* •	*	

[†] The comparison group was NHS primary health care teams
* Hospital A
• Hospital B

Table 10.3 Attitudes of doctors and nurses from the Emergency Department (ED) teams towards CPOE (n = 140#)

Attitudes to CPOE†	Hospital A ED (n = 60)			Hospital B ED (n = 80)			Significance
Using CPOE:	Agree % (n)	Neutral % (n)	Disagree % (n)	Agree % (n)	Neutral % (n)	Disagree % (n)	
Results in cookbook medicine	23 (14)	22 (13)	55 (33)	7 (5)	50 (38)	43 (33)	$X^2 = 14.841$ df = 2 p = 0.001‡
Helps in the process of deciding which tests are appropriate to order for each patient	51 (30)	17 (10)	32 (19)	47 (37)	32 (25)	22 (17)	$X^2 = 4.466$ df = 2 p = 0.107
Improves the practice of medicine	73 (44)	22 (13)	5 (3)	51 (40)	37 (29)	13 (10)	$X^2 = 7.600$ df = 2 p = 0.022+
Results in over ordering of tests	45 (27)	27 (16)	28 (17)	37 (29)	34 (27)	29 (23)	$X^2 = 1.211$ df = 2 p = 0.546
Depersonalises medicine	5 (3)	13 (8)	82 (49)	6 (5)	31 (24)	63 (49)	⊗
Alienates doctors from patients	2 (1)	12 (7)	87 (52)	5 (4)	24 (19)	71 (56)	⊗

total n = 140 with 4 missing from 'cookbook medicine'; 2 missing from 'helps decide appropriate tests'; 1 missing from 'improves the practice of medicine' and 1 missing from 'results in over ordering.'
† attitudes were measured on a five-point Likert scale collapsed to a three-point Likert scale with 'agree' including 'strongly agree' and 'disagree' including 'strongly disagree'
+ significant at p<0.05
‡ significant at p<0.01
⊗ significance could not be tested as the views were strongly held by the respondents

Haematology ward teams' satisfaction with, and attitudes to CPOE

Respondents from the Haematology ward teams were satisfied with computerized viewing of test results (91%). The majority of respondents thought computerized viewing was reliable (89%), improved productivity (82%) and did not hinder communication between health professionals (73%). However only half the respondents from both sites felt that computerized viewing of test results reduced patient care errors (50%).

Respondents in both hospitals had similar positive responses to computerized test ordering work practices with the majority agreeing that work was easier (84%) and was completed more quickly (81%) and more accurately (72%).

A large number of respondents from the Haematology Ward at Hospital B had neutral responses to the attitude questions, whereas the respondents from Hospital A were more definite in their attitudes (Table 10.4). The majority disagreed that computerized ordering depersonalizes medicine (67%), and agreed that it helps in deciding which tests are appropriate to order (57%) and improves the practice of medicine (63%). Respondents from

Table 10.4 Attitudes of doctors and nurses from the Haematology teams towards CPOE (n = 49#)

Attitudes†	Hospital A Haematology ward (n = 30#)			Hospital B Haematology ward (n = 19#)		
	Agree % (n)	Neutral % (n)	Disagree % (n)	Agree % (n)	Neutral % (n)	Disagree % (n)
Results in cookbook medicine	33 (10)	17 (5)	50 (15)	6 (1)	50 (8)	44 (7)
Depersonalises medicine	17 (5)	17 (5)	67 (20)	6 (1)	41 (7)	53 (9)
Helps with the process of deciding which tests are appropriate to order	57 (17)	20 (6)	23 (7)	39 (7)	33 (6)	28 (5)
Alienates physicians from patients	7 (2)	17 (5)	77 (23)	11 (2)	50 (9)	39 (7)
Improves the practice of medicine	63 (19)	27 (8)	10 (3)	17 (3)	73 (13)	11 (2)
Results in over ordering of tests	37 (11)	23 (7)	40 (12)	22 (4)	50 (9)	28 (5)

Total n = 49 with 3 missing results from 'cookbook medicine'; 2 missing results from 'depersonalises medicine' and the remaining attitude variables with 1 missing result each
† attitudes were measured on a five point Likert scale collapsed to a three-point Likert scale with 'agree' including 'strongly agree' and 'disagree' including 'strongly disagree'

both Haematology wards were mixed in their responses regarding whether computerized test management systems result in over ordering of tests.

When asked whether they would replace the computerized ordering or viewing and ordering system with paper the majority of respondents from both hospitals said they would not revert to the manual system (97%).

Discussion

Our study showed that a positive team climate in terms of support for innovation was associated with high levels of satisfaction with computerized viewing of test results and positive attitudes towards CPOE systems generally. High levels of team interaction, voiced and practical support for innovation, ideation and safety are all critical factors for the acceptance and uptake of a new clinical information system like the computerized provider order entry system. High scores for interaction frequency would be expected in an ED where there are generally high levels of interaction between clinicians given the nature of the department (Chisholm et al., 2000; Coiera et al., 2002; Spencer and Logan, 2002). In terms of the relationship between innovation support and team members having a sense of safety, our findings are supported by others. Gosling and colleagues also found 'a significant association between team functioning and the effective use of an online evidence system where team members with higher safety scores reported improved patient care' (Gosling et al., 2003: 250).

The ED team at Hospital B showed high results on fewer sub-scales of the TCI than at Hospital A. It is important to note, however, that CPOE had been used in Hospital A (both ordering tests and viewing results) since 1991 but, at the time of the study, only the test viewing function was used in Hospital B. The more positive culture in terms of uptake of innovations at Hospital A could be due to the more advanced stage which Hospital A was at in terms of the life cycle of implementation of clinical information systems.

In relation to work practice satisfaction, the majority of respondents believed that work was completed more quickly, more accurately and was easier with the computerized system. These findings are supported by a previous survey at Hospital A which examined the early implementation of the computerized system and found high levels of satisfaction with 83% reporting that they would not revert back to the manual system (Soar et al., 1993).

Other studies show complementary results to those reported here, with most reporting mixed responses from clinicians highlighting both negative and positive aspects of electronic test ordering (Doolan et al., 2003; Hawkins et al., 1999; Lee et al., 1996; Murff and Kannry, 2001; Mekhjian et al., 2002). Although computerized test management systems have been in existence since the 1970s (Hasman et al., 2003; Kuperman and Gibson, 2003), their adoption has been slow with numerous studies reporting barriers to uptake which include changes to work practices; time taken to use the system compared to manual ordering; cultural and organizational issues; non involvement of clinicians; cost; no value perceived by users; no demonstrated links to improved patient outcomes; and resistance to change (Ash et al., 2003a; Ahmad et al., 2002; Callen et al., 2006; Ash et al., 2003b; Ash et al., 2001; Bates et al., 2003; Doolan et al., 2003; Massaro, 1993; Callen et al., 2007; Callen et al., 2008). Our study extends this work to emphasize the relationship between a positive team climate and attitudes to, and satisfaction with, clinical information systems.

Limitations of research methods and procedures

The four teams studied were doctors and nurses working in the same clinical area. Other studies have shown that doctors and nurses working together in one clinical area may not necessarily work as a cohesive team (Ummenhofer et al., 2001; Braithwaite and Westbrook, 2005). If the participants had been asked to self-allocate into teams the groups, may have been different. Team size has also been shown to affect team functioning (Williams and Laungani, 1999). In this study the number of teams was small (4) and the size of each team was large (mean = 44). The impact of team size is not known and further studies need to be undertaken on hospital teams of various sizes and compositions (Ouwens et al., 2008).

Conclusion

Clinical information systems support communication and information sharing between health professionals and therefore multidisciplinary health care teams which work well together will be likely to use these systems. This chapter has shown that team climate is an important factor determining the implementation of new information systems. We suggest that team climate should be examined prior to implementation to ascertain if the team is 'ready' for or orientated toward innovations. Teams that favour the uptake of new innovations will likely be more receptive and positive towards clinical information systems. Productive team climates are related to satisfaction with, and positive attitudes towards, clinical information systems.

References

Ahmad, A., Teater, P., Bentley, T.D., Kuehn, L., Kumar, R.R., Thomas, A. and Mekhjian, I.S. (2002) 'Key attributes of a successful physician order entry system implementation in a multi-hospital environment', *Journal of the American Medical Informatics Association*, 9, 16–24.

Anderson, J.G. and Aydin, C.E. (1994) 'Theoretical perspectives and methodologies for the evaluation of health care information systems', in Anderson, J.G., Aydin, C.E. and Jay, S.J. (eds), *Evaluating Health Care Information Systems: Methods and Applications*. London: Sage, 5–29.

Anderson, N. and West, M. (1999) *Team Climate Inventory. User's Guide*. Berkshire, UK: NFER-Nelson.

Ash, J.S., Gorman, P.N., Lavelle, M., Lyman, J., Fournier, L., Carpenter, J. and Stavri, P.Z. (2001) 'Physician order entry: Results of a cross-site study', presentation at the IT in Health Care Sociotechnical Approaches 1st International Conference, Rotterdam, September, 6–7.

Ash, J.S., Gorman, P.N., Lavelle, M., Stavri, P.Z., Lyman, J., Fournier, L. and Carpenter, J. (2003a) 'Perceptions of physician order entry: Results of a cross-site qualitative study', *Methods of Information in Medicine*, 42, 313–23.

Ash, J.S., Stavri, P.Z., Dykstra, R. and Fournier, L. (2003b) 'Implementing computerized physician order entry: The importance of special people', *International Journal of Medical Informatics*, 69, 235–50.

Bates, D.W., Kuperman, G.J., Wang, S., Gandhi, T., Kittler, A., Volk, L., Spurr, C., Khorasani, R., Tanasijevic, M. and Middleton, B. (2003) 'Ten commandments for effective clinical decision support: Making the practice of evidence-based medicine a reality', *Journal of the American Medical Informatics Association*, 10, 523–30.

Borrill, C., West, M., Shapiro, D. and Rees, A. (2000) 'Team working and effectiveness in health care', *Bristish Journal of Health Care Management*, 6, 364–71.

Braithwaite, J. and Westbrook, M. (2005) 'Rethinking clinical organisational structures: An attitude survey of doctors, nurses and allied health staff in clinical directorates', *Journal of Health Service Research & Policy*, 10, 10–17.

Callen, J.L., Braithwaite, J. and Westbrook, J.I. (2007) 'Cultures in hospitals and their influence on attitudes to, and satisfaction with, the use of clinical information systems', *Social Science & Medicine*, 65, 635–9.

Callen, J.L., Braithwaite, J. and Westbrook, J.I. (2008) 'Contextual implementation model: A framework for assisting clinical information system implementations', *Journal of the American Medical Informatics Association*, 15 (2), 255–62.

Callen, J.L., Westbrook, J.I. and Braithwaite, J. (2006) 'The effect of physicians' long-term use of CPOE on their test management work practices', *Journal of the American Medical Informatics Association*, 13 (6), 643–52.

Chisholm, C.D., Edgar, K., Collision, B.A., Nelson, D.R. and Cordell, W.H. (2000) 'Emergency department workplace interruptions: Are emergency physicians interrupt-driven and multitasking'? *Academic Emergency Medicine*, 7, 1239–43.

Coiera, E., Jayasuriya, R.A., Hardy, J., Bannan, A. and Thorpe, M.E.C. (2002) 'Communication loads on clinical staff in the emergency department', *Medical Journal of Australia*, 176, 415–18.

Doolan, D.F., Bates, D.W. and James, B.C. (2003) 'The use of computers for clinical care: a case series of advanced US sites', *Journal of the American Medical Informatics Association*, 10, 94–107.

Gerowitz, M.B., Lemieux-Charles, L., Heginbothan, C. and Johnson, B. (1996) 'Top management culture and performance in Canadian, UK and US hospitals', *Health Services Management Research*, 9, 69–78.

Gosling, A.S., Westbrook, J.I. and Braithwaite, J. (2003) 'Clinical team functioning and IT innovation: A study of the diffusion of a point-of care online evidence system', *Journal of the American Medical Informatics Association*, 10, 244–51.

Hasman, A., Safran, C. and Takeda, H. (2003) 'Quality of health care: Informatics foundations', *Methods of Information in Medicine*, 42, 509–18.

Hawkins, H.H., Hankins, R.W. and Johnson, E. (1999) 'A computerized physician order entry system for the promotion of ordering compliance and appropriate test utilization', *Journal of Health care Information Management*, 13, 63–72.

Hearn, J. and Higginson, I.J. (1998) 'Do specialist palliative care teams improve outcomes for cancer patients? A systematic literature review', *Palliative Medicine*, 12, 317–32.

Kuperman, G.J. and Gibson, R. (2003) 'Computer physician order entry: Benefits, costs, and issues', *Annals of Internal Medicine*, 139, 31–9.

Lee, F., Teich, J.M., Spurr, C.D. and Bates, D.W. (1996) 'Implementation of physician order entry: User satisfaction and self-reported usage patterns', *Journal of the American Medical Informatics Association*, 3, 42–55.

Massaro, T.A. (1993) 'Introducing physician order entry at a major academic medical center: Impact on organizational culture and behavior', *Academic Medicine*, 68, 20–5.

Mekhjian, H., Kuman, R.M., Kuehn, L., Bentley, T., Teater, P., Thomas, A., Payne, B., and Ahmad, A. (2002) 'Immediate benefits realized following implementation of physician order entry at an academic medical center', *Journal of the American Medical Informatics Association*, 9, 529–39.

Meterki, M., Mohr, D.C. and Young, G.J. (2004) 'Teamwork, culture and patient satisfaction in hospital', *Medical Care*, 42, 492–8.

Murff, H.J. and Kannry, J. (2001) 'Physician satisfaction with two order entry systems', *Journal of the American Medical Informatics Association*, 8, 499–509.

Nagi, S.Z. (1975) 'Teamwork in health care in the US: A sociological perspective', *Health and Society*, Winter, 75–91.

Ouwens, M., Hulscher, M., Akkermans, R., Hermens, R., Grol, R. and Wollersheim, H. (2008) 'The Team Climate Inventory: Application in hospital teams and methodological considerations', *Quality and Safety in Health Care*, 17, 275–85.

Risser, D.T., Rice, M.M., Salisbury, M.L., Simon, R., Jay, G. and Berns, S. (1999) 'The potential for improved teamwork to reduce medical errors in the emergency department', *Annals of Emergency Medicine*, 34, 373–83.

Soar, J. Ayres, D. and Van der Weegen, L. (1993) 'Achieving change and altering behaviour through direct doctor use of a hospital information system for order communications', *Australian Health Review*, 16, 371–82.

Sommers, L.S., Marton, K., Barbaccia, J.C. and Randolph, J. (2000) 'Physician, nurse, and social worker collaboration in primary care', *Archives of Internal Medicine*, 160, 1825–33.

Spencer, R. and Logan, P. (2002) 'Role-based communication patterns within an emergency department setting', in Ribbons RM., Dall V. and Webb R. (eds), *Handbook of Abstracts*. Tenth National Health Informatics Conference. Health Informatics Association of Australia, 53–4.

SPSS Version 11.5 for Windows. SPSS Inc. Chicago, USA. http://www.spss.com.

Tierney, W.M., Overhage, J.M., McDonald, C.J. and Wolinsky, F.D. (1994) 'Medical students' and housestaff's opinions of computerized order-writing', *Academic Medicine*, 69, 386–9.

Ummenhofer, W., Amsler F., Stutter, P.M., Martina, B., Martin, J. and Scheidegger, D. (2001) 'Team performance in the emergency room: Assessment of inter-disciplinary attitudes', *Resuscitation*, 49, 39–46.

West, M.A. and Wallace, M. (1991) 'Innovation in health care teams', *European Journal of Social Psychology*, 21, 303–15.

Williams, G. and Laungani, P. (1999) 'Analysis of teamwork in an NHS community trust: An empirical study', *Journal of Interprofessional Care*, 13, 19–28.

11
Health Network Culture and Reform

Rod Sheaff, Lawrence Benson, Louise Farbus, Jill Schofield,
Russell Mannion and David Reeves

Networks, their culture and climate

For policy-makers who favour health system marketization, that is the re-structuring of health systems to mimic the organizational structures and inter-organizational relationships found in markets, networks offer a surrogate governance structure in those parts of a 'hollowed-out state' where direct hierarchical control of individuals or organizations has been removed (Etzioni, 2001; Rhodes, 1997), supplementing hierarchies and markets as a 'third way' governance structure. Health care networks have correspondingly proliferated and now include professional ('expertise') networks: clinical referral ('care') networks; project networks; programme ('linkage') networks such as WHO-style programmes; 'experience' networks of users and carers; policy networks (including policy 'communities' as a special case); learning networks; and interest networks which promote particular policy or interest-group (Southon, Perkins and Galler, 2005). Meantime, 'reforms' of health-care bureaucracies have proceeded apace in many countries as have attempts to re-introduce or extend health-care markets.

England fits this pattern, and the National Health Service (NHS) sometimes leads it. New Labour governments have consistently maintained a hierarchical, centralizing approach towards controlling the NHS but also, despite some substantial differences to the equivalent policies of the Thatcher governments, increasingly favoured quasi-market and market-based health reforms. Yet alongside these reforms, the UK government also continues to mandate NHS managers to maintain professional and clinical networks. These networks are mainly either professional ('expertise') or clinical referral (or 'care') networks, although some also function as programme or 'linkage' networks (aimed at locally implementing national health policy or guidance') and as learning networks disseminating evidence-based practice (Southon et al., 2005) addressing such NHS priorities as coronary heart disease, mental health and services for children. These officially mandated networks coexist with non-mandated networks created voluntarily by patients, clinicians, local health organizations or others. Thus the English NHS now uses not only hierarchical and market, but also network governance structures.

Networks can be defined as relatively stable sets of working relationships between individuals, organizations or a combination, typically undertaking shared but distributed tasks requiring inputs from several members. Many networks have a central managing 'core' (committee, secretariat, website etc.), but governance through networks rests less upon property-rights and contracts, hierarchical status and contracts than upon persuasion, help-in-kind, ideological commitment and reciprocity. One would therefore expect its culture and climate to be an important medium through which a network coordinates its activities. Schein defines 'organizational culture' as:

> A pattern of shared basic assumptions that the group learned as it solved its problems of external adaptation and internal integration, that has worked well enough to be considered valid and, therefore, to be taught to new members as the correct way you perceive, think, and feel in relation to those problems. (Schein, 1997).

Such a culture has three levels:

1. artefacts, that is, the empirically observable language, technology, products, style (clothing, manners of address, myths, stories) typical of an organization (Schein, 1997).
2. espoused values. An organization's leaders' stated 'values' become shared assumptions, socially validated and promulgated across the organization.
3. basic underlying assumptions, that is, what organization members pay attention to; what things mean to them; how they react (including emotionally) to events; and what actions they think it proper to take and when. These assumptions are not always expressly formulated but often reflect repeatedly-applied practical solutions to recurrent problems, becoming so internalised as hardly to be conscious (Schein, 1985).

Organizational values can thus be divided between espoused, negotiable values and taken-for-granted, non-negotiable values. When the observed artefacts and the espoused values conflict, any resolution of the conflict stems from the underlying assumptions.

Organizational culture is often described as a single entity which 'exists when members share identity and mission' (Schein, 1997). But most organizations with any developed stratification or division of labour have organizational cultures (plural) differentiated by (e.g.) occupation, hierarchical level and practical function besides 'informal' criteria such as age, sex, ethnicity or religion (Scott, Mannion, Davies and Marshall, 2003; Morgan and

Ogbonna, 2008). These non-managerial 'subcultures' often subvert those espoused values and assumptions which put employees (or other groups) at a disadvantage *vis-a-vis* managers. As the primary embedding-mechanisms of culture, Schein mentions the ways in which leaders: select what to monitor, measure and control; react to critical incidents and organizational crises; allocate scarce resources; model roles and coach staff; allocate rewards and status; recruit, select, promote, retire and excommunicate organizational members (Schein, 1985; 1996). These observable behaviours constitute the 'climate' which manifests and reproduces an organizational culture.

Like policy-makers, certain organizational theorists (e.g. Granovetter, 1983; Jones, Hesterly and Borgatti, 1997) have differentiated networks from both markets and hierarchies (organizations), raising the question of what differences, if any, there are between the cultures of hierarchical bureaucracies ('organizations') and the cultures of networks (which are organized but which are not in the foregoing sense a single organization). Within networks whose member organizations have different cultures but also pursue shared goals or tasks, or face a common problem, one might expect to find 'cultural blending' (Cutcher-Gershenfeld et al., 1998) or a 'cultural mosaic' (Chao and Moon, 2005)).

If networks' cultures do indeed differ from those of hierarchies and markets (including quasi-markets), one would nowadays expect to see in NHS networks a heightened tension between the network's own culture and the artefacts, espoused values and assumptions entailed by implementing recent NHS reforms which re-introduce quasi-market governance structures. Using case studies of four English health networks, this chapter therefore explores how recent NHS reforms have affected the networks' existing culture (artefacts, espoused values, underlying assumptions), how network cultures adapted and how, therefore, would Schein's account of organizational culture have to be adapted for application to health networks in these circumstances.

Patterns of network development

Network 1: Mental health care for young children

The small provincial city which network 1 serves has a relatively high proportion of families vulnerable to mental health problems in children under five. Compared with many care networks, network 1 is quite a complex, long-established referral network, which has evolved piecemeal since the late 1980s and links NHS, local government and 'third sector' organizations in the city. Whilst the referral routes by which children or families entered the network were relatively few, they become more complex and fragmented as patients proceed from primary care towards a wide range of specialized services provided by diverse organizations. In 2005, some of these organizations held a conference to put the network onto a more systematic footing.

The network is now coordinated by a group containing representatives of the organizations whose most important concern is child mental health. An NHS manager provides the main day-to-day managerial support.

With the aforementioned NHS reform policies came a flow of policy guidance about mental health services (e.g. a *National Service Framework on Mental Health* (Department of Health, 1999). National Service Frameworks are long-term strategies for improving specific areas of care) and the care of children (the *Common Assessment Framework, Every Child Matters* (Department for Education and Skills, 2008)). Both the network itself and some of its member-organizations were now jointly commissioned by the local NHS Primary Care Trust (PCT) and the city council, whose Local Area Agreement provided the criteria by which the commissioners attempt jointly to manage network 1.

We began fieldwork in network 1 by examining its coordination functions. Across the occupational groups (although not uniformly within each) our informants showed some reluctance to enter the 'dangerous territory' of diagnosing, providing or referring children for mental health care. Although the network's central role was care coordination, artefacts relating to it were until recently conspicuous by their absence. For instance, there was no formal description of the network's remit and few common protocols for working practices. During 2006–7 however more such artefacts began to appear, some internally generated (e.g. care pathways) and others extracted from central guidance (e.g. the Common Assessment Framework). Responses to recent short-term policy initiatives were also in evidence. The most substantial artefact was a new children's advice and support centre in a new but rather deprived housing estate.

Short-term service contracts, project and policy 'initiative' funding meant that collaboration with local government and NHS commissioners became preoccupations in a hitherto mainly practice-oriented network. The network responded to these external dependencies and uncertainties by commissioning formal evaluations and by collecting data to legitimate the whole network, its current managerial activity and its recent artefacts (e.g. the aforementioned children's centre). Concomitantly, more formalized, documented self-definitions of the network, its remit and working practices began to appear. By 2006 network 1's espoused values expressly included collaboration, network integration, and seeking an agreed common function and activity for the network as a whole. The network's coordinating group maintained the importance of preventing mental health care for young children becoming submerged in more generic mental health services.

Basic assumptions found among network members included, for some occupational groups (e.g. midwives), a strong professional identity which pre-dated their role in network 1. Yet within each of the main occupational groups we discovered disagreements about the definition of child mental health problems, indeed about whether children under five can

meaningfully be said to have mental health problems at all. Many informants, all of whom in fact collaborated in caring for young children, did not
perceive themselves as network members. They found network 1 complex
and opaque. Few informants appeared to know or understand the underlying care pathway structure as a whole. Whilst they understood quite
clearly their own professional roles and *de facto* contributions to the wider
activity of coordinating mental health care for young children, the fundamental property of having an explicitly-defined membership was largely
absent from network 1.

Network 2: Health promotion for adults with long-term mental health problems

This network was set up in 2006 in a provincial city to coordinate the activities of three organizations and some individuals who were already promoting the physical health of adults with long-term mental health problems.
A worker in the PCT Public Health Development Unit began encouraging
these groups and individuals to collaborate, which had not happened before
due to differences in funding sources and these actors' lack of knowledge
of other support groups and services. Another important interaction was
that the National Institute for Mental Health in England (NIMHE) 'Let's get
physical' initiative provided £5000 (€8000) to assist the groups' participation in the pilot scheme. This scale of support meant that network activities
would depend on volunteers. The network seeks support from any outside
bodies, not just public funders.

Up to April 2008, the NHS reforms of practice-based commissioning,
'patient choice' and payment by results had no effect on network 2 at all.
Network members, even the most active, were largely oblivious to NHS
reform.

Network 2's artefacts were nearly all for its members' own use and included
food hygiene and preparation training sessions; aerobics and other exercise
sessions; volleyball games and tournaments; walks; trips to the coast; and
contributions to a local time-bank and skill-swap scheme. The latter was a
mechanism for rewarding network members in kind for helping each other.
A side-effect of these events has been recruiting people to network 2, which
is essential for the network's sustainability. The network has displayed its
activities at PCT-sponsored events, and – its sole managerial artefact to
date – produced an evaluation report for NIMHE.

The network's espoused values are, above all, to increase opportunities for
health and well-being for people with long-term mental health problems.
The latter are defined broadly, expressly not limited to psychoses. The network's explicit index of success is to increase the number of people with
long-term mental health problems eating healthy food, doing moderate exercise, stopping smoking and gaining an increased sense of well-being. Where
possible, the network's activities should be available in non-stigmatizing

settings. Their other main value was to encourage the individual participants to feel empowered through doing more for others and over time to develop trust between the individuals and organizations involved. In particular, the network aims 'to encourage those users stuck in "serviceland" to make use of other opportunities' (pilot scheme evaluation report).

A fundamental underlying assumption is that network 2 relies entirely on self-help. It is therefore critical to retain contact and involvement with existing members, and to recruit and retain more members. Although welcome, practical or financial help from outside bodies is taken as a bonus. The network also assumes that it undertakes relatively modest activities and requires correspondingly modest support: its core members regarded a £500 (€800) donation from a charitable trust as a large grant. At network 2's health and exercise events any level of participation was acceptable, even just turning up and doing little physical exercise itself. We take this as evidence of an underlying assumption that the network exists more for the members' use than to impose expert norms of what constitutes healthy exertion.

Network 3: A cardiac network

Activity to establish network 3 began in 2001, aiming to create a common strategy for cardiac heart disease services across two counties served by four main acute hospitals. Soon afterwards two of these hospitals found themselves struggling to meeting their waiting list and waiting time targets, a problem exacerbated by Norwalk and MRSA outbreaks. The local PCTs responded by commissioning extra cardiac inpatient capacity in London and another city outside the network's territory. The 'Payment by Results' reform meant that the PCT also shifted the payment for these episodes to the extra-territorial hospitals. Increasingly, advising a Strategic Health Authority commissioning group became the network's main activity. Besides various technically-oriented subgroups network 3 also set up a patient participation group with 14 members with a part-time coordinator. Although by NHS standards its annual budget (£80,000/€130,000) was modest, network 3's main artefacts were demand management tools, activities to promote workforce development (in particular to address the shortage of cardiac physiologist technicians) and clinical practice guidelines. The network's budget was mainly spent on a database supporting clinical audit by developing an infrastructure for collecting data across the network. Besides an extensive website, the main artefacts for public consumption have been talks, organized through the patient involvement group, to 'educate' patient representatives (e.g. about infection control). NHS reforms have resulted in other bodies (e.g. NICE) producing similar guidance to that of network 3. A standing sub-group on IM&T and the service improvement sub-group ceased because other NHS bodies took over their functions. At the time of writing, it is uncertain what future network 3 has.

Network 3 documents espouse four main 'values': evidence based practice and professional development; developing the infrastructure for cardiac services, for instance by gaining additional funding for coronary heart disease (CHD) services; implementation of national policy for cardiac services (as 'achievements' the network's documents mention meeting waiting time targets, introducing PBR for revascularization); and patient participation in the network, regarded as legitimate, indeed welcome. Of the network's underlying assumptions, the most obvious is medical, specifically hospital medical, dominance. Hospital consultants were seen as – and were – the network's leadership and effectively its key decision-makers. Liaison with SHA management was partly via another (public health) doctor. Leading network members assumed that their role was 'mainly to prevent bad commissioning decisions'.

In summary, NHS reforms made the network's artefacts partly redundant. Its espoused values were becoming managerialized, although not to the extent of subverting medical dominance.

Network 4: A nested CHD network

Network 4 was established as a clinical network mandated by the then Health Authority to improve services and access to services in an area with a very high incidence of CHD. There were already long-established close working relationships between primary and hospital based clinicians (both for secondary and tertiary care). With the publication of the National Service Framework (NSF) for coronary heart disease (Department of Health, 2002) the network was charged with implementing it. The network's membership consists of commissioners, senior hospital and primary care clinicians and managers, but network 4 was also nested within a sub-regional CHD network with a similar mandate. Between 1998 and 2005 the local commissioning agencies changed from Health Authorities to much smaller Primary Care Groups (PCGs), then to PCTs, followed by four local PCTs merging into one. Despite these repeated reorganizations both the local and sub-regional networks maintained continuity of leadership.

The artefacts which our informants most cited as network 4's achievements were:

1. A new primary angioplasty service for the sub region.
2. Ensuring more equitable care for patients at the interface between secondary and tertiary care.
3. Adaptation of national guidelines and standards, for example, NICE guidelines, to the local situations.
4. Increasing uptake of cardiac rehabilitation.

In addition, the network made 'process maps' of existing CHD patient routes through the local health system, 'benchmarked' the performance of these services against similar services elsewhere, and then redesigned these pathways to comply with NSF recommendations. The redesigned care processes were then commissioned across the network's member-organizations which implemented them. 'Process mapping', 'benchmarking' and the application of evidence-based protocols are typical of 'new public management' techniques in the NHS.

A prominent espoused value was, quite simply, the scope for collaboration which network 4 offered. Members of the local network commented that the well-organized nature of the steering group and its subgroups was important in signalling to new and existing members that this was a focused, reliable and well-led network which made concrete progress to visible, clear goals. The value of this collaboration lay, network members said, not only in promoting service improvements but also in making those improvements equitable across the network; and, more generally, 'trying to achieve clinical excellence in the network' Members valued the continuity in the local network's membership. By organizing the network around one of the main hospitals they hoped somewhat to insulate the network from its unstable environment.

Interviewees suggested that people were motivated to join a CHD network because 'that's just what sensible people do to improve the service they provide for their patients'. They assumed that clinical, especially medical, participation would enable network 4 to influence the design and commissioning of local cardiac services. Whilst some assumed that clinicians 'know best', other interviewees questioned whether networks composed of clinicians would always focus upon patient interests. Interviewees implied that it was desirable but difficult to involve patients in the governance of networks. Patients could be most meaningfully engaged when subgroups of the network were working on specific tasks, for example reviewing cardiac rehabilitation.

Patterns of network culture and their apparent implications

Differences between the networks appear to reflect differences, first, between lay and professional, in particular clinician, network leadership. The lay leadership of network 2 was rather indifferent to NHS reforms. They did not depend on government or NHS management for resources, goodwill or legitimation. Unlike networks 1 and 3, network 2 produced almost no managerial artefacts. This difference reflects their different degree of resource dependency on public bodies. Even within network 2, a tangible effect of public funding was the creation of one (managerial) artefact which was markedly atypical of that network's artefacts in general. All three networks that were, or became, mandated, displayed a similar move towards a managerial formalization of network culture, irrespective of the quite different care groups served (CHD vs. mental health patients) and the concomitant differences in content and readerships for the guidance (artefacts) they produced for practitioner use.

Our data, while not representative or definitive, suggest that the larger a network, the more likely to develop a 'mosaic' of localized cultures as network 1 did. But network 3, with wider geographical coverage, showed less tendency to do so. This suggests that heterogeneity of membership in terms of occupational and organizational membership affiliation (greater in network 1 than 3) is more influential than scale. The repeated re-structuring of NHS commissioning organizations (Department of Health, 2007) and the continual appearance and cessation of short-term policy initiatives with their equally short-term funding had decidedly disruptive effects (Smith, Walshe and Hunter, 2001). Changes to service commissioning was the aspect of NHS reforms which most affected the networks, either as an important way in which networks obtained funding or as an activity in which they participated. Involvement in commissioning let the networks to produce more formalized, managerial artefacts (reports, monitoring tools, practice guidelines). In general these networks' espoused values tended to endorse these new activities, and NHS reform policies more widely, rather than comply under duress or challenge the reforms. Even for the networks most involved with NHS commissioning, however, their underlying assumptions seemed little affected. Thus the impact on the affected networks' cultures, at least in the relatively short-term studied here, appeared uneven. Artefacts changed most, espoused values less markedly, and underlying assumptions least. Network 2 and its culture was the most resilient in face of health system reform because its external resource dependencies were few. Pro-market reforms were largely irrelevant to its core activity and it was not integrated into NHS policy-communication channels anyway.

Networks, their cultures and health reforms

Applying Schein's 'artefacts – espoused values – underlying assumptions' schema to an empirical analysis of health networks proved straightforward, without having to force either categories or data. That artefacts changed most, espoused values less markedly, and underlying assumptions least is as Schein would predict. However, this observation also suggests that underlying assumptions adapt in the light of changes in artefacts and espoused values, a point less easy to reconcile with Schein's schema. The foregoing evidence suggests it would be simplistic to think that the three levels of network culture develop synchronically or that there is a simple one-to-one relationship between them. Even in network 1, where relationships between artefacts, espoused values and assumptions were clearest, there was no simple one-to-one mapping. In response to external imperatives, a network's artefacts change more readily than its espoused values, and the latter change more readily (and sooner) than the underlying assumptions. In three of the study sites a relatively stable set of espoused values accommodated a shift to producing new types of artefact. One might infer that, at least in networks, the relationship between espoused values and artefacts, and perhaps also between these two and their underlying assumptions, is one of mutual constraint (under-determination) with each level accommodating a (specific) range of possibilities in the other two.

The formation, and if it is possible at all the management, of cultures and sub-cultures would appear to be still more complex in networks than in organizations; and less well understood. The foregoing evidence suggests that the production of artefacts is the least, and the underlying assumptions the most, resilient of Schein's three elements of network culture in the face of health system reform. Stable, consistent reform policies would therefore be required to change the underlying culture of health-care networks, which on the above evidence appear in that respect little more responsive to health reform policies than conventional hierarchies are. Indeed they may prove less responsive because the networks' culture derives from that of its member-organizations and occupational groups and would therefore only change following changes there. In these respects large-scale, professionally controlled health networks may not have all the clear-cut governance advantages that 'third way' reformers anticipated.

Acknowledgement

This research was funded by the English National Institute for Health Research NHS Service Delivery and Organisation research programme (project SDO104). The views expressed here are not necessarily those of the funders but of the authors only.

References

Chao, G.T. and Moon, H. (2005) 'The cultural mosaic: A metatheory for understanding the complexity of culture', *Journal of Applied Psychology*, 90 (6), 1128–40. doi: Article.

Cutcher-Gershenfeld, J., Nitta, M., Barret, B., Belhdi, N., Chow, S. and Inaba, T. et al. (1998) *Knowledge-Driven Work: Unexpected Lessons from Japanese and United States Work Practices*. Oxford: Oxford University Press.

Department for Education and Skills C. Y. P. A. F. D. (2008). *Every Child Matters. Change For Children*. UK government official website. Retrieved 7 February from http://www.everychildmatters.gov.uk/

Department of Health (1999) National service framework for mental health: Modern standards and service models. Guidance document. Retrieved 18 September from http://www.dh.gov.uk/en/Publicationsandstatistics/Publications/PublicationsPolicyAndGuidance/Browsable/DH_4096400

Department of Health (2002) *A National Service Framework for Coronary Heart Disease*. London: Department of Health.

Department of Health (2007) *World Class Commissioning: Vision.* London: Department of Health.

Etzioni, A. (2001) 'The third way to a good society', *Sociale wetenschappen*, 44 (3), 5–40.

Granovetter, M. (1983) 'Economic action and social structure: The problem of embeddedness', *American Journal of Sociology*, 41, 481–510.

Jones, C., Hesterly, W. and Borgatti, S. (1997) 'A general theory of network governance: Exchange conditions and social mechanisms', *Academy of Management Review*, 22 (4), 911–45.

Morgan, P. and Ogbonna, E. (2008) 'Subcultural dynamics in transformation: A multi-perspective study of health carehealth care professionals', *Human Relations*, 61 (1), 39–65.

Rhodes, R. (1997) *Understanding Goverance.* Buckingham: Open University Press.

Schein, E. (1996) 'Culture: The missing concept in organization studies', *Administrative Science Quarterly*, 41 (2), 229–40.

Schein, E. (1985) *Organisational Culture and Leadership.* San Francisco, CA: Jossey-Bass.

Schein, E. (1997) *Organizational Culture and Leadership.* Retrieved from http://www.tnellen.com/ted/tc/schein.html

Scott, T., Mannion, R., Davies, H. and Marshall, M. (2003) *Health Care Performance and Organisational Culture.* Oxford: Radcliffe Medical.

Smith, J., Walshe, K. and Hunter, D.J. (2001) 'The "redisorganisation" of the NHS.' *BMJ*, 323 (7324), 1262–3. doi: 10.1136/bmj.323.7324.1262.

Southon, G., Perkins, R. and Galler, D. (2005) 'Networks: A key to the future of health services', *Australian Health Review*, 29 (3), 317–26.

12
Primary Health Care Innovation Sites: Learning to Create New Cultures of Care

Ann Casebeer, Trish Reay, Karen Golden-Biddle,
Bob Hinings and Kathy Germ

Introduction

In order to understand how natural 'experiments' move from new possibilities to the next 'standard way of doing things' – we have to observe what is actually happening – and we have to watch long enough to see if new ways really emerge and sustain. As a team of researchers our primary objective is to understand how organizations learn to spread and institutionalize good ideas about providing primary health care[1]. This Chapter describes results from a comparative study of ten primary health care innovation sites. Based on in-depth empirical data we show how organizational learning occurred within the sites and across multiple levels.

Background

The history of primary health care reform in Canada is littered with a legacy of special funding initiatives, time-limited natural experiments and demonstration pilots. Learning to change the nature of primary health care provision through this potpourri of short-term, add-on reform options has been difficult at best and counter productive at worst (Hutchinson et al., 2001). Primary health care innovation has essentially had to limp forward alongside but outside of larger reform initiatives such as regionalization.

A new mechanism with potential for significantly altering the face of primary health care has emerged within Alberta's health system that merits observation and interrogation. In 2005, a provincial framework for 'Primary Care Networks' (innovation sites) was launched (Alberta Health and Wellness, 2008). What makes this initiative different from others is the partnership arrangements it enshrines, linking funding to trilateral govern-ance among physician practices, regional health authorities[2] (RHAs) and the provincial health system (see Figure 12.1). Instead of creating the condi-tions for these new innovation sites, the partners opted to create local plan-ning processes that culminated in the production of business plans that were negotiated and agreed to collaboratively. Overall, each of these 'innov-ation sites' was expected to develop long-term arrangements for new ways of providing primary health care and new ways for linking to other levels of care – both within the health system and also intersectorally within and with communities served.

As a team of organizational change researchers, we have been watching attempted health care innovation for over a decade (Casebeer and Hannah, 1998; Hinings et al., 2003; Casebeer et al., 2006; Pablo et al., 2007; Reay et al., 2006). With the collaborative development of innovation sites, we see a promising avenue for improving primary health care and the possi-bility of a sustainable culture shift in the delivery of care and the capacity for change. Since the first innovation sites were launched in February 2005, we have been watching a purposeful sample of eight innovation sites in the province of Alberta and two sites in British Columbia.

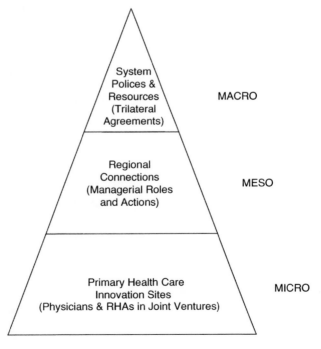

Figure 12.1   Levels of organizational action and learning

Research objectives and methods

Our research objective was to understand how organizations learn to spread and institutionalize good ideas about providing primary health care. We identified how participants made sense of the changes they were involved with, how learning evolved and led to new ways of 'doing' primary health care. We employed a longitudinal case study design consisting of three phases (Pettigrew, 1990; Stake, 1995). In each phase, researchers visited all 10 sites to conduct in-depth interviews. A total of 109 interviews were conducted, tape-recorded and transcribed. Findings reported here are summarized from a total of 55 interviews at the completion of Phase One (2006) and 54 interviews at the completion of Phase Two (2007). All data were coded with the use of qualitative data analysis software (NVivo). Analysis was based on a grounded theory approach with iterative attention to data and the extant literature (Glaser and Strauss, 1967).

How learning occurred

We wanted to understand how organizations learn to provide services in new ways. We found that organizational learning took place through activities performed by individuals, groups, and organizations as they gathered and digested information, imagined and planned new actions, and implemented change (Carroll, 1998). However, the process was more than individuals gaining new knowledge and using it within their organization. Consistent with established theory (Argyris, 1999; Crossan et al., 1999), we observed that the overall organization changed over time. For example, routines, procedures and other organizational systems were altered as people attempted to accomplish new things. Based on comments from our interviewees, we see that learning is occurring in at least three different categories or levels – (1) Learning within the innovation sites, (2) Learning within the RHA, and (3) Learning within the provincial health system (Table 12.1). After two years of observations and interviews, we found that learning at all levels was critical to ongoing successes.

Learning within the innovation sites (micro level data)

We asked interviewees to tell us about learning that occurred over time. Below we discuss key points related to learning within their site.

Developing inter-disciplinary teams

A founding principle of all innovation sites was the development of an inter-disciplinary approach to service provision where health professionals worked collaboratively to provide care. People told us that this was not

Table 12.1   Levels and categories of organizational learning

Levels	Categories
Within Innovation Sites:	Developing inter-disciplinary teams Valuing management Utilizing strategic management techniques Improving knowledge transfer Creating local solutions
Within Regions:	Providing structure for innovation sites Developing physician/RHA relationships Designating individuals to share learnings Managing resources
Within Systems:	Accepting environmental jolts: – Physician recruitment – Funding Attempting evaluation & knowledge transfer

easy to accomplish. In every site, we heard about ongoing efforts to get the right people working on the team – and maintaining the team over time. The following excerpt from one of our interviewees explains the process.

> We gradually learn[ed] more about each other, and we saw each other as individuals not as a regional person or physician. And I think what happened, this grew into respect for each other and trust in each other and I mean that would only benefit us whichever way we go…I think this is the most important thing that's been going on in the months that I've been involved.

As part of establishing inter-disciplinary teams, there was a strong emphasis on cultivating a positive physician-RHA relationship. Sites with strong, focused and attentive directors were much more successful in developing these positive relationships. In the sites without a dedicated manager, or where the manager changed several times, relationships between physicians and others tended to become more distant, and in one case the relationship was severed.

We observed that developing and maintaining a positive physician-RHA relationship took time and determination and requires ongoing effort from all individuals involved. It has also been challenging. In some sites, the development of these relationships was viewed as making a significant difference in how work is accomplished. The following quote illustrates this point.

> What is different about this initiative is that we're doing things together…When you do that in collaboration it's learning to link arms

and walk together and do it together. And that's huge. That is really huge. It's a whole new way of doing health care. And I think it's very exciting.

Valuing management

There have been different approaches to managing the sites. Most are managed by individuals with health care experience combined with credentials in business or management. Interviewees repeatedly indicated that these site managers are crucial to the success of innovation site development. '[Site managers], particularly in the bigger networks, are very valuable and important.' With the large number of doctors in [sites], having dedicated [site managers] creates a 'conduit to discuss issues' and introduce changes at a regional level. We also heard that these managers have facilitated the development of trusting relationships with physicians; they 'genuinely appreciate that [physicians are] trying to deliver good care in the [sites]'. This recognition helped create the conditions for local site management to be valued and to support learning and innovation activity.

Utilizing strategic management technique

Most physicians are over-booked with patient appointments, making it difficult for people to see a physician on short notice. We heard from many interviewees that the sites were learning better ways to manage patient flow by building on strategies from the business world. For example, many sites have introduced an established office management program that protects a certain number of appointments for medical concerns arising 'over night'. Several sites tested and subsequently implemented telephone systems to connect urgent patients with an on-call family physician, and to make appointments with family physicians for less urgent patients. More remote sites have hired locums in order to provide continuous service and improve physician retention. Others have established an after-hours clinic to serve commuter patients unable to see a physician until evening. Interviewees told us they believed the purposeful use of strategic management techniques was an important aspect of learning within their site.

Improving knowledge transfer

Interviewees told us they were learning how to gather new knowledge and use it to provide better care for their patients. They noted this was especially a concern for patients requiring more than a short doctor's visit, or for those patients requiring frequent visits – patients with mental health concerns, patients with chronic diseases, pregnant women. Because of the resulting strain put on physicians, particularly in rural areas, there was also great concern for patients with high on-call requirements – making arrangements for women giving birth, palliative care patients, or other urgent calls were high priorities for several innovation sites.

To improve services for patients with chronic needs, we heard that people began gathering information from conferences, articles, and their informal networks. This enabled them to test out the ideas within their site. For example, sites have experimented with different roles for nurses, nurse practitioners, dieticians, counsellors, rehabilitation providers or others. Site managers follow these trials and adjust or abandon experiments that do not give satisfactory results. Sites with dedicated managers have a greater ability to gather information, decide what knowledge they can use, and actually put trials into place.

Creating local solutions

In response to our question about the sources of ideas for the innovation sites, people identified three sources: (1) internal experience of people in the region; (2) new ideas from conferences or colleagues; and (3) new information found through publication or internet searches. We heard about a process of learning that could be labelled 'bricolage.' That is, people gathered bits and pieces of information, discussed these ideas and related them to their local experiences. They had many conversations with each other, and eventually came to consensus about the appropriate innovations to develop and implement.

Although everyone told us about a mix of sources for the good ideas that were ultimately used, we noted that physicians tended to identify their personal professional experiences as most important in determining the appropriate ways to change primary health care. They also were open to hearing about initiatives elsewhere, and in some cases took time to visit other innovation sites before deciding how to proceed in their own sites. Interviewees who held RHA managerial responsibilities, tended to search the literature for evidence about what worked and what didn't. They were not always successful in finding useful materials, but they viewed it as their responsibility to ensure that planning committees had all available information. They relied on the committee processes to determine strategies that would be appropriate for local use.

Learning within the RHAs (meso level data)

In addition to learning within the innovation sites, we also heard how individuals within the RHA attempted to spread the 'good ideas' to other sites. Below, we identify some of the structuring arrangements and strategies being used to facilitate that process.

Providing structure for innovation sites

Across the RHAs, we see that there have been different strategic approaches to setting up innovation sites. Some RHAs established a relatively large number of sites quickly, planning to learn from multiple experiences concurrently. In other RHAs, the focus was on developing a small number of innovation sites and learning as much as possible from them before expanding. In this approach, the success of one project is critical to the ability to spread the innovation. Thus, 'getting it right the first time' should provide the foundation for rapid (but later) spread to other locations. We observed that both strategies have been successful, although some interviewees expressed frustration in holding back future sites in order to work out details with early sites.

Developing physician/RHA relationship

In addition to the importance of the physician/RHA relationship within sites, we heard about potentially long-lasting changes that have occurred at the regional level. Physicians told us that prior to these initiatives, they had little trust of RHA intentions. This has changed dramatically during the first years of the innovation sites, to the point where physicians tell us they now hold respect for RHA managers and the work they do. Similarly, RHA managers told us they had come to understand and appreciate family physicians. This 'new' relationship has been recognized as an important foundation for advancement and learning in relation to primary health care reform. The following quotes capture the sentiments we heard.

> Coming from the RHA perspective, even though I see myself as partnering with the physicians all the time, we really haven't been. Now, we really see them as partners who have an interest in providing quality care, and we're starting to see where they're coming from when they talk about quality care. (RHA manager)

> Most of the planning was really physicians and the regional health authorities feeling each other out... And that was actually the most useful thing, even if nothing comes out of it at the end... Both sides have recognized some of the limitations of the other and the realities of the other group. (Physician)

Designating individuals to share learnings inside RHA

In some regions more than others, we observed that specific individuals have been designated to transfer information about what works and what doesn't work from one site to another within their region. In other RHAs, individuals purposefully fill this knowledge-sharing role because they are personally intrigued and committed. In other regions, we observed that this role of purposeful sharing seemed to be distributed among a number of people, and may be written into work responsibilities or left more open. We observed that any of these approaches may provide the desired transfer of knowledge.

Managing resources

Managing resources is deemed an important strategy to support learning in a number of different ways. For example, some RHAs and PCNs have jointly focused on the use of a 'gap-analysis' to determine the appropriate needs and therefore expenditure of funds within particular communities. Together they gather information about 'what programs are in place' and 'what needs are not currently being met.' Resources are then matched to meet the identified needs. As each site has flexibility within the business plan guidelines to provide programs and hire appropriate employees, they can leverage resources to target their learning needs as they introduce new or enhanced services. Sometimes additional regional resources are also expended to facilitate PCN activities. Many innovation sites use incentive bonuses to encourage involvement in activities. These incentives appear to encourage sustained learning and change.

When it comes to managing resources, most of the mechanisms are developed at the innovation site (micro) level with support at the RHA (meso) level. However, the long-term sustainability of what is seen as hopeful progress depends substantially on continued System (macro) level support. Flexibility at the local site level within a stable funding supply from the provincial level seems to spell success for organizational learning and innovation.

Learning within the health care system (macro level data)

Our interviewees also offered their views about how learning was taking place at the macro level. Many of them pointed out that even though innovation sites may be making good progress, they remain at risk from environmental jolts that impact physician clinics or the broader health system. In spite of a delivery model that was designed to meet physician need and encourage multidisciplinary care, at various points, the future of some sites has been threatened by the inability to attract sufficient numbers of physicians.

Accepting environmental jolts

An important learning is that innovative models of Primary health care cannot provide protection against all environmental threats. In addition to learning how to deliver primary health care in better ways, health regions and physicians also need to learn how to adapt to, or react to untoward events as they arise. That is, they need to develop resilience. Currently, two significant impacts hold the potential to derail current initiatives. First, it remains difficult in many regions to attract and retain sufficient numbers of physicians to provide services in accordance with the model. This is particularly difficult in non-urban regions and in regions experiencing exponential population growth. Second, consistent and predictable government funding is always desired and seldom the case.

> We don't have guaranteed funding. We have funding for another two years and then after that we don't know if there is going to be any more

money for the projects we've set up. And that creates a certain tenuousness to the whole situation. That's probably the biggest question. Is there funding for the projects?

Attempting evaluation and knowledge transfer

Although province-wide evaluation is mandated, this area has been slow to develop. There are some examples of regional evaluation initiatives and/or individual innovation site action. Although there have been many conferences and workshops for site managers, physicians and other professionals to share experiences across sites, we heard only partial support that learning occurs. Moreover, whereas some participants find these opportunities to be beneficial, others consider them a waste of time.

How do these roles and mechanisms and actions facilitate organizational learning?

Negotiating and creating solutions and 'filling the gaps' identified requires a high level of participation from all parties involved. Site directors play a critical managerial role, especially in engaging physicians and other health professionals to create and participate in solutions. For example, we heard from several site managers that strengthening communication through regular face-to-face meetings was critical, providing a forum for physicians to keep up to date with programs available and learn more about multidisciplinary teams.

Site managers, together with RHA leaders for primary health care learned how to develop new programs or new innovation sites by keeping track of experiences and specifically using those to inform the next efforts. That is, they used their experiential knowledge to create systems and structures that made it easier to repeat or modify the process. They shared their 'how to' knowledge with others verbally or in written formats. This spreading of 'know-how' is occurring regularly at both the micro and meso levels and is beginning to emerge at the macro (system level) through systematic and regular committee work and early evaluative review and data sharing provincially, as well as the dissemination of early research efforts.

At the regional (meso) level, primary health care manager roles often include two important tasks: (1) creating strategies for the overall region and (2) encouraging the PCN employees to realize those strategies. These managers share knowledge, information and know-how among innovation sites and communities. Discussion of the managerial roles at the system (macro) level was sparse; most study participants saw the system level responsibility as keeping the resources flowing rather than managing the change process.

At the system level, our data suggest that policies and mechanisms for managing resources are 'double-edged'. At times, the lack of adequate mechanisms for managing resources has reduced the opportunities for organizational learning, making it difficult to move ahead with planned programs.

Whereas, when available, mechanisms for managing resources, especially flexible incentives, have proven highly supportive of learning and diffusion of new and improved ways of providing primary heath care. Appropriate and sufficient mechanisms for managing resources, combined with dedicated and collaborative managerial roles have emerged as two critical supports for learning at the micro and meso levels and appear to be impacted by the actions or inactions at the macro level. Where both are in place, innovation site teams are learning and innovating.

Implications for future research and practice

Early findings suggest that some aspects of primary health care are being fundamentally altered, and that contextual factors are key variables enabling or inhibiting the degree of shift. Further, the initial expectations and subsequent experiences of innovation site providers and champions are that they are truly changing the cultures of care and enhancing capacity for sustained change in the direction of positive health gains for communities who are involved and served.

The findings of this research make a significant contribution to the understanding of implementing organizational change, and in particular, the roles that organizational learning play in conceiving, diffusing and sustaining change in multi-jurisdictional public sector contexts. Using our data collected over two years, we see that findings to date fall into four distinct categories of learning.

First, primary health care innovations are evolving differently in different local environments but all sites are achieving progress in terms of understanding key factors enabling professionals to work in multidisciplinary environments. Innovations must be tailored to the local context and flexibility to adapt is crucial to success at each site.

Second, although it has taken a lengthy period of time, in almost all sites, primary care physicians report satisfaction with the new ways of working. For example, physicians believe the innovations are resulting in improved patient care and improved working conditions. While Phase One showed that physicians were initially resistant to multidisciplinary teams, in Phase Two we heard that a cooperative community of practitioners has emerged in most sites, which incorporates physicians, nurse practitioners, registered nurses, administrators and other health care professionals into patient care. This has created a collaborative learning environment for health care professionals that promotes learning and also improves health care delivery to patients.

Third, knowledge transfer, both internally and externally, has been slow but invaluable in creating an environment of learning and establishing new clinics. Within innovation sites, knowledge transfer allows health care professionals to share experiences and learnings with fellow colleagues.

Across sites, some learnings are being shared both formally and informally. Interestingly, we see that in all sites, people are more likely to conduct their own experiments than to adopt learnings from other sites. The sharing of experiences at or through the macro level of the system may be worth watching for in future studies.

Finally, and probably most intriguingly, at the micro level and the meso level, we observe that two key organizational structures seem to be critical in the process of organizational learning: managerial roles at the innovation site (micro level), and resource management mechanisms at both the innovation site (micro) and RHA (meso level). The managerial role for each innovation site and for overall management of primary health care within each RHA is facilitating the development of a positive working relationship between family physicians and the RHA. One RHA chose not to formally designate an innovation site manager, and this initiative is struggling. The mechanisms developed within each innovation site for managing financial and non-financial resources are leading to accepted organizational systems that influence how health professionals (including physicians) deliver primary health care services in new ways.

The implications for both practice and research of our findings to date suggest an imperative to continue collecting data, and analyzing and sharing how learning is occurring in and among our participating sites and subsequently with other primary health care innovation initiatives. Our empirical findings concerning how organizational learning occurs demonstrates how new cultures of care are emerging – creating enhanced arrangements for those who practise and, ultimately, new benefits for the patients and communities that are better served. This experience is likely transferable and of relevance to research and practice efforts elsewhere, particularly when capturing how such learning moves experimental activity into mainstream normalized ways of working – moving from innovative learning to normal practice. There is substantial potential to advance theoretical understanding of the micro, meso and macro level contributions required to learn 'organizationally' and to share and diffuse this learning more widely.

Acknowledgments

We express gratitude to our research participants for the insights, sharing and contributions that made this work possible. We thank the Canadian Institutes for Health Research and the Alberta Heritage Foundation for Medical Research for funding this research project.

Notes

1. Primary health care is defined as: 'essential health care based on practical, scientifically sound and socially acceptable methods and technology made universally

accessible to individuals and families in the community through their full participation and at a cost that the community and the country can afford to maintain
at every stage of their development in the spirit of self-determination' [1] (Alma
Ata international conference definition).
2. Regional health authorities are entities within a provincial health system, managing and providing health care to geographically defined populations. At the time
of this research, Alberta had nine RHAs and British Columbia had six RHAs.

References

Alberta Health and Wellness (2008) Primary health care initiatives: http://www.
health.gov.ab.ca/key/primary-health-care.html (accessed 10 January).
Argyris, C. (1999) 'Introduction: The evolving field of organizational learning', *On
Organizational Learning*, Oxford: Blackwell, 1–15.
Carroll, J.S. (1998) 'Organizational learning activities in high-hazard industries: The
logic underlying self-analysis', *Journal of Management Studies*, 35 (6), 699–717.
Casebeer, A.L. and Hannah, K.J. (1998) 'The process of change related to health
policy shift: Reforming a health care system', *International Journal of Public Sector
Management*, 11 (7), 566–82.
Casebeer A.L., Reay T., Golden-Biddle, K., Pablo, A., Wiebe, E. and Hinings, C.R.
(2006) 'Experiences of regionalization: Assessing multiple stakeholder perspectives
across time', *Health care Quarterly*, 9, 32–43.
Crossan, M.M., Lane, H.W. and White, R.E. (1999) 'An organizational learning frame-
work: From intuition to institution', *Academy of Management Review*, 24, 522–537.
Glaser, B.G. and Strauss, A.L. (1967) *The Discovery of Grounded Theory: Strategies for
Qualitative Research*. Hawthorne, NY: Aldine de Gruyter.
Hinings, C.R., Casebeer, A.C., Golden-Biddle, K., Greenwood, R., Reay,T. and Pablo,
A. (2003) 'The regionalization of health care in Alberta: Legislated change, loose
coupling and uncertainty', *The British Journal of Management*. 14 (s1), S15–S30.
Hutchinson, B., Abelson, J. and Lavis, J. (2001) 'Primary care in Canada: So much
innovation, so little change', *Health Affairs*, 20 (3), 116–31.
Pablo, A.L., Reay, T., Dewald, J.R. and Casebeer, A.L. (2007) 'Identifying, enabling
and managing dynamic capabilities in the public sector', *Journal of Management
Studies*, 44 (5), 687–708.
Pettigrew, A. (1990) 'Longitudinal field research on change: Theory and practice',
Organization Science, 1, 267–92.
Reay, T., Golden-Biddle, K. and GermAnn, K. (2006) 'Legitimizing a new role: Small
wins and micro-processes of change', *Academy of Management Journal*, 49 (4),
977–98.
Stake, R.E. (1995) *The Art of Case Study Research*. Thousand Oaks, CA: Sage.

Part III

Research into Practice

13

A Shared Vision: Using Action Research for Work Culture Change in a Cardiology Department

Susan Long, Dan Penny, Stanley Gold and Wendy Harding

Introduction

Participative Action Research (PAR) is a collaborative process in which members of an organization work with researchers in a process of exploration and change. In contrast to traditional research processes, PAR employs a cyclical and iterative process of exploration, discovery, action to implement change and evaluation. This chapter reports on a participative action research project in the Department of Cardiology at the Royal Children's Hospital in Melbourne. The Department worked with the Creative Organisational Systems (COS) Group at RMIT University in Melbourne between August 2006 to March 2008 to explore and improve the organizational culture of the Department.

The project aimed to explore the underlying group and organizational dynamics of the Department of Cardiology and to discover ways to improve the work culture. A project steering committee, comprised of members of the Department and the University researchers, provided the vehicle for this collaborative research.

The chapter describes the key issues raised in action research and learning for work culture improvement. It also describes some interventions made in a process of cultural change.

Action research and learning

Action research and action learning processes are different to the typical research models employed in much health and medical research and there is little understanding of them in this research community. Unlike the experimental research design used in clinical randomized controlled trials action research tends to be naturalistic and does not necessarily adhere to rules of inferential measurement. In essence, action research is a research management process, rather than a research method. It often relies on qualitative and descriptive data collection and analysis, although it does not preclude quantitative methods, and it tends to use inductive and abductive rather than deductive logic.

There are three aspects to be considered in this research management process.

1. Action research involves social change or quality improvement processes alongside research. It aims for planned change as well as exploration and study. It is therefore inherently a political process, and in action research, these politics and the desire for change are overt.
2. Because action research involves managing a process within a social system made up of groupings of individual 'players' it engages with collective subjectivities. The research setting is not a pure objective space, but an arena of subjective processes: emotions; motivations, changing perceptions, diverse understandings and collective group dynamics. Some of these subjective processes will be overt and consciously available to the players, others may be more subtle, covert and unconscious.
3. Action research, by virtue of the fact that it is enacted within a dynamic social system, recognizes that the process of research, of observation and intervention, whether for collecting or analysing data or for implementing change, will have an effect on the system.

One basic model of action research is the Plan-Do-Study-Act cycle (Berwick, 1998). The cycle may be continual as successive changes bring about new effects. We adapted this model to include a reflective component thus:

Study

A work culture analysis was carried out by the university researchers using interview, discussions and observations. A report was provided describing key themes and working hypotheses about the organizational culture. This focused on work roles and groups of roles and individual data were grouped and thus made anonymous.

Plan

Plans were developed based on outcomes and working hypotheses derived from the work culture analysis. These plans were made by the project steering group through a consultative process with staff. All staff were invited to come to feedback forums where the cultural analysis was discussed, validated and implications drawn out.

Act

Improvements to the culture or to work practices were implemented through appropriate means. Here the university researchers acted as consultants to the process and supported the implementation of plans.

Reflect

Various groups within the organization were given the chance to reflect on their learning within the project and the effects of the changes as they were implemented.

Change ('Do')

The outcomes of the first cycle of action research and learning were examined and integrated into broader systemic changes where possible.

Action learning

Action learning is a process where people learn through doing (Long, 2000; Carroll and Edmonson, 2002). It is highly appropriate for supporting the work of managers and others dealing with the changing and sometimes unpredictable environments such as found in hospitals and health services. New technologies requiring multidisciplinary team work, and the increasing complexity of the organization of health services requires strategic and often novel thinking from change managers. The skills involved include: dealing with ambiguities and uncertainties; weighing up situations with multiple influences (for example, managing multiple stakeholders); problem solving in an increasingly complex economic, political and social climate; and dealing with the life and death situations that the clinical task brings, together with the emotions that this work gives rise to.

The project described here included all of these complexities and the action learning approach provided a 'container' for members to explore not only their thinking about problems, but also their feelings about the situations involved and how such feelings often interact with decision-making.

Working in the cardiology department

The Department consists of several different professional groupings, all of whom have to work together for the smooth running of clinics and associated work. These include: Cardiologists, Technologists, Nurses, Secretaries, Administrative staff members, Receptionists and Cardiology Fellows.

The project steering group identified several areas where continuous quality improvement was required which included changes to the efficiency and effectiveness of work practices as well as organizational culture improvements associated with communication and interactions between subgroups. The desire was to have a department that worked optimally across its various subdivisions, that had a friendly, lively and research oriented climate while continuing to maintain its high quality service function to families.

As with most hospital departments, there was a top-down culture in which doctors led the clinical and research efforts. However, increasingly the Department was moving toward a more team-based culture with recognition of the need for all roles to have optimal input to decision-making about how the Department operates.

The cultural analysis identified areas for improvement, some of which the steering group had originally identified and others that became evident through detailed examination. At a strategic level, the Department had an excellent reputation for teaching, research and clinical work and attracted local and international cardiology fellows. But the patient lists were high, the cardiologists had only minimal time for teaching and the technologists less for research. In addition, the departmental Director was clearly overloaded. Alongside his leadership, teaching and research duties, he also retained a heavy clinical load. It became clear that roles required a re-examination in terms of duties, workload and the ways in which heavy patient demand was handled so that the aims of research, teaching and clinical work could all be met.

At a more procedural level, for example, it was clear that the system used to book patients into sessions with the technologists required improvement. Long waiting times between echocardiographs and seeing the specialist regularly occurred. But the problems were not simply administrative. Improvements could only be achieved through challenging old assumptions about the roles of cardiologists, cardiology fellows and technologists. Some of these old assumptions involved a hierarchy-in-the-mind about who could do what, rather than a rational assessment of professional skills. Following feedback of the results of the cultural analysis to all department members, plans were made for interventions.

The intervention processes

Two main interventions were used. These were a modified Open Space technology (Owen, 1997) and Organisational Role Analysis (Newton, Long and Sievers, 2006) with Departmental sub-specialization teams. These interventions were suggested by the university researchers following the cultural analysis outcomes and in discussion with the steering group.

Open space

With much effort, a regular weekly time was set aside on Thursday mornings to work on the theme of 'Change in the Cardiology Department'. Open space methodology or technology is a process where people voluntarily attend to work on a theme or issue that they feel is important. 'Open Space' refers to the open space in the centre of a circle – the circle being a form of equality of membership. This is the space for dialogue. A facilitator presents the theme and invites individuals to convene meetings on issues about which *they feel strongly and about which they are prepared to take some responsibility*. It is solely up to the individual whether or not they convene a group meeting. People coming forward as conveners are asked to state to the group the issue that they wish to work with. The issue is written up on a card and posted on a bulletin board together with the time and place that the convenor wishes to hold the meeting. People may convene one or many meetings and can choose the time and place for the meeting within the overall time available. Seeing times posted for other meetings will help with this decision.

When all themes are posted, members can sign up to attend the meetings. Although initially signed up, members can come and go to various meetings at will given adherence to the major rule that they stay at a meeting as long as they believe they are learning or usefully contributing and leave if they believe they are no longer learning or not contributing.

Conveners write and post notes on the outcomes of their meetings. Sometimes conveners find that no-one signs up or turns up to his/her meeting. In that case, the meeting may be cancelled or the convenor may wish to write up and post his/her own ideas on the issue.

Outcomes and decisions about changes may be negotiated with those who have the authority to implement the suggested changes.

Basically, the process provided for departmental members to bring forward ideas for change and to discuss these in a democratic and open atmosphere. The values and mind-sets promoted included:

- We cannot know the outcomes at the start;
- Be prepared to be surprised;
- Everyone has an equal voice;
- You can take up leadership or followership as you please;
- You can be involved with something you feel strongly about.

Authorizing the projects

An Open Space Executive team was formed consisting of the Department Director and representatives from each of the professional groupings. This Executive team had the authority to approve changes and improvements decided by the open space project groups and to ensure that they were put into practice. This was critical because although the open space is a democratic process where anyone can begin a project, to get the outcomes translated into practice requires that they are formally authorized.

The open space projects that were developed in the Department included several that dealt with procedures within the department. For example, developing a health questionnaire for pre operative and pre catheter patients; working with the cardio-base electronic database; improving outpatient departments and the backlogs of appointments. An advantage of the open space was the immediate availability of all the relevant staff members to make acceptable and workable decisions. One staff member said that previously it had taken her several months to formulate a questionnaire that in open space took only a few days because the staff members were there to make the decisions promptly. Although the accomplishment of such practical issues might seem easily achieved, it is only in an agreed and authorized space they are actually achieved.

But such procedural issues were easy to deal with in comparison to cultural change. Other projects were developed to deal with more entrenched difficulties around workplace culture. For example, one project was aimed at improving social interaction within the department, another at developing reasonable expectations that staff might have of one another during work interactions and another about managing inappropriate behaviour. The cultural analysis and open space allowed these issues to be openly discussed, whereas previously the discussion had been covert. While all organizations need to develop agreements about interpersonal interactions among staff members, medical organizations tend to adhere to implicit 'rules' within the medical hierarchy – for instance, with regard to style of communication, about whether one should 'ask' or 'command' another to carry out a particular task. It then becomes difficult to discuss, for instance, communication styles, because the discussion threatens to challenge the authority of roles within the hierarchy. Entrenched cultural assumptions had to be addressed and re-evaluated.

The open space created in the Department was a reminder that each staff member was able to bring forward work issues of concern and ask others to work with them for resolution or improvement. This was at times difficult to take up by staff members who felt they had little authority in the medical system, especially some of the secretarial and administrative staff, because they did not see themselves as clinicians. However, for many improvements, their input was crucial. At one stage, they were reminded by us that they were in fact 'medical people': in the sense that they were *medical* administrators. This was to aid them in taking the authority they did have through their identification with the primary task.

The Department has continued with the open space as a process for continuous improvement. A weekly time slot is devoted to this process.

Role analysis

At the time of the institution of the open space, the Department Director identified improvements required for what became known as sub-specialization teams. These were existing teams of sub-specialists led by a specialist Cardiologist. The improvements were designed to encourage a more team-based approach through having a leadership team of people from across disciplines. It also allowed a spread of responsibilities across a range of quality objectives for which the teams were responsible, such as: education, research, clinical quality, task effectiveness and efficiency and inter-liaisons with other teams, thus relieving busy doctors from leadership responsibilities in all these areas. It meant that most sub-specialization teams were led by a combination of doctor, technologist and nurse. In addition, a new outpatient team was introduced. Importantly, these new sub-specialization leadership teams allowed for an improved recognition of roles taken up by team leaders and members.

Continuous improvement of role definitions, of who does what, when and why, was important for optimal teamwork across specialized roles. In order to better understand these roles, each sub-specialization team undertook role analysis sessions (Newton, Long and Sievers, 2006). These not only described and articulated roles as they were currently configured but allowed for new agreements to be forged between team members. For instance, the teams, previously led by a specialist cardiologist, developed a collaborative leadership between cardiologist, nurse and technologist. In addition, a new role of Deputy Director was developed. This role was able to support the Director whose role had become overloaded in recent times. A cross-disciplinary management team was developed and each of its members was able to discuss their own views and experiences with regard to the development of this role.

What is organizational role analysis?

Organizational role analysis is not a simple exploration of role descriptions, but involves looking at how the role-holders understand the broader system within which they work.

Role is the place where the person and the system meet and overlap. Role consultation works in this space. In considering the system (the organization-in-the-mind/experience of the client) the exploration is through the role and the role as a part of the system. Questions addressed are: How does the system look from this role? What does the system demand of this role? What does the system 'put into' this role through its structure and dynamics?

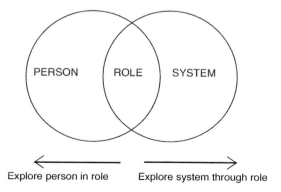

Figure 13.1   Person – Role – System

In considering the person, we can explore how the role affects the person and what the person brings to the role. Questions addressed are: What thoughts, motives and emotions are generated by the role? What skills and capacities does the person bring from their training, personality and history? How is the role shaped by these?

When considering system, role and person we see the effects on the system of how the person takes up and shapes and works with the authority of the role. We may also see how the system shapes the role and fills the person so that they experience issues that are *in* them but not *of* them.

What does the method involve?

Through the use of role drawings, an image of the 'organization-in-the-mind' and the 'roles-of-others-in-the-mind' is gained. The process allows for team members to discuss how they see each others' roles and how they understand their own authority and the authority of others-in-role. It aids in an understanding of how each role-holder takes up their role and how this influences the work of others. In this regard, a strong systemic approach is taken, where the work of individual role-holders is seen to affect and be affected by the broader system of work.

The process is guided by an experienced consultant, able to ask questions that aid the exploration in a safe non-judgmental environment.

Rules or Constraints

1. The method involves a **collaborative exploration** of role by the consultant(s) and staff member. The role consultant works as co-explorer. Together, consultant and staff member explore the staff member's role and system (in-the-mind). This exploration may at times lead to some exploration of personal issues, skills, training, competency, history etc. However, the focus is on role and the role relations between the staff member and other system role-holders rather than on the person.
2. The exploration involves the use of **working hypotheses**. The working hypothesis is a temporary device for understanding. Unlike an interpretation or assertion it recognizes that although partial meaning may be usefully discovered this may change as new data and experience emerge. The working hypothesis tends to focus the exploration. *If* it holds, then certain implications follow that might be explored. If these are unfounded then new hypotheses should be explored.
3. It is assumed that we all work from implicit and hidden hypotheses (or implicit theories about role, system and behaviour). These guide the role-holder *and* the consultant(s). They need to become explicit in order that they be examined and tested against reality and experience. To support this exploration, questions about the role need to be accompanied by a

working hypothesis so that the direction of questioning and the assumptions underlying the question are surfaced. The work thus becomes collaborative and exploratory rather than directive and inquisitorial.

4. Because role analysis explores the role as a part of the wider system, a systemic perspective is taken. This is to be borne in mind by all participants. The exploration is primarily about **role** rather than person, even though at times the exploration may involve how the person **finds, makes and takes** up a role. However, roles are performed by role-holders and it is their **experience within the role** that leads to an understanding of the sociological and psychological dynamics at play. Consequently, the exploration involves:

- The organization/system-in-the-mind of the role-holder as it is formed through experience in the role;
- The role as given (to the role-holder *by* the system) and the role as taken (by the role-holder *in* the system);
- Experiences with other roles in the broad system (organization) and its subsystems;
- The place of the role in the organizational task, political, emotional, economic/financial, technical and other systems;
- The social/emotional/behavioural effects of the demands and pressures of role on the role-holder. What it is that the role *holds* for the system.

Exploration of these aspects sometimes requires methods for understanding psycho-social, psycho-dynamic, political and unconscious processes in organizations in support of the development of working hypotheses about the system. Interpretation is to be avoided, lest 'wild analysis' occur. But it should always be held in mind that dynamics from one part of the system may be played out through displacement in another part of the system (Long, 2001).

During the role analysis, staff members learned more about the work of others from different disciplines. The built-in time for reflection and the safe atmosphere of working with a disinterested consultant who was able to question and critically address organizational issues, generally allowed for a franker appraisal of organizational roles. For example, the sometimes frustrating work of administrative staff in handling bookings and referrals and the nursing staff in having to deal with anxious parents awaiting treatment for their child became more broadly appreciated.

Problems

No process of cultural improvement or change goes smoothly. There are always reasons why work practices evolve as they do, only some of which are logically and consciously articulated. For instance, people tend to persevere with some practices out of habit. It is often thought that combining change and training to assist improvements will work against habits and routines. However, people often have strong emotional investment in 'doing things as they have always been done' even if this is a tacit or unconscious attachment. This means that a deeper exploration is required in order to understand the emotional investment in current practices. This may uncover conflict between different professional groups and disciplines, or between the tacit and stated assumptions about the primary purpose of the work. This can be further complicated by the emotional context of the clinical task, which induces anxieties and other unpleasant feelings which may be denied, disguized or deflected into unnecessary or distorted interactions with others.

In order to explore these kinds of conflicts, trust must be developed between team members, and this takes time. Moreover, the development of trust requires a mutual understanding of the shared task and each roleholder's contribution. This trust must also be developed in relation to the structure and process of the organization. Members must trust that authority will be fairly exercised despite individual emotional investments. All this requires good communication and a stable and responsible leadership at all levels. Some of these aspects of leadership may be learned as part of general medical training but organizational leadership is not formally taught (Fruge and Horowitz, 2005), instead it is learned through experience, in context. The medical model has a form of 'heroic' leadership where the doctor acts independently making decisions, carrying responsibility alone and not requiring – or at least not showing – a need for emotional support or emotional self knowledge (Meier et al., 2001). This model can no longer hold in medicine, let alone in medical administration. Decisions must be made with consultation; teamwork and reflective practice are essential.

In this project, such issues were addressed through the development of cross-disciplinary sub-specialization leadership; the development of a departmental management team to assist the Director and through work done in the projects, democratically developed in the open space. The continuation of Thursday morning reflective time, which now also involves education sessions, discipline and sub-specialization meetings, demonstrates a move toward a more consultative culture. This may be difficult to maintain, however, in the absence of a wider consultative culture in the hospital and health system as a whole – something this project was unable directly to assess or address.

References

Berwick, D. (1998) 'Developing and testing changes in the delivery of care', *Annuals of Internal Medicine*, 128 (8), 651–6.

Carroll, J.S. and Edmondson, A.C. (2002) 'Leading organisational learning in health care', *Quality and Safety in Health Care*, 11, 51–6.

Long, S.D. (2000) 'Participative action research, action research and action learning', in Y. Gabriel (ed.), *Organizations in Depth*. London: Sage.

Long, S.D. (2001) 'Co-operation and conflict: Two sides of the same coin', in R. Weisner and B. Millett (eds), *Management and Organisational Behaviour: Contemporary Challenges and Future Directions*. Australia: Wiley and Sons.

Fruge, E. and Horowitz, M. (2005) 'Leadership dimensions of the physician's role', in G. Amado and L. Vansina (eds), *The Transitional Approach to Action*. London: Karnac.

Meier, D.E., Back A.L. and Morrison R.S. (2001) 'The inner life of physicians and care of the seriously ill', *JAMA*, 286, 3007–14.

Newton, J., Long, S. and Sievers, B. (eds) (2006) *Coaching in Depth: The Organizational Role Analysis Approach*. London: Karnac.

Owen, H. (1997) *Open Space Technology: A User's Guide*. San Francisco, CA: Berrett-Koehler.

14
Creating a Climate for Service Improvement through Role Structures

Aoife McDermott and Mary A. Keating

Introduction

The huge challenges in implementing service improvement are well recognized in the international literature. Overtveit and Gustavson (2002) have called for the development of theory to explain why quality and service improvement is often unsuccessful. While Ferlie et al. (2005) identified professional, social and cognitive *barriers* to the spread of innovations in health care this chapter focuses on how service improvement may be *enabled* by organizational climate.

In Ireland, an exponential increase in both public and private health care expenditure was evident from 1995 to 2004 (Department of Health and Children, 2005). However, in line with international experience, the national health care strategy and specific initiatives such as the national cardiovascular and cancer strategies have proved difficult to implement (National Health Strategy Consultative Forum, 2001). This chapter draws on a study which identified the impact of contextual factors on the capacity and climate for service improvement.

Capacity for change is an organizational level construct that refers to the ability of an organization to undertake service improvement activities. As such, it is a measure of potential, influenced by the extent of organizational autonomy in accounting, service-planning and governance systems. Following Schneider et al. (1998) the climate for service improvement refers to the level of support for service improvement in the organization, in the present. This concept can be likened to 'receptivity for change', identified by Pettigrew, Ferlie and McKee (1992). Our findings demonstrated that climate is affected by levels of strategic distraction in the organization, the extent of senior management support for service improvement and the role structures in place. Counter-intuitively, capacity was not directly linked to climate. It had been anticipated that organizations with a high capacity for change would have a supportive climate. Therefore, this paper focuses on climate as a tool to augment levels of service improvement, independent of the underlying capacity. In particular, the chapter focuses on role structures – the way in which roles are arranged – which emerged as the discriminating factor in creating a supportive climate for service improvement.

Methodology

The research design was influenced by the particularities of the Irish health care system and the exploratory nature of the research. These choices were (1) to adopt a processual analysis framework; (2) to undertake case studies within this frame; and (3) to adopt a part-operational replication of Fitzgerald et al. (2006).

The processual framework is commonly used in health and change management studies. It focuses on establishing and understanding the influence of context, systems and change process on quality and service improvement outcomes, a focus identified as lacking to date in health care by Solberg (2000). In turn, this framework led to the decision to undertake case studies.

The three case studies comprised interviews with senior managers, managers, clinical managers and clinicians. Between 12 and 20 interviews were conducted in each case, in accordance with the scale of each organization. Respondents are detailed in Table 14.1. The interview schedule and case-study template had role, relationship, context and change sections. Following Fitzgerald et al. (2006), respondents were asked to describe 'tracer' issues, which were significant service improvements enacted. This approach allowed questions to be directed at concrete situations which encouraged respondents to report their own personal observations and experiences (Alvesson, 2003). Non-participant observation and secondary data analysis were also undertaken. In the wake of the National Cardiovascular Strategy (Department of Health and Children, 1999), cardiology was chosen as a high change context in which to conduct the research.

This research was a part-operational replication (Kelly, Chase and Tucker, 1979) of Fitzgerald et al. (2006). The direct application of their UK findings to Ireland was precluded by significant contextual differences. An iterative process of data analysis led to the identification of underlying dynamics across the cases, explored in the ensuing section.

Introduction to the cases and key findings

A contextual overview of each case is presented in Table 14.1 to orientate the reader.

Data analysis led to the counter-intuitive identification of variations in capacity and climate across the cases (see Table 14.2). Most interestingly, the case with the least capacity had a supportive climate, with more and significantly better outcomes than would have been reasonably expected.

Table 14.1   Overview of the structure and context of the three cases

	Hospital 1	Hospital 2	Hospital 3
Management structure	Senior management team comprises; CEO, head of finance and director of nursing	Senior management team comprises; general manager, director of finance, nursing and medical director	Executive management group of CEO, deputy CEO, director of nursing, finance and consultant representatives. Also medical board.
Accounting and service-planning systems	Organizational accounting system flexible. Service-planning done on basis of defined financial criteria rather than formal planning cycle	Accounting systems environmentally determined by receipt of govt funding; unable to plan for depreciation. Inefficient service-planning due to annual planning cycle	Similar to Hospital 2 but with greater discretion
Strategic distractions	Tax breaks for the development of private hospitals have led to competition for patients and staff; expansion planned	Scare re down grading; ongoing capital development; decreasing autonomy due to health service restructuring	Resource constraints with increasing demand for services; major capital development; attempt to consolidate strategic position post health service restructuring
Senior Management support for service improvement	High (proactive support)	High – moderate (reactive support)	Moderate (high for policy or senior management led initiatives, lower for emergent or non resource neutral initiatives)
Number of interviews	12 staff and 2 former staff – 6 managers – 3 clinical managers – 3 clinicians	13 staff – 6 managers – 6 clinical managers – 1 clinician	16 staff and 2 contextual interviews – 1 board member – 6 managers – 7 clinical managers – 2 clinicians

Table 14.2 The capacity, climate and role structures across the cases

	Hospital 1	Hospital 2	Hospital 3
Capacity for service improvement	High	Poor	Moderate
Climate for top-down service improvement	Proactively Supportive	Reactively Supportive	Moderately Supportive (Strategically proactive but distracted)
Climate for bottom-up service improvement	Proactively Supportive	Supportive	Poor for non-consultant-led service improvements
Role structures	Devolved	Partially-devolved	Consultant-centred
Consultant's role in service improvement	Bypassed	Figurehead	Gatekeeper

Role structures emerged as the primary discriminating factor and are hence the focus of the remainder of the chapter. An important caveat to this is that the climate for individual service improvements was augmented by the provision of resources.

Overview of findings

Case overviews of the climate for service improvement

This section depicts the climate for service improvement and discusses the role structures in place in each case. Role structures mediated the extent to which (1) there was a clear line of accountability for service improvement and (2) the extent to which responsibility for and leadership of service improvement was dispersed. In turn, the extent of dispersed leadership affected the level of consultation with multidisciplinary stakeholders. These issues are used to elucidate the cross-case differences.

In Hospital 1, a proactively supportive climate for service improvements meeting financial and quality-oriented criteria was created through innovative and devolved role structures. Responsibility for service improvement was devolved to individual department heads, who were supported by a quality manager and an overall department manager. These two supportive roles were explicitly oriented towards assisting service improvement. In Hospital 2, a regional-level network (introduced to identify regional priorities in the national cardiovascular strategy) distributed resources, monitored the implementation of the national cardiovascular strategy and facilitated the development of relationship groupings and peer-mentoring within and across professions and organizations. In conjunction with the partial devolution of responsibility for service improvement to departmental heads, these relationships led to the unanticipated development of a supportive, albeit reactive, climate. The network group interactions also led to the perceived legitimacy of front-line staff initiating and implementing change. In Hospital 3, a regional implementation network was also in operation. However, highly centralized and consultant-centred role structures undermined the potential benefit of the network, by failing to empower or support front-line staff in their service improvement endeavours. In this instance a poor – and in fact disinterested – climate emerged. The role structures and their effects are now explored more fully.

Role structures in Hospital 1

In Hospital 1, remuneration structures encouraged consultants to focus on service provision rather than departmental management. Consultants' concerns or service improvement ideas were addressed in consultant-focused meetings.

A meaningful formal invitation to engage in bottom-up change was extended to non-consultant staff through innovative role structures, which provided a clear line of accountability for service improvement. These role structures focused on devolution. Responsibility for local service improvement was given to individual departmental heads. Department heads all had clinical backgrounds, were provided with relatively significant autonomy and also had responsibility for Human Resources (HR). Service improvements were required to meet clear quality and financially oriented criteria. Cases were submitted by department heads on this basis. The overall departmental manager (DM) presented the cases from within their department for ratification. For larger projects, they also assisted with project management. In addition, an innovative quality manager (QM) role was introduced to harness emergent initiatives organization-wide. This provided a clear and structurally embedded liaison point for department heads and other staff engaged in service improvement initiatives.

> It is a very interesting role because I liaise with everybody. I don't have responsibilities for anything as such. I am a facilitator. So I work with the staff – with everybody about change and I try and give them, empower them with the information, with the expertise, that they can bring about change themselves. Because otherwise it won't last. (Quality Manager, Hospital 1)

The devolved role structures bypassed the consultant in Hospital 1. These role structures proactively encouraged service improvements meeting defined criteria. Responsibility was devolved to department heads and was supported by the quality and department manager. These structures led to high multidisciplinary involvement and, in conjunction with senior management support – despite significant strategic distractions (detailed in Table 14.1), – the emergence of a highly supportive climate.

However, while this structure displays significant advantages and is of particular potential benefit to organizations attempting to manage dysfunctional relationships between consultants and other staff, some caveats arise. Specifically, the lack of contact between consultants and departments, and between departments, may reinforce the social and cognitive boundaries which can hinder change (Ferlie et al., 2005).

Role structures in Hospital 2

In Hospital 2, service improvements were initiated by consultants and clinical managers. A broad vision for the department was established through a consultant-led consultation process, after which responsibility for the implementation of initiatives and the further development of the sub-units was devolved to unit heads, most of whom held clinical-management roles. While the consultant generally ratified emergent initiatives, often late in the planning stages, the implementation of changes occurred in a devolved and local manner.

> We just said we'd do it. Told [the consultant] at a meeting and he said 'ok, that's brilliant'. (Cardiac rehabilitation co-ordinator, Hospital 2)

Once an initiative was ratified, the consultant liaised with management, as required, to progress initiatives. Hence, the consultant adopted a figurehead role in service improvement.

A cardiology user's group provided a further multidisciplinary forum for the negotiation and ratification of developments, meaning that the final decision on implementing an initiative did not solely rest with the consultant.

Two key issues emerged from this front-line involvement in service improvement. The first was the importance of slack. In the majority of cases, respondents had no direct responsibility for service improvement and undertook this in addition to their primary – and often pressing – core job role. One allied health professional reconfigured the manner in which she saw patients, to create sufficient slack to consider necessary service improvement. Slack has previously been identified as a facilitating factor in strategic change (Greenwood and Lachman, 1996) and it is particularly important for service improvement, which tends to be implemented as an extra-discretionary responsibility (Fitzgerald et al., 2006). Second, networks emerged as highly important. A network set up under the national cardiovascular strategy facilitated peer mentoring, knowledge sharing and acted as what Addicott et al. (2006) described as a 'sustained platform of joint activity and local learning.' This further augmented the climate for service improvement in Hospital 2.

Overall, the partially-devolved role structures and the figurehead role adopted by the consultant in Hospital 2 facilitated service improvements. Notably those led by non-consultants progressed easily. The role structures also led to high multidisciplinary contact and involvement and, in conjunction with senior management support, the emergence of a supportive climate. This occurred despite significant strategic distractions (detailed in Table 14.1) and a poor capacity for service improvement in the organization.

Role structures in Hospital 3

There were no formal roles or organizational processes dedicated to harnessing service improvements in Hospital 3. As a result, the unit managers had less control over service improvement than that evident in Hospital 2. Non-consultant respondents needed to acquire support from a sponsor to progress their initiatives. This sponsorship role was predominantly filled by the consultant. This was unanimously justified on the basis that even very minor initiatives progressed much more speedily with the support of a consultant, rather than a line-manager.

The consultants presented initiatives which they supported to management for ratification, if necessary. Overall, consultants had significant influence over those changes which progressed; they had both a gate-keeping and figurehead role. The gate-keeping role pertained to both the changes supported by them, and the level of multidisciplinary involvement. Although adopting a 'clinical representative' role in liaising with management, the consultants failed to proactively engage in consultation with multidisciplinary staff. In describing their involvement in the actual implementation of bottom-up service improvements, a majority of multidisciplinary respondents articulated their desire for greater and meaningful participation and information.

Problems arose in Hospital 3 when consultants did not embrace a potential initiative, because the informal system provided no basis for redress. Hence, service improvements that failed to receive consultant support got lost in the organization. The absence of formal responsibility for service improvement also led to a failure to recognize change as a component of the role of department heads, who lacked formal structures through which to progress their initiatives. Interestingly, Hospital 3 was the only hospital where completely unsuccessful change initiatives were discussed. Lack of success in each instance was linked to the absence of consultant support. Overall, significant issues were encountered in Hospital 3, with regards to both the progression of non-consultant-led changes, and the level of multidisciplinary involvement evident throughout the process. These issues led to the emergence of a poor climate for service improvement in the organization, in spite of senior management support and a good capacity for service improvement.

Discussion

Role structures – the way in which roles are arranged – are a key determining factor of the climate for service improvement. The cases described above have provided evidence that a supportive climate is achieved through role structures which (1) provide a clear line of accountability for service improvement and (2) the structural devolution and dispersion of responsibility, providing an imperative for multidisciplinary inclusion.

Three themes emerged from these findings. The first is the contribution that the findings make to the literature on context, the second is the key actors in service improvement and the third is the contribution of role structures in health care to professional segregation, which has been identified as a barrier to the spread of innovation and service improvement (Ferlie et al., 2005). These are discussed below.

Context is a configurational and interactive process, rather than a backdrop to service improvement (Jones, 2007; Dopson and Fitzgerald, 2005). In detailing the interplay between the capacity and climate for service improvement in the organizations studied, these findings provide insight into the combinations of contextual factors that can facilitate service improvement. The fact that climate can be independent of the underlying capacity illustrates the impact of role structures in practice. This aligns with the findings from Fitzgerald et al.'s (2006) UK based study, which found that greater success was evident in service improvement where dispersed leadership was evident. However, role structures – in which change-related responsibility and accountability are *embedded* in the way roles are arranged – were not identified as a discriminating factor in that context.

Of the five roles identified as central in service delivery (Boss, 1989; Mintzberg, 1997; Johnson, 1979; Fitzgerald et al., 2006), namely the board, doctors, nurses, management and clinical managers, two emerged as particularly central in service improvement in Hospitals 2 and 3. These were doctors, specifically consultants, and clinical managers. In Hospital 1, clinical managers and general managers were most important. While the relationships between the collaborating actors were generally positive, changes tended to be implemented by individual clinicians or clinical managers in conjunction with the consultant (Hospitals 2 and 3) or quality manager/ department manager (Hospital 1). Hence service improvements were generally implemented within discipline silos, by heads of departments who liaised as necessary.

These findings indicate fewer actors than similar research conducted in the UK, where service improvement was found to be most effective when centred upon management trios such as the general manager, the head of a clinical unit and another senior manager (Fitzgerald et al., 2006). The UK findings mirror the need for collective leadership in strategic health care change (Denis et al., 2001; Denis et al., 1996; Pettigrew et al., 1992;

Shortell et al., 1990), which has generally taken the form of a leadership trio of a manager, physician and nurse. However, in the Irish case, the findings presented suggest that fewer and different actors may be required to deliver service improvement rather than strategic change. An explanation for the presence of leadership duos rather than trios in Ireland may be the absence of clinical-directorate-type structures. Second, the successful duos presented were located at lower organizational levels than those found in prior studies.

While service-delivery and improvement are ostensibly provided through multidisciplinary teams, the change-related roles and relationships evident in this study emphasized professional segregation and fragmentation. Service improvements were generally implemented by silo-based professionals, liaising with a consultant or significant other as required. This may be problematic in the light of Ferlie et al.'s (2005) finding that social and cognitive barriers between professions impede the spread of innovations in health care. In Hospital 2, where inter-professional relationships were most successfully managed, relationships were engendered by the cardiology users group and an external networking initiative. Nonetheless, stratification between professional groups was evident across all of the cases. While the role structures in Hospital 1 were highly effective in supporting service improvement, they reinforced stratification by creating an intra-unit focus. Similarly, the role structures and the role adopted by consultants in Hospital 3 failed to address the silo-type nature of hospital working. Finally, while the role structures in Hospital 2 were most successful in engendering multidisciplinary engagement, this tended to occur in dyads between the consultant and individual heads of departments, although it was supported by the cardiology users group and staff involvement in regional-implementation groups. The role stratification evident across the three hospitals is a structural, rather than individual, issue.

In Hospital 1 we found that the consultant was bypassed and excluded from inter-professional relationships on the basis of fully devolved role structures. As Fitzgerald et al. (2006) have found that where relationships between clinical groupings are problematic they impact the provision of care and the implementation of change, bypassing the consultant in this manner may be of significant benefit where relationships are dysfunctional. In Hospital 3, the patterns of inter-professional relationships evident, associated with consultant-centred role structures, can be classified as 'knotworking', as per Engestrom et al. (1999). Knotworking entails establishing and re-establishing links via brief interactions. In contrast, more sustained inter-professional relationships were evident in Hospital 2, associated with a partial devolution of responsibility for service improvement to departmental heads, in conjunction with multidisciplinary forums. Drawing from these differences, specific role structures may be of benefit in overcoming social and cognitive boundaries (Ferlie et al., 2005) and establishing sustained collaborative relationships in the longer term. This outcome may be supported by the introduction of a partial-devolution strategy, multi-professional forums and an associated clear role structure for change.

Concluding remarks

The case for formalizing supportive role structures is implicitly supported by the prior work of Buchanan et al. (2007). He found that the structural independence of a target service, in combination with articulated goals and priorities and the presence of change champions in key positions, led to the continuance of change in a hospital, even with changes to the CEO, a key leadership figure. In the Irish context, our findings explicitly highlight the importance of supportive role structures in creating climates that facilitate service improvement. The provision of clear lines of responsibility and accountability for service improvement and the embedding of dispersed leadership and multidisciplinary involvement are paramount. While the role structures in Hospital 1 were highly successful in supporting service improvement in the short term, the structures adopted in Hospital 2 are advocated. Hospital 2 devolved responsibility for service improvement to department heads, in conjunction with generating an agreed agenda for change and hosting multidisciplinary meetings. In the longer term, such a model could contribute to improved inter-professional relationships and may assist in overcoming the professional silos which can impede service improvement in health care.

Notes

* The first author would like to acknowledge funding received from the Irish Research Council for the Humanities and Social Sciences for this research.

References

Addicott, R., McGivern, G. and Ferlie, E. (2006) 'Networks, organisational learning and knowledge management: NHS cancer networks', *Public Money and Management*, 26 (2), 87–94.

Alvesson, M. (2003) 'Beyond neo-positivists, romantics and localists: A reflexive approach to interviews in organizational research', *Academy of Management Review*, 28 (1), 13–33.

Boss, W.R. (1989) *Organization Development in Health care*. Reading, MA: Addison-Wesley.

Buchanan, D., Addicott, R., Fitzgerald, L., Ferlie, E. and Baeza, J. (2007) 'Nobody in charge: Distributed change agency in health care', *Human Relations*, 60 (7), 1065–90.

Denis, J., Lamother, L. and Langley, A. (2001) 'The dynamics of collective leadership and strategic change in pluralistic organizations', *Academy of Management Journal*, 44 (4), 809–37.

Denis, J., Langley, A. and Cazale, L. (1996) 'Leadership and strategic change under ambiguity', *Organization Studies*, 17 (4), 673–99.

Department of Health and Children (1999) *Building Healthier Hearts: The Report of the Cardiovascular Health Strategy Group*. Dublin: Department of Health and Children.

Department of Health and Children (2005) *Health Statistics*. Dublin: Department of Health and Children.

Dopson, S. and Fitzgerald, L. (2005) 'The active role of context', in Dopson, S. and Fitzgerald, L. (eds), *Knowledge to Action: Evidence-Based Health Care in Context*. Oxford: Oxford University Press, 79–103.

Engestrom, Y., Engestrom, R. and Vahaaho, T. (1999) 'When the center does not hold: The importance of knotworking', in Chalkin, S., Hedegarrd, M., and Jensen, U. (eds), *Activity Theory and Social Practice*, Aarhus: Aarhus University Press.

Ferlie, E., Fitzgerald, L., Wood, M. and Hawkins, C. (2005) 'The nonspread of innovations: The mediating role of professionals', *Academy of Management Journal*, 48 (1), 117–34.

Fitzgerald, L., Lilley, C., Ferlie, E., Addicott, R., McGivern, G. and Buchanan, D. (2006) *Managing Change and Role Enactment in the Professionalised Organisation*. London: SDO Board.

Greenwood, R. and Lachman, R. (1996) 'Change as an underlying theme in professional service organisations: An introduction', *Organization Studies*, 17 (4), 563–72.

Johnson, R.L. (1979) 'Revisiting the "wobbly three legged stool"', *Health Care Management Review*, 4 (3), 15.

Jones, J.L. (ed.) (2007) *Sustaining and Spreading Change: The Patient Booking Case Experience*, Oxon: Routledge.

Kelly, C.W., Chase, L.J. and Tucker, R.K. (1979) 'Replication in experimental communication research: An analysis', *Human Communication Research*, 5 (4), 338–42.

Mintzberg, H. (1997) 'Towards healthier hospitals', *Health Care Management Review*, 22 (4), 9–18.

National Health Strategy Consultative Forum (2001) Subgroup Report: Service Delivery and HR. Dublin: Department of Health and Children.

Overtveit, J. and Gustafson, D. (2002) 'Evaluation of quality improvement programmes', *Quality and Safety in Health care*, 11 (3), 270–5.

Pettigrew, A.M., Ferlie, E. and McKee, L. (1992) *Shaping Strategic Change. Making Change in Large Organizations: The Case of the National Health Service*. London: Sage.

Schneider, B., White, S. and Paul, M.C. (1998) 'Linking service climate and customer perceptions of service quality: Test of a causal model', *Journal of Applied Psychology*, 83 (2), 150–63.

Shortell, S., Morrison, E. and Friedman, B. (1990) *Strategic Choices for America's Hospitals*. San Francisco, CA: Jossey-Bass.

Solberg, L. (2000) 'Guideline implementation: What the literature doesn't tell us', *Journal on Quality Improvement*, 26 (9), 525–37.

15

Accountability and Transparency through the Technologization of Practice

David Greenfield

Introduction

In the last 20 years, professional accountability has evolved significantly (Rose, 1999). Professionals in practice communities (Webb, 2005), public organizations (Hindle et al., 2006) and private enterprises (Blomgren, 2007) have been publicly called to account for their conduct. This is true for health care as for many other industries. Improving the governance and administration of health organizations has for many clinicians, managers and policy makers become a critical issue. This goal has involved addressing the appropriateness, quality and safety of clinical services; the term clinical governance has been coined to encompass this focus (Flynn, 2002).

While important steps have been taken, for example the expansion of evidence-based practice (Timmermans and Berg, 2003) and the growth of quality and accreditation programs (Greenfield and Braithwaite, 2008), success in improving clinical governance has been slow and not easy to accomplish (Braithwaite et al., 2007). A key issue is changing the culture and climate of professional practice in an organization. Changing 'the way we do things around here' to increase accountability and transparency continues to be a challenge for many organizations. Examining this issue, this chapter adopts the following understanding of organizational climate and culture. Climate is behaviourally orientated, that is, the actions of people on a daily and ongoing basis (Svyantek and Bott, 2004). Culture is a set of shared values and norms that guide their interactions, it is 'an interactive ongoing process operating between individuals and structures' (Tyrrell, 2004: 85).

The study described here explains how a clinical group evolved a collaborative practice. The group through collectively defining, monitoring and disciplining their own conduct – a process termed the technologization of practice – instigated a collaborative practice climate and culture characterized by transparency and accountability; they enacted a communal self-governance – governmental duality.

The exploration of the technologization of clinical care is an undertaking that is noted as underdeveloped in the health care field (Heath et al., 2003) and one that has previously been called for (Timmermans and Berg, 2003). Illuminating the interaction between people and the artefacts they construct, refine and are shaped by makes visible how practice is constituted and mediated by technologies (Araujo, 1998; Latour, 1986). Furthermore, expanding understanding of how people act in collaboration with materials (Heath et al., 2003) and the practices and processes by which technologies come to be stabilized and take on an unremarkable character (Heath et al., 2003; May and Ellis, 2001), are important goals.

The study described in this chapter utilized qualitative methods that are complimentary (Fontana and Frey, 1994) and appropriate, as they allow an investigation of the culture (Kilduff and Corley, 2004), climate (Wiley and Brooks, 2004) and dynamics of health organizations (Fessey, 2002), and the examination of developmental and historical processes within organizations and communities (Sofaer, 1999). Similar methods have been used in research that investigated the introduction of new technologies into health settings (Blomgren, 2007) and change in organizations (Chreim, 2007), including health services (Greenfield, 2007).

The chapter is structured as follows. The next section details the method followed by the findings and discussion. The conclusion draws the chapter to a close.

Method

The study comprised one year of ethnographic fieldwork, undertaken during 2001–2 in a community health service in Sydney, Australia. It focused on an early childhood nursing team providing clinical care. The team consisted of 13 members. The study utilized an ethnographic methodology comprising ethno-document analysis (Lincoln and Guba, 1985), non-participant observation (Spradley, 1980) and interviews. The study totalled 960 hours. The documents examined were the organizational and clinical policies and procedures that applied to the clinical team. Observations covered all aspects of the team's work, that is, their formal meetings, clinical assessments and social interactions. Interviews were of two types: informal or natural interviews (Davies, 1999) and formal semi-structured interviews (Hammersley and Atkinson, 1995). Informal interviews ranged from several minutes to half an hour depending on the circumstance. Note taking was by hand at the time of the interviews and observations.

The findings were analysed and structured through constructing a narrative strategy, constructing a detailed account from the data, with temporal bracketing, using time, to structure the account (Langley, 1999). The narrative strategy was formed through the integration of 'experience-near' and 'experience-distance' concepts (Geertz, 1983); for example, the former being the clinicians' team and in-service meetings, and the latter being the notion that these together are a 'sense-making structure' (Choo, 1998) for the team. Patterns, issues and themes are considered in relation to theoretical material; the empirical data were integrated with theories from the literature to construct the discourse of the technologization of practice.

Findings and discussion

The clinicians changed their practice climate and culture, enacting a collaborative community through two actions. First, by assigning responsibility for the service and enacting a collective 'sense-making structure' (Choo, 1998) the clinicians established a 'community of practice' (Wenger, 1998). Second, the community's 'assemblage' (Rose, 1996) and 'appropriation' (Suchman, 1987) of resources, or 'technologies' (Rose, 1999), standardized how the clinicians conceptualized and enacted their work.

Assigning responsibility and enacting a collaborative sense-making structure

The community health team from which the clinicians were drawn for this study, provided a range of complex services including early childhood and palliative care. A continual expansion of services over time had stretched the skills and knowledge of the clinicians beyond their capacities; as a result the quality of care was compromised. These clinicians did not share the same practice model. Individually they were responsible for the service they provided. There was not a practice culture of transparency and no climate of collaboration. The clinicians confronted the problems with this situation by defining a clear boundary, separating early childhood nursing from generalist community health nursing. This process of evolution has been explored elsewhere (see Greenfield (2007)).

The manager of community health selected from the existing staff a small group of clinicians, with a clinical manager, and assigned them the responsibility to provide the specialized early childhood service. By constructing a small team and collectively handing them responsibility to determine their service created a break with past practice. The new organizational context imposed new responsibilities, roles and relationships, and was one step towards affecting change in conduct (Worren et al., 1999). However, being placed in a new organizational structure was not in itself going to change the practice climate and culture. The clinicians still had to learn to work collaboratively together and leadership by the clinical manager was required. The manager actively set out to engage the clinicians in organizing the work and delivering services. She strove to facilitate collaborative relationships within the team, moving the emphasis away from the traditional hierarchal structure. The manager aimed to achieve this through negotiating the purpose, direction and activities of the work, rather than directing or ordering what should, or should not be, the work of the team (Bolton, 2003).

The manager utilized two formal meetings, the team meeting and the in-service meeting, to share responsibility with the team for the organizing and delivery of the service. Inclusion in organizing activities such as these has been found to build commitment and ownership to the work (Worren et al., 1999). The team meeting became the place to collectively establish a common purpose for, and approach to, the clinical work. The team meeting was used to disseminate and discuss organizational material – memos, notices and administration issues, to monitor the general management of resources – cars, phones and clinical items, and ensure the coverage of clinics and home visits, when staff were away – at meetings, holidays, sick or conferences. Negotiating aspects of the work the clinical team became a collective effort where participation was encouraged, supported and indeed necessitated (West, 1990). In addition, through participating in the reviewing of clinical policies and developing their own policies and procedures, the clinical team developed and aligned their communal practice culture and climate with their colleagues throughout the area health service (Kilduff and Corley, 2004). The outcome is the conceptualization and enactment of appropriate practice is simultaneously disciplined and realized through these activities. Through their conduct the clinicians demonstrated belonging, locally to their immediate team, and more distantly to the practice of their professional colleagues within the larger organization; in this way the local culture was directly influenced by the ties to other organizational actors (Kilduff and Corley, 2004).

The participatory approach adopted by the manager encouraged the clinicians to assume collective ownership of their work built on trust and collaboration (Zajac and Bruhn, 1999). The team's work became the enactment of different, but interrelated, clinical and the bureaucratic roles. While the clinicians provided the clinical service – the home visits and clinics, one clinician accepted responsibility for managing the occupational health and safety issues, conducting audits as required by the organization. Another clinician monitored the physical resources, reordering the physical supplies as necessary. A third acted as the fulltime 'intake officer' and two others provided expertise and resources for specific client health problems. In this way, membership of the team was expressed as collaborating in the organizing and management of the work, and was integrated its enactment. The clinicians engaged in a common clinical role and distributed the other clinical and bureaucratic tasks across the team. A collaborative team has been shown to encourage people to take risks and learn (Hoskins et al., 1998), whereby individually and collectively they are rewarded through their interactions and they develop their common knowledge (Smith et al., 1995).

The clinicians used their other formal meeting, the weekly in-service meeting, to identify the knowledge and skill areas where they required further professional development. This meeting became part of the clinicians' formal reflection, which enabled them to develop personal development plans. By collectively identifying the requirements of the work, the clinicians were able to individually assess their skills and knowledge, and take responsibility for professional development. This required greater openness about their skills and capabilities and encouraged greater accountability and transparency within the team. This collaborative endeavour meant that the clinicians were participating in their own disciplining and control (Sewell, 1998).

The two meetings together provided the clinicians with a 'sense-making structure' (Choo, 1998) by which to enact communal responsibility and accountability (Schweikhart and Smith-Daniels, 1996). The formal structures engaged the clinicians so that their work expanded beyond just providing clinical services to establish a practice culture and climate defined by participating in the defining, organizing, managing and reflecting upon their clinical activities, skills and capabilities. The meetings provided a routine by which the community enacted communal surveillance and self-governance (Scally and Donaldson, 1998). The team meetings were part of the 'web of tension' (Rose, 1996) that united the clinicians into their community across their daily, weekly and monthly activities. The clinicians collectively disciplined each other with the expectation that they will be in a certain place, at a certain time, for a certain purpose, for example being expected to attend and participate in the in-service meeting. Through their collaboration and participation, or surveillance and discipline, the clinicians learnt to enact responsibility and accountability for themselves and one another about a common endeavour; they became a collaborative community of practice (Wenger, 1998).

Assembling and appropriating resources

The clinical team collectively 'assembled' (Rose, 1996) and 'appropriated' (Suchman, 1987) resources – organizational and professional knowledges, vocabularies, systems of judgement and technical devices – to define and enact their practice; they did so through their collective sense-making structure. These resources are those of the State (for example, clinical assessment artefacts), those originating in the area health service (for example, the identification tag which represented authority to practise), those located in the division of community health (for example, physical assets and local policies), and those specific to childhood nursing (for example, clinical equipment). The resources are 'technologies' (Rose, 1999) that accord the clinicians the capacity to know, judge and govern themselves and their client population. They construct standardized routines which manipulate their social and physical world thereby making practice transparent and accountable (Rose, 1999). In other words, the assemblage and appropriation of the technologies enacts a standardized practice climate and culture, creating and strengthening extended relationships of accountability.

The resources are technologies with one or two dimensions; the dimensions are 'organizing' and/or 'transforming'. A technology has an organizing dimension when it directs or shapes the conduct of people and the physical artefacts they use; that is, it regulates the thought, expectations and actions of people individually and collectively (Gilbert, 2003). A technology has a transforming dimension when it enables clinicians to 'transform' (Barley, 1996) and 'translate' (Schultze, 2000) experience of the physical world into a written form. They create standardized indices and symbols to be transcribed and transported, via artefacts or 'immutable mobiles' (Latour, 1986), to other contexts for examination by other people. The technologies normalize and standardize the clinical environment for the clinicians, their use brings order to the chaotic unordered world (Henderson, 1994). A resource can be a technology, that is either 'organizing' or 'transforming', or alternatively it may combine these dimensions and be 'organizing- transforming'. Examples of each of these possibilities follow.

Organizing technologies: The organizational code of conduct and uniform policy

The clinicians' extended relationships of accountability are strengthened by resources such as the organizational code of conduct or the policy about uniform. These resources or organizational artefacts are technologies that shape how the clinicians will act and present themselves as representatives of the health service. These technologies dovetail with the clinicians' expectations that they should present themselves as 'professionals'. In their formal and informal interactions the clinicians' survey and comment on each other's appearance and behaviours, comparing and contrasting themselves against one another. In this way they collectively discipline, adopting conduct and a standard of dress as a community they deem appropriate for the workplace. These are but two examples of organizational administration policies that regulate the organizing and enactment of the collaborative practice climate and culture (Gilbert, 2003). Furthermore, they highlight the multidirectional nature of power, impacting upon, and taken up by, the clinicians, simultaneously manifesting submission and institutional status (Manias and Street, 2000).

Transforming technologies: The staff identification tag

The health service by marking out a geographical territory defines the conditions upon which a professional can call him or herself an organizational member. To this end the 'staff identification tag', worn by all organizational members, is an artefact that symbolizes, making visible and mobile, the organization and its boundaries. The staff identification tag is a transforming technology that makes visible and explicit the clinician's accountability to their immediate team, the larger health organization and their wider professional community; for example, Mary Smith, Community Health Nurse,

Southern Sector, Area Health Service. Making the clinician visible is a mechanism by which to control their conduct (Gordon, 2002) and reinforce the practice culture and climate when the clinician is alone, with a client or professional colleagues.

Organizing and transforming technologies: The Edinburgh Postnatal Depression Scale

The Edinburgh Postnatal Depression Scale (EPDS) is an artefact appropriated from the discipline of mental health that allows the clinicians to assess, but not diagnose, postnatal depression. The EPDS is an organizing and transforming technology which is completed by the mother and then 'scored' by the clinician. The clinician uses the artefact to therapeutically explore with the mother her experiences and current psychological-emotional state. The mother is encouraged, and where needed assisted by the clinician, to reflect and then describe her experiences, in both written and verbal form, to the expert professional. Through this interaction, the mother and clinician are enacting their identities (Gilbert, 2001; Gordon, 2002). The EPDS is a transforming technology that allows the clinician and mother to make visible the mother's experience and compare and measure this against the maternal population; that is, the EPDS is a governmental technology that seeks the normalization of the individual within a client population (Holmes, 2002).

The technology enables the clinician to exercise 'pastoral power' (Holmes, 2002) engaging with the mother to jointly construct savoir, or knowledge, about the mother, the governed subject. Using this knowledge the clinician is then required to act as a 'buffer' (Barley, 1996), suggesting to the mother that she be referred on to other professional services when the possibility or likelihood of depression is identified. The EPDS, similar to other clinical artefacts, is an immutable mobile and also a coordinating device (Timmermans and Berg, 2003) between the immediate clinician and other health and welfare professionals. It is an expansive technology that makes practice transparent and strengthens the extended relationships of accountability. Furthermore, the clinician is made visible and accountable within her practice community as the health file can be audited to see if she has completed the artefact and fulfilled her responsibilities (Flynn, 2002; Gilbert, 2001). Aware of this possibility the clinician self-governs to ensure this artefact, and all others within the file are completed, so that if her file is audited she will be judged professionally competent. The potential, and actuality, of being governed in this way reinforces the self-governance of the individual clinician and the collaborative practice climate and culture.

Conclusion

This study has demonstrated how a collaborative practice culture and climate is achieved via the technologization of practice. The technologization enables the team to collectively define, monitor and discipline their individual and collaborative conduct. The clinicians used technologies – artefacts (clinical forms and physical items), conduct (expectations and tasks) and processes (team meetings) – to standardize how they conceptualized and enacted their work. The team became a community as they developed trust, emotionally engaged with one another, formed a shared history of learning, constructed and enacted overlapping roles, and collaborated to pursue knowing (Wenger, 1998). The clinical team became a community that enacted subtle, but extensive, control through collaboration and participation; accountability is a negotiated and choreographed set of practices (Webb, 2005). Through their increasingly intense collaboration the clinicians' conceptualization and enactment of practice became increasingly standardized and accountable. They enacted a collaborative practice climate and culture (Gilbert, 2003).

The team, through the technologization of practice, enacted a communal self-governance-governmentality duality. The clinicians' practice community in the ongoing action of collectively defining what their practice expertise is, simultaneously monitor their own conduct thereby disciplining themselves to ensure they met their own standards (Scally and Donaldson, 1998). The effect of these actions is increased transparency and accountability personally and collectively, to their professional colleagues and to their organization. They enact self-governance. Simultaneously, the clinicians' practice community through the use of their technologies makes visible and 'knowable' the population to whom they provide services. In doing so the population becomes countable, and accountable, to themselves, the clinicians and the state. The effect of this is the population can be shaped to meet the expectations of all three, that is, they can be governed (Rose, 1999).

Routinization is the process by which cultural change is achieved (Hatch, 2004); the technologization of practice changed the practice culture and climate of the team. Individual conduct was replaced by collaboration and participation within a community. The practice culture changed to acknowledge that explicit knowledge is distributed within the practice technologies and tacit knowing is distributed across, and is continually enacted by, the collaboration of the practice community. The practice climate changed to recognize the necessity of interaction and collaboration of individuals within their community to practice effectively. The technologization of practice fused individual professional expertise within a collaborative community, with a practice climate and culture defined by transparency and accountability.

References

Araujo, L. (1998) 'Knowing and learning as networking', *Management Learning*, 29 (3), 317–36.

Barley, S. (1996) 'Technicians in the workplace: Ethnographic evidence for bringing work into organisational studies', *Administrative Science Quarterly*, 41 (3), 404–41.

Blomgren, M. (2007) 'The drive for transparency: Organisational field transformations in Swedish healthcare', *Public Administration*, 85 (1), 67–82.

Bolton, S. (2003) 'Multiple roles? Nurses as managers in the NHS', *The International Journal of Public Sector Management*, 16 (2), 122–30.

Braithwaite, J., Westbrook, M., Travaglia, J., Iedema, R., Mallock, N., Long, D., Nugus, P., Forsyth, R., Jorm, C. and Pawsey, M. (2007) 'Are health systems changing in support of patient safety? A multi-methods evaluation of education, attitudes and practice', *International Journal of Health Care Quality Assurance*, 20 (7), 585–601.

Choo, C. (1998) *The Knowing Organisation: How Organisations Use Information to Construct Meaning, Create Knowledge, and Make Decisions*. New York, NY: Oxford University Press.

Chreim, S. (2007) 'Social and temporal influences on interpretations of organisational identity and acquisition integration', *The Journal of Applied Behavioural Science*, 43 (3), 449–80.

Davies, C. (1999) *Reflexive Ethnography: A Guide to Researching Selves and Others*. London: Routledge.

Fessey, C. (2002) 'Capturing expertise in the development of practice: Methodology and approaches', *Learning in Health and Social Care*, 1 (1), 47–58.

Flynn, R. (2002) 'Clinical governance and governmentality', *Health, Risk & Society*, 4 (2), 155–73.

Fontana, A. and Frey, J. (1994) 'Interviewing: The art of science', in Denzin, N. and Lincoln, Y. (eds), *Handbook of Qualitative Research*, Thousand Oaks, CA: Sage, 361–76.

Geertz, C. (1983), *Local Knowledge*. New York: Basic Books.

Gilbert, T. (2001) 'Reflective practice and clinical supervision: Meticulous rituals of the confessional', *Journal of Advanced Nursing*, 36 (2), 199–205.

Gilbert, T. (2003) 'Exploring the dynamics of power: A Foucauldian analysis of care planning in learning disabilities services', *Nursing Inquiry*, 10 (1), 37–46.

Gordon, N. (2002) 'On visibility and power: An Arendtian corrective of Foucault', *Human Studies*, 25 (3), 125–45.

Greenfield, D. (2007) 'The enactment of dynamic leadership', *Leadership in Health Services*, 20 (3), 159–68.

Greenfield, D. and Braithwaite, J. (2008) 'Health sector accreditation research: A systematic review', *International Journal for Quality in Health Care*, 20 (3), 172–83.

Hammersley, M. and Atkinson, P. (1995) *Ethnography: Principles in practice*. New York: Routledge.

Hatch, M. (2004) 'The cultural dynamics of organising and change', in Ashkanasy, N., Wilderom, C. and Peterson, M. (eds), *Organisational Culture and Climate*. London: Sage, 245–60.

Heath, C., Luff, P. and Svensson, M. (2003) 'Technology and medical practice', *Sociology of Health and Illness*, 25 (Silver Anniversary Issue), 75–96.

Henderson, A. (1994) 'Power and knowledge in nursing practice: The contribution of Foucault', *Journal of Advanced Nursing*, 20 (14), 935–9.

Hindle, D., Braithwaite, J., Travaglia, J. and Iedema, R. (2006) 'Patient safety: A comparative analysis of eight inquiries in six countries', Center for Clinical Governance Research, UNSW, Sydney.

Holmes, D. (2002) 'Police and pastoral power: Governmentality and correctional forensic psychiatric nursing', *Nursing Inquiry*, 9 (2), 84–92.

Hoskins, M., Liedtka, J. and Roseblum, J. (1998) 'Beyond teams: Towards an ethic of collaboration', *Organisational Dynamics*, Spring, 34–50.

Kilduff, M. and Corley, K. (2004) 'Organisational culture from a network perspective', in Ashkanasy, N., Wilderom, C. and Peterson, M. (eds), *Organisational Culture and Climate*, London: Sage, 211–21.

Langley, A. (1999) 'Strategies for theorising from process data', *The Academy of Management Review*, 24 (4), 691–710.

Latour, B. (1986) 'Visualisation and cognition: Thinking with eyes and hands', *Knowledge and Society: Studies in the Sociology of Culture Past and Present*, 6 (1), 1–40.

Lincoln, Y. and Guba, E. (1985) *Naturalistic Inquiry*. Beverly Hills, CA: Sage.

Manias, E. and Street, A. (2000) 'Legitimation of nurses' knowledge through policies and protocols in clinical practice', *Journal of Advanced Nursing*, 32 (6), 1467–75.

May, C. and Ellis, N. (2001) 'When protocols fail: Technical evaluation, biomedical knowledge and the social production of "facts" about a telemedicine clinic', *Social Science & Medicine*, 53 (11), 989–1002.

Rose, N. (1996) *Inventing ourselves: Psychology, Power and Personhood*. Cambridge: Cambridge University Press.

Rose, N. (1999) *Powers of Freedom: Reframing Political Thought*. Cambridge: Cambridge University Press.

Scally, G. and Donaldson, L. (1998) 'Clinical governance and the drive for quality improvement in the new NHS in England', *British Medical Journal*, 317 (1), 61–5.

Schultze, U. (2000) 'A confessional account of an ethnography about knowledge work', *MIS Quarterly*, 24 (1), 3–41.

Schweikhart, S. and Smith-Daniels, V. (1996) 'Reengineering the work of caregivers: Role redefinition, team structures and organisational redesign', *Hospital & Health Services Administration*, 41 (1), 19–36.

Sewell, G. (1998) 'The discipline of teams: The control of team-based industrial work through electronic surveillance', *Administrative Science Quarterly*, 43 (2), 397–429.

Smith, K., Carroll, S. and Ashford, S. (1995) 'Intra- and interorganisational cooperation: Toward a research agenda', *Academy of Management Journal*, 38 (1), 7–23.

Sofaer, S. (1999) 'Qualitative methods: What are they and why use them?' *Health Services Research*, 34 (5), 1101–18.

Spradley, J. (1980) *Participant Observation*. Rinehart and Winston, NY: Holt.

Suchman, L. (1987) *Plans and Situated Actions: The Problem of Human-Machine Communication*. Sydney: Cambridge University Press.

Svyantek, D. and Bott, J. (2004) 'Organisational culture and organizational climate measures: An integrative review', in Thomas, J. (ed.), *Comprehensive Handbook of Psychological Assessment: Industrial and Organisational Assessment*. Wiley, NJ: Hoboken, 507–24.

Timmermans, S. and Berg, M. (2003) *The Gold Standard: The Challenge of Evidence-Based Medicine and Standardisation in Health Care*. Philadelphia, PA: Temple University Press.

Tyrrell, M. (2004) 'Hunting and gathering in the early Silicon age: Cyberspace, jobs and the reformulation of organisational culture', in Ashkanasy, N., Wilderom, C. and Peterson, M. (eds), *Organisational Culture and Climate*. London: Sage, 85–99.

Webb, P. (2005) 'The anatomy of accountability', *Journal of Education Policy*, 20 (2), 189–208.

Wenger, E. (1998) *Communities of Practice: Learning, Meaning and Identity*. Cambridge: Cambridge University Press.

West, M. (1990) 'The social psychology of innovation in groups', in West, M. and Farr, J. (eds), *Innovation and Creativity at Work: Psychological and Organisational Strategies*, Brisbane: John Wiley and Sons, 309–33.

Wiley, J. and Brooks, S. (2004) 'The high performance organisational climate', in Ashkanasy, N., Wilderom, C. and Peterson, M. (eds), *Organisational Culture and Climate*. London: Sage, 177–209.

Worren, N., Ruddle, K. and Moore, K. (1999) 'From organisational development to change management', *The Journal of Applied Behavioural Science*, 35 (3), 273–86.

Zajac, G. and Bruhn, J. (1999) 'The moral context of participation in planned organisational change and learning', *Administration & Society*, 30 (6), 706–33.

16
The Role of Cultural Performance in Health Care Commissioning

Helen Dickinson, Edward Peck, Joan Durose and Elizabeth Wade

Introduction

New Labour acceded power in 1997 much influenced by a 'third way' ideology (Giddens, 1998) and promised an approach which lay between the 'Old Labour command and control' and the internal market approach of the Conservatives (Ham, 2004). Central to their vision was a commitment to public services, but services which were much modernized and delivered in different ways from the past. This government's ten-year reform plan for the National Health Service (NHS) was set out in *The NHS Plan* (Secretary of State for Health, 2000) which promised unprecedented amounts of investment in health services, but in return for a radical overhaul of the system. Since the publication of this document much effort – and investment – have been expended in England in an attempt to change a health service that was 'failing to deliver' into one driven by cycles of 'continuous improvement'. Leatherman and Sutherland (2004: 288–9) describe these improvement efforts as being the 'most ambitious, comprehensive, systematic and intentionally funded effort to create predictable and sustainable capacity for improving quality of a nation's health care system'.

Characterized by a turbulent policy environment, this period of reform focussed initially on major supply-side transformation. Over time, however, as the rate of improvement failed to match either political aspirations or public expectations, it became apparent that the government saw ongoing poor performance of the health care system as partially due to failure of the commissioning process to elicit the desired service changes from providers (Department of Health, 2005b). It was recognized that despite (or perhaps because) of several reorganizations of local health care commissioning infrastructure, little had been put in place locally to actually strengthen the demand-side of the system in terms of capacity and capability. Woodin (2006: 203) defines the term commissioning stating that it, 'tends to denote a proactive strategic role in planning, designing and implementing the range of services required, rather than a more passive purchasing role. A commissioner decides which services or health care interventions should be provided, who should provide them, and how they should be paid for, and may work closely with the provider in implementing changes'. In England, the organizations who are predominantly charged with this commissioning role in health care are Primary Care Trusts (PCTs). Although the precise functions of health care commissioners are relatively unique to the English NHS, this focus on the 'steering', rather than 'rowing' is illustrative of a wider international trend of New Public Management where governments were being encouraged to drive improvements by separating out service delivery from determining what sorts of services should be delivered and by whom (see for example, Peters and Waterman, 1982).

Of course, the very limited impact of these initiatives driven by primary care based commissioning on the performance of secondary care providers is scarcely surprising given the international evidence (see Smith et al., 2004). Faced with this combination of experience and evidence, New Labour's perseverance with local and collective yet nationally tax-funded public commissioning as a central component of health care reform may lead to it becoming one of the government's distinctive contributions to public management. This may mean that previous accounts of these contributions (e.g. 6 and Peck, 2004) will have to be updated. Of course, as Powell (2007) demonstrates, the underlying commitment to markets in public services which the approach exemplifies is characteristic of the impact of new public management across most democratic capitalist states over the past 20 years.

Indeed, during 2007, there was a burst of policy time and attention devoted to the development of demand-side capacity and capability in England. During 2006, as a prelude to this attempt to move from a 'provider-driven' to a 'commissioning-driven' service (Department of Health, 2005a: 2), all PCTs underwent a so-called 'Fitness for Purpose' review to assess their ability to take forward this new agenda. This assessment process was designed and delivered by McKinsey & Company under contract from the Department of Health and consisted of two tools: an organizational assessment to review the overarching competencies of PCTs across a range of activities; and a commissioning diagnostic to benchmark PCTs against best practice commissioning (measures for both these tools are summarized in Table 16.1).

The organizational assessment tool was intended to measure PCTs against 'objective minimum performance goals' focusing on outcomes. The results were aggregated into a rating for each category and were argued to give an 'objective' view of the PCT's ability to meet baseline performance goals over the short-term (six to twelve months). Whilst being prospective rather than retrospective, in many respects it was similar to a number of previous assessment regimes applied by the UK government to public services in recent years (see 6 and Peck, 2004). The accompanying commissioning diagnostic tool described the activities needed for 'good' PCT commissioning, so that any gaps could be identified and high-level development plans designed.

Table 16.1 Measures for fitness for purpose diagnostic tools

Organizational assessment tool	Commissioning diagnostic tool
Financial assessment	Strategic planning
Strategy assessment	Care pathway management
Governance assessment (including financial governance, clinical and health governance and quality of patient experience)	Provider management
External relations	Monitoring
Emergency planning	

The Fitness for Purpose assessment represents a specific kind of performance management regime, which suggests that high-performance is determined on an objective basis by comparison with benchmark data and intelligence about commissioning best practice. Thus, a high-performing PCT is judged to be so, almost irrespective of context, in comparison with a set of measures concerning solely the efficiency of the organization and the effectiveness of its commissioning function.

McKenzie's general theory of performance

Since the end of the Second World War, the concept of performance has come to constitute a pervasive force within modern societies. Kershaw (2006) suggests that recent decades have seen the emergence of 'performative societies' where 'the human is increasingly constituted through performance' (p. 30). McKenzie (2001) suggests that there are three predominant types of performance: organizational (efficiency); technological (effectiveness); and cultural (efficacy). He goes on to generate a general theory of performance, which is an emergent confluence of these distinct forms of performance. According to this thesis, performance is not a simple, coherent and stable concept; rather it is dynamic, responding to changes in dominant socio-cultural forces. Thus, the parameters of 'high' performance will alter according to the values and norms prevalent in social, political and organizational systems. The Fitness for Purpose assessment – and the high-performance organizational literature more generally – reflect the bureaucratic tendency in much organizational theory and practice. Much more emphasis is therefore given to efficiency and effectiveness than efficacy; indeed, this latter aspect is almost entirely absent from previous accounts.

Methodology

This chapter reports on a group of PCT Chief Executives (CEs) who created a co-productive network to develop a set of practical characteristics relevant to high-performing commissioning organizations in health care. This chapter reports on an early stage of this project where CEs were interviewed to garner their perceptions of what PCT high-performance would look like five years hence. CEs were interviewed using a semi-structured format according to a pre-determined schedule in December 2006/January 2007; at this stage, these PCT CEs were still awaiting the outcome of the Fitness for Purpose Assessment. The software application NVivo was used to code and analyse interview transcripts; this was further supplemented by data collected in the form of notes taken at meetings of the network.

Organizational performance – efficiency

McKenzie's general theory of performance links organizational performance with the challenge of *efficiency*. Input efficiency, in the form of strict cost control, was certainly a preoccupation of the government during the period preceding the interviews (e.g. Health Service Journal, 2007). Indeed, the recent reconfiguration of PCTs had itself been driven (at least in part) by a perceived need for PCTs to improve their efficiency through achieving better economies of scale (this despite a lack of evidence that any 'ideal' size for commissioning organizations exists Bojke et al., 2001; Smith et al., 2004). One of the explicit objectives of the re-organization was a reduction of 15% in management and administrative costs; priority had also been given to financial management in the Fitness for Purpose assessment; arguably, this represented the nationally tax-based aspect of the approach to commissioning.

Perhaps unsurprisingly in this context, most CEs highlighted financial issues as a key indication of their organization's ability to perform. The majority linked financial imperatives – and other centrally defined, national targets (the promulgation of which is another characteristic of New Labour highlighted by 6 and Peck, 2004) – as 'must-do' indicators against which Government will assess the performance of PCTs. However, in spite of the recent assessment criteria and the contemporary financial pressures, a number of CEs were aware of the dangers of simply representing to their local public their performance in terms of financial issues. This public – and patients in particular – were viewed as being less interested in the stewardship of national tax spend and more interested in the quality of local services.

A number of CEs recognized the importance of meeting short-term, output related and financial targets set and monitored by government in order to be viewed as high-performing (in line with the McKinsey organizational assessment tool). So doing, it was believed, would bring them freedom to get to grips with more local, varied and potentially long-term issues. That is, by being seen to perform efficiently on the 'must-dos', PCT CEs argued that they could earn autonomy to act locally; this underlines 6 and Peck's (2004) account of the extent to which New Labour's paradoxical formulation of 'earned autonomy' has entered the language of English public management.

This local – and collective – dimension was articulated by CEs as relating to the particular health status of and health outcomes for their resident populations.

The interview data suggested a need for PCTs to be 'ambidextrous' in terms of demonstrating their organizational performance; that is, capable of balancing short-term national targets with long-term local outcomes. In other words, whilst central Government viewed high-performance in a purposive sense (focusing on cost, short-term tasks, quantity, risk avoidance, etc.), local communities, CEs believed, would be much more likely to judge PCT performance according to long-term outcomes, quality, innovation etc. The ambidexterity of PCTs comes in the ability to manage these competing, and often conflicting, demands in ways that satisfied divergent stakeholders. Of course, this account is also consistent with findings in the policy implementation literature of the concerns of the local agent faced with perceived national imposition (see Peck and 6, 2006).

Technological performance – effectiveness

McKenzie (2001: 97) describes technological performance as 'the technical "carrying-out" of prescribed tasks, successful or not'. Much of the CEs' discourse around commissioning tended to treat it as just such a technical task. Unlike references to, say, civic leadership or community engagement (see below), commissioning was continually referred to as something to 'get right' or that can be 'honed'; perhaps unsurprisingly, this largely reflected the premise of the commissioning diagnostic tool. They did not think that there was necessarily one way to commission that was 'correct'. Most commissioning decisions tended, they argued, to reflect the position typically described as bounded-rationality; that is, perfectly rational decisions are often not feasible in practice due to the finite computational resources available for making them. In practice, commissioning was typically seen as the result of a long and open series of negotiations and compromises. Nonetheless, there were aspects of this process which were suggested to be akin to technological performance.

Department of Health policy has described the role of commissioning services as 'crucial' within the reform programme (Department of Health, 2005b: 2), yet a number of commentators have suggested that NHS commissioning has so far 'failed to deliver' (Bramley-Harker and Lewis, 2005; Walshe et al., 2004). This was reflected during the interviews. A number of CEs referred to the inability of PCTs in general – and the NHS as a whole – to commission effectively. The majority of CEs viewed the technical aspect of commissioning as one where they needed to be seen to deliver and that this aspect of performance would be judged within relatively short time spans.

Smith et al. (2006) illustrated four key elements of effective health commissioning within the NHS: the identification of need and demand; the shaping of markets; holding the market to account; and, holding commissioners to account. Underpinning most of these factors is a requirement for good information and information analysis (Woodin, 2006) – the generation of commissioning intelligence – and a number of CEs discussed this aspect broadly in terms of what McKenzie considers technological performance. For example, most CEs talked about information collection and analysis as a technical task. Indeed, a number pointed to the ability of commercial sector companies (for example large supermarkets) to routinely collect and analyse data well, contrasting the NHS unfavourably in this regard.

Most CEs could see some potential role for private sector involvement within PCT commissioning and this predominantly related to information collation or market intelligence. Actively promoted as such by the Department of Health in line with New Labour's general enthusiasm for information technology as a lever for reform (see 6 and Peck, 2004), the commercial sector was generally viewed as a higher-performer in this technical area. In line with this explicit government policy, some CEs saw no problem with hiring in such organizations as it was self-evident that they would improve the technological performance of PCTs. Other CEs were slightly more circumspect, being prepared to involve the commercial sector provided that it was done in a co-productive way; that is, they would hire in the commercial sector to do a particular task but the external company would be required to pass on expertise to PCT staff order to enhance the organization's internal technical ability.

A small group of CEs were, however, more hesitant about offering up commissioning functions to private sector organizations. They were concerned with the effect that outsourcing core functions might have on external perceptions of their own organization's performance and also feared this could undermine rather than enhance their technical competence. Furthermore, some were wary of the commercial sector actually doing (as opposed to advising on) PCTs' commissioning due to what they saw as the inherently political nature of this task.

Interestingly, a high proportion of CEs suggested that the commercial sector should not be involved in the decision making role of PCTs as their unique purpose was to introduce – and be seen to introduce – a distinctive local flavour to national tax-based health care commissioning. This line of argument moves towards the final, cultural, aspect of performance.

Cultural performance – efficacy

Concepts of cultural performance are largely absent from the PCT diagnostic tools outlined above. McKenzie (2001: 30), however, views cultural performance as being as crucial as organizational and technological performance, distinguishing it from these other forms by its challenge of *efficacy*. This theory suggests that in order for a PCT to demonstrate high-performance it must be perceived to act in a culturally efficacious manner; that is, it must reflect and affirm local social values and priorities when exercising its responsibilities. This research showed strong CE support for this position. The vast majority of CEs indicated the importance of cultural legitimacy at some point during their interviews and suggested that this would become increasingly important. The strength of this belief is at first sight surprising given that it is virtually absent from previous accounts of organizational high-performance, and certainly not emphasized in PCT guidance up to that date.

These aspirations tended to be particularly prevalent during discussions of civic leadership and of engagement with local communities. The vast majority of CEs considered themselves civic leaders, partially as they were invited to a range of civic functions in their local areas but also because they spent large amounts of public money on behalf their local population. Many CEs recognized that in order to be able to deliver in terms of organizational efficiency they would need to have cultural efficacy; for example, in order to make substantial changes to hospital services the local public would have to trust the PCT CE. Without such legitimacy as a local leader, CEs recognized that their ability to deliver on health care reform would be limited.

Civic leadership was often highlighted as being what PCTs had lacked in previous years. CEs suggested that they suspected very few members of the public were even aware of the existence of PCTs – or what they did – and this posed problems in gaining local credibility. Where they are recognized, PCTs are often portrayed in the media as 'rationers' of expenditure, that is, they exemplify the stewardship of national tax revenue rather than the primacy of the local perspective. Indeed, when they do stand-up for a local priority – such as the non-funding of new (and expensive) pharmaceutical treatments – they can be overruled by national politicians concerned with avoiding the so-called 'postcode lottery' (even when just such a lottery is a consequence of creating PCTs).

CEs acknowledged that they cannot commission services that will satisfy all the people, all of the time; however, most saw an imperative to engage in dialogue with local communities if they were ultimately to become more effective commissioners. Many gave examples of where local media had approached hospital sector colleagues for their reaction to events or had named these colleagues within lists of most influential local people whereas PCT leaders were typically overlooked. A number of the CEs talked about the importance of creating visibility for themselves as leaders – and for their organizations – within their localities.

CEs also discussed their lack of local legitimacy in comparison to elected members of local authorities. A number highlighted the importance of creating a vision for 'place' and of engaging in processes of 'place-shaping' with partner organizations from the locality; these picked up on the suggestion of local authorities as place-shapers that had been raised by the Lyons review (Lyons, 2006). It would appear, therefore, that for some CEs the conception of the local dimension of their role relates to shaping the broader determinants of health status in the resident population in a context where the more direct healthcare provision is largely determined by national policy and regulation.

At the same time, the introduction of practice-based commissioning – where local GPs act to manage demand – and the presence of local authorities – with many generations of visible civic leadership – offer alternative ways in which the government's ambitions for healthcare commissioning could be delivered. Both approaches – and they are mutually compatible – could engage in healthcare commissioning local actors (GPs and Councillors) who already possess a significant degree of cultural efficacy.

Discussion

The Fitness for Purpose assessment which evaluated PCT performance in relation to their new priorities and functions as commissioning organizations focused on financial efficiency and commissioning effectiveness. This assessment largely related to short-term performance and measured them against sets of objective benchmark data and indicators of best practice. However, in subsequent discussions, CEs highlighted all three aspects of McKenzie's framework being relevant to becoming high-performance; that is, not just efficiency and effectiveness but also efficacy.

This discourse of high-performance was underpinned by another important theme prevalent at network meetings, which focused more on whether PCTs would be performing at all in three years time. In other words, behind all three aspects of performance, the spectre of organizational extinction could be discerned.

Whilst the CEs saw that PCTs would and could need to show efficiency – and there is evidence at the time of writing that NHS expenditure is currently much more under control (Gainsbury, 2007) – they understood that this would be closely enforced. Indeed, in terms of simple financial efficiency, the top-slicing approaches to financial control that helped to achieve this financial balance suggest that, in transactional terms, PCTs may never be the most efficient way of channelling taxpayers' money from treasury to healthcare providers. Furthermore, much hospital-based activity is commissioned through PCT consortia; after all, the needs of a patient requiring a hernia repair in one locality are much like those of a hernia repair patient from anywhere else. There are clear threats here to the continued importance of localness in current approaches to commissioning in a setting where any accusation of a 'postcode lottery' is politically damaging.

The CEs' ambivalence about the best approach to technological performance in the collection of information and use of intelligence also seemed to reflect concerns about survival. Whilst there were different views amongst CEs about the appropriateness of utilizing the private sector to deliver these functions, it was generally agreed that their perceived expertise would have a positive impact on technological performance. However, there was some concern that this approach might serve to further undermine the relevance of PCTs if it was expanded too far (and thus the importance attributed by some CEs to the transfer of skills); after all, it might suggest to government that local, tax-based and collective healthcare commissioning could be entirely entrusted to the commercial sector.

So, it would appear that it is in the realm of cultural performance that the future of PCTs may reside: to deliver significant changes to services, PCT CEs of high-performing PCTs will have to build legitimacy through community engagement; and to shape the wider determinants of health, these PCT CEs will have to exhibit civic leadership in their dealings with partner agencies.

Overall, the research suggested a clear set of characteristics of high-performance healthcare commissioners from the perspective of PCT CEs. These are summarized in Table 16.2.

Following the end of the first stage of this research project, and perhaps in some ways influenced by its findings, the UK government put in place an ambitious programme to enhance local capacity and capability under the rubric of 'world-class commissioning' (Department of Health, 2007). This identifies 11 competences that PCTs must possess (see Table 16.3). It represents a high-profile re-commitment to the future of PCTs as the vehicles for local, tax-based and collective healthcare commissioning which seeks to deal with the ambitions and anxieties revealed in this research. Furthermore, it seems to re-affirm that this approach to public service reform has become one of the enduring – and perhaps genuinely distinctive – motifs of New Labour's approach to the modernization of healthcare.

Table 16.2 Indicators of PCT high-performance

Efficiency	Effectiveness	Efficacy
Resolving issues related to the future of PCT provider services	Achieving technical competence in commissioning	Demonstrating civic leadership
Achieving financial balance	Creating a vibrant organization	Creating new conversations with communities
Demonstrating value for money		Influencing policy
Demonstrating quality services		

Table 16.3 Competencies for 'World Class' commissioners

Works collaboratively with local people and partners as a key 'community leader'
The PCT leads continuous, meaningful engagement with its communities, partners to develop a shared ambition with key partners
Engage with public and patients, being responsible for investing funds on behalf of communities
Leads strong, continuous clinical engagement across the whole economy to shape strategy, design services and contract for clinical quality
Has outstanding knowledge management capability
Prioritize investment by having a thorough understanding of different sections of the local population along with partners to develop a set of clear, outcome-focused, strategic priorities and investment plans
Stimulate the market to produce a choice of responsive providers in place to meet the health and care needs of the local population
Promote improvement and innovation
Has world class contracting and procurement skills
Applies market management techniques to maintain quality and encourage improvement in standards as appropriate
Has a clear financial strategy and demonstrates excellent financial management

Source: Department of Health, 2007

Conclusion

The aim of this research was to use empirical data from current PCT CEs to synthesize the key characteristics of high-performing healthcare commissioning organizations of the future. Notwithstanding that the Fitness for Purpose assessment process was concerned largely with issues of organizational efficiency and commissioning effectiveness, the more recent world-class commissioning framework gives equal attention to aspects that could be defined as relating to cultural efficacy. This seems to confirm McKenzie's (2001) framework of performance, and his suggestion that any notion of performance is an emergent property made up of the three specific types of performance. This is the first occasion that characteristics that can be seen as relating to cultural efficacy have appeared overtly in a performance framework for healthcare emanating from the UK government (and neither do they appear in the broader review conducted by Powell, 2007); this may become another contribution of New Labour to the development of twenty-first century public management.

Of course, the world-class commissioning initiative may not enable PCTs to be perceived to be high-performing quickly enough for them to survive. Further, if performance is emergent and negotiated (as opposed to 'objective' and non-contextual), then arguably a central priority for PCTs is to shape

Department of Health (and perhaps public) perceptions of performance towards measures correlated with efficacy. This is especially crucial given the lack of evidence that primary care based healthcare commissioners can increase the efficiency and effectiveness of hospitals through their own efficiency and effectiveness (Smith et al., 2004). Thus, for PCTs to flourish, their being judged at least partially on the grounds of efficacy is vital.

The importance of a simple measure of high-performance for health care systems (as suggested by Collins, 2001) which stresses the importance of the central role of PCTs becomes crucial in these circumstances. The PCT CEs network alighted upon 'Increasing life expectancy' as the key foundation underpinning PCT high-performance as they believed it had high public resonance and potentially served to reduce the currently dominant profile of hospitals in political and public perception. Its adoption would represent a meta-narrative that might represent high-performance upwards to the Department of Health but also outwards to stakeholders in the local community.

In other words, for PCTs to be high-performing, they need to re-construct the criteria of performance for the healthcare system deployed by government...now that would be quite a cultural performance. Perhaps, nonetheless, it can be done; the vision for world-class commissioning suggested by the Department of Health at the end of 2007 was: 'World class commissioning will add life to years and years to life' (Department of Health, 2007).

References

6, P. and Peck, E. (2004) 'New Labour's modernization in the public sector: A Neo-Durkheimian approach and the case of mental health services', *Public Administration*, 82, 83–108.

Bojke, C., Gravelle H. and Wilkin D. (2001) 'Is bigger better for primary care groups and trusts?' National Primary Care Research and Development Centre, Manchester.

Bramley-Harker, E. and Lewis, D. (2005) *Commissioning in the NHS: Challenges and Opportunities.* London: NERA.

Collins, J. (2001) *Good to Great: Why Some Companies Make the Leap and Others Don't.* London: Random House.

Department of Health (2005a) *Commissioning a Patient-Led NHS.* London: Department of Health.

Department of Health (2005b) *Health Reform in England: Update and Next Steps.* London.

Department of Health (2007) *World Class Commissioning: Vision.* London: Department of Health.

Gainsbury, S. (2007) 'NHS underspends by £1.8bn', *Health Service Journal.* Available from www.hsj.co.uk.

Giddens, A. (1998) *The Third Way: The Renewal of Social Democracy.* Cambridge: Polity Press.

Ham, C. (2004) *Health Policy in Britain.* Basingstoke: Palgrave Macmillan.

Health Service Journal (2007) 'Trusts face 15 public productivity rankings', *Health Service Journal*. Available online from www.hsj.co.uk.

Kershaw, B. (2006) 'Performance Studies and Po-Chang's Ox: Steps to a Paradoxology of Performance', *NTQ*, 22, 30–53.

Leatherman, S. and Sutherland, K. (2004) 'Quality of care in the NHS of England.' *British Medical Journal*, 328, 288–90.

Lyons, M. (2006) 'National prosperity, local choice and civic engagement: A new partnership between central and local government for the 21st century', Lyons Inquiry into Local Government, Lyons Inquiry/HMSO, London.

McKenzie, J. (2001) *Perform or Else: From Dicipline to Performance*. London: Routledge.

Peck, E. and 6, P. (2006) *Beyond Delivery: Policy Implementation as Sense-Making and Settlement*. Basingstoke: Palgrave MacMillan.

Peters, T.J. and Waterman, R.H. (1982) *In Search of Excellence: Lessons from America's Best-Run Companies*. New York: Harper & Row.

Powell M. (2007) *Understanding the Mixed Economy of Welfare*. Bristol: Policy Press.

Secretary of State for Health (2000) The NHS plan: A plan for investment, a plan for reform. London: HSMO.

Smith J., Lewis R., and Harrison T. (2006) 'Making commissioning effective in the reformed NHS in England', The Health Policy Forum, London.

Smith J., Mays N., Dixon J., Goodwin N., Lewis R., McClelland S., McLeod H. and Wyke, S. (2004) 'A review of the effectiveness of primary care-led commissioning and its place in the NHS', The Health Foundation, London.

Walshe, K., Smith, J., Dixon, J., Edwards, N., Hunter, D.J., Normand, C. and Robinson, R. (2004) 'Primary care trusts – premature reorganisation, with mergers, may be harmful', *British Medical Journal*, 329, 871–2.

Woodin, J. (2006) 'Health care commissioning and contracting', in K.Walshe and J.Smith (eds), *Healthcare Management*. Maidenhead: Open University Press, 201–23.

Conclusion: Culture and Climate in Health Care Organizations – Evidentiary, Conceptual and Practical progress

Paula Hyde, Catherine Pope and Jeffrey Braithwaite

In this final chapter we bring the range of contributions to a conclusion. To accomplish this, we provide a synthesis of the terrain we have covered and offer some suggestions about where this might lead us in the future. Health care organizations involve a diverse mix of managerial, professional and ancillary groups of workers the result of which is that health services are made up of culturally complex organizations. This diversity encapsulates multiple value systems, beliefs and attitudes as well as considerable power differentials. Therefore, health care organizations offer a rich landscape for study. 'Culture' and 'climate' have been central themes in this volume, which has included broad ranging studies that are of interest to health care professionals, managers, policy makers and the informed public as well as the community of health care organizational researchers.

Constructs of culture and climate have been used to attempt to understand and account for the success or failure of organizational changes. The challenge for researchers has been how to identify and track changing values that underpin managerial thinking and how to explore the implications of these changes for patients, health care organizations and local health care communities. This volume has provided a variety of examples of this field of endeavour across international borders. The authors have explored these concepts to illuminate policy orientations, in situ interactions of health care workers and their various effects on health service delivery. Thus, the international scholars included in this volume have attempted to expose for examination, using a diversity of methodologies, values, and meanings underpinning participants' actions in organizational settings.

Each of the three sections of the book identified important aspects of research in this field. The book began by examining concepts of both culture and climate in health care organizations in Part I. It continued with papers that identified the importance of relationships and collaboration in health service delivery in Part II. The book culminated in an examination of novel research methodologies available to researchers of culture and climate in Part III. We now conclude by identifying some of the theoretical, conceptual and methodological points of convergence and divergence the compendium suggests to us.

Conceptual and practical views of culture and climate

A fundamental concern of many authors included in this volume lay with the problem of elucidating how culture or climate might affect large-scale organizational change and or the performance for health service organizations. Given that both culture and climate are contested concepts, it may be surprising to see that there is a proliferation of assessment tools for measuring culture and climate. Braithwaite et al drew upon existing metrics to identify similarities and differences between the two constructs using empirical data from Australian hospitals. They concluded with the suggestion that culture and climate, if not one and the same, were at least related with a considerable degree of overlap. Their study illustrated the potential utility of such research for providing increasingly refined assessment tools.

Measures of culture and climate have also been shown to offer the opportunity to explore organizational phenomena that are more commonly associated with individuals, for example, bullying. McMahon et al. found several common factors linking measures of culture to experiences of being bullied and suggested that such metrics may form one means of identifying both problematic and beneficial aspects of shared features encompassed in organizational cultures.

A recurring theme throughout the book was a question about the extent to which cultures are susceptible to management influence or manipulation. Rather than being a static feature of organizations, cultures change over time as Mannion et al. illustrated. Their exploration of senior management cultures in National Health Service (NHS) hospital trusts demonstrated longitudinal culture shifts, with clan cultures in decline but remaining dominant overall. These changes in culture as measured by standardized tools are important, and they may reflect international trends to institutional arrangements for care provision.

In contrast, Freeman and Peck questioned the nature of culture implied by prescriptive policy reforms, particularly the degree to which cultures might be thought of as homogenous and the extent to which cultures might be managed. Their application of Butlerian notions of performativity suggested that more subtle reading of organizational culture(s) was required.

Culture change, policy reforms and relationships between workers

Whilst the degree to which culture and climate is susceptible to managerial reform remains open to question, it is nevertheless apparent that culture change has increasingly formed a central feature of policy reform (see Freeman and Peck). Many papers explored the challenges confronted by health services management researchers in linking between the different worlds of policy and practice. Internationally, policymakers have become increasingly interested in culture change as a means of driving health services performance improvements. Policy reforms have led to concomitant challenges for professional and organizational groups. For example, Human Resource Management (HRM) has become a central function responsible for creating culture change and deriving performance improvements. However, some chapters suggested that changes to functional arrangements for HRM, for example, can change the nature of operating relationships for better or worse as illustrated in the competing accounts of Hyde and Rondeau and Wagar. Further, whilst recognizing the questionable susceptibility of cultures to being managed or manipulated, Schaeff et al. argue that network cultures may be even less susceptible to manipulation than organizational cultures. In addition, Pope et al. elucidate interconnections between culture and place in shaping organizational change. They argue that the geographical and physical environment provides a powerful signal to organizational actors in making sense of organizational change and in shaping decision-making.

Much international health policy is conceptualized in a functionalist frame. This view tends to suggest cultures are features of health care organizations amenable to simple manipulation and adaptation. Chapters by Fitzgerald and Dadich and Hyde illustrated how simplistic policies aimed at overcoming organizational problems may exacerbate rather than ameliorate team climate. This was also evident in the chapter by Callen et al. who drew together ideas about diffusion of innovations and team climate. More complex policies promoting networking may make culture change more rather than less problematic.

Interpersonal relationships and collaborations between work groups formed a common theme in many empirical studies, offering a counterpoint to considerations of formal power and organizational structure. Eljiz et al. explored elements of mutually reinforcing subcultures that had a powerful effect on decision-making about patient care. They used the concept of culture to elucidate how tacit knowledge was sustained and transmitted between organizational members and Casebeer et al. offered comparative case examples to illustrate how cultures of care may be formed and sustained over time. So culture may be susceptible to change, but those changes may be difficult to predict or manipulate using simplistic managerial approaches.

Developing a richer theoretical and empirical research base

While there has been a strong international flavour to the edition, we note that the authors are from predominantly English speaking countries with little or no contribution from continental European or BRIC (Brazil, Russia, India and China) or developing countries. Organizational behaviour is a key issue in these countries, too, and its analysis has much to offer, as it can consider change and illuminate issues within different systems of health care provision. Future OBHC conferences, and SHOC research initiatives, ought to address this deficit, because it can enrich our understandings.

We were pleased that many chapters went beyond a narrow focus on culture change that might have been expected in the purely managerialist literature, but instead employed a broad range of social science theories applied to the study of health care organizations. Which theoretical positions were most prevalent? Much work fell within organizational analytic tradition. Eljiz et al., for example, used stakeholder class theory. Sociology of the professions was evident in Fitzgerald and Dadich's illustration of how appointments of professionals as managers could amplify organizational professional conflict. Political science has been an influential base discipline (see for example Schaeff et al.) and systems dynamics formed the base for Long et al.'s action research. Organizational change and development and diffusion of innovations approaches were the theoretical constructs of choice of Callen et al. There remains little usage of neo-Marxist perspectives such as labour process theory, or of perspectives drawn from organizational economics such as principal agent theory. Many of the papers were representative of single disciplines or traditions.

As this volume has illustrated organizational culture and climate lends itself to both qualitative and quantitative study (Scott et al., 2003). This volume has demonstrated a diversity of methodological approaches from quantitative statistical analyses of established metrics (see Braithwaite et al. and Mannion et al.) mostly dominated by survey designs (see Fitzgerald and Dadich and Callen et al.) through to process oriented qualitative studies (see Freeman and Peck, Hyde, and Casebeer et al). Quantitative empirical studies tended to be broadly functionalist, summarizing culture as relatively stable, multidimensional and shared by organizational members. The dominant methodologies were broadly process-based, especially case study designs, sometimes of a comparative nature (see McDermott and Keating). In-depth methods such as ethnography (see Pope et al.) also featured as did action research (see Long et al.). Long et al. offered a novel example of empirical work where culture change was the research objective. Through the use of organizational consulting methods derived from Tavistock principles, the purpose of the research was to enable a move towards shared understanding between organizational members.

Culture and climates for change

Some of the chapters touched on management issues likely to be of increased importance in the future. Not least are the problems as well as the possibilities of network modes of organizing explored by Schaeff et al. and the nature of possible long term changes in modes of governance and control of health care organizations. As attempts to improve health service organizations tended to involve large-scale changes, it could be argued that capacity for change is dependent upon aspects of organizational climate. McDermott and Keating suggested that role structures – the way in which roles were arranged – emerged as a discriminating factor in creating a supportive climate for service improvement. Greenfield described how one group of health workers deliberately formed a collaborative practice climate to establish communal self-governance. Both Schaeff and Greenfield suggested that one of the major effects of culture change has been the stripping out of middle management functions through cultural adaptations necessitating self-governing modes of functioning. Most of the chapters illustrated a policy preoccupation with cultures for performance (see for example, Dickenson et al.).

Changing culture seems to have been a central feature of governmental reforms with profound practical consequences for planning organization and delivery of local health services. The rising challenges threaded through many of the chapters concerned questions of whether culture enabled or interfered with change? Whether cultures could be managed? Did cultures arising from professional value systems recommend particular approaches to change, that is, by attempting to change professional values? In addition, organizational relationships were a key issue. Several chapters illustrated attempts to unite views by merging work groups, for example, professionals and managers. However, it would seem that these attempts may have been less successful than first hoped.

We offer this edition as a further contribution towards building an international knowledge base drawing on the social sciences for theory and the practice of health care management for inspiration. We hope that readers will find the edition useful in stimulating their own thoughts on current themes in national and comparative health care organizational behaviour.

Reference

Scott, J.T., Mannion, R. Marshall, M.N. (2003) *Healthcare Performance and Organisational Culture.* Oxford: Radcliffe Medical Press.

Index